Unveiling Coptic Liturgy: Exploring Roots in Jewish Second Temple Texts

Revised Edition

Emile Tadros

AGORA
UNIVERSITY
PRESS

Emile Tadros ii

Unveiling Coptic Liturgy: Exploring Roots in Jewish Second Temple Texts

Copyright © 2024 by Agora University Press
All rights reserved. Printed in the United States of America. No part of this book may be used or reproduced in any manner whatsoever without written permission except in the case of brief quotations embodied in critical articles or reviews.
For information contact: aupress@agora.edu
Agora University Press: aupress.org
ISBN 978-1-950831-47-0
Printed in the United States of America

HIS HOLINESS POPE TAWADROS II *118th*
Pope and Patriarch of the great city of Alexandria and the See of St. Mark

HIS HOLINESS PATRIARCH IGNATIUS APHREM II
Patriarch of Antioch and All the East

Abstract

This exploration is an initial attempt to shed light on the mutual interaction between Coptic and Jewish traditions by demonstrating a Jewish impact on the early stage of the Alexandrian Church as seen in the Coptic Morning Service. It explores the possible influence of the Jewish liturgies and prayers, including the writings of the late Second Temple era (200 BCE–70 CE) on some of the origins of fundamental Coptic rituals. The Coptic Morning Service holds almost identical texts and order of prayers, along with many major Jewish thematic interrelations.

This study argues for an important lacuna in the spirituality of the contemporary Coptic worshiper. The mystifications surrounding many Coptic liturgical components prevent parishioners from praying with understanding (1 Cor. 14:15). The twenty-first century Copt needs a sort of "Halakah" guidance towards their worshiping practices.

This research hopes to offer a potential reconstruction of the early history of the Alexandrian Church through liturgy that could open a new scholarly field of Judeo-Coptic studies.

To my knowledge, this is the first book that deals with a liturgical study between early Egyptian Christianity and Judaism, detailing research that reflects the continuance and evolution of Jewish liturgy in the early stages of the Coptic Church. According to the latest

Emile Tadros iv

studies, the Second Temple texts had an exceptional impact on early Christianity: This book is a contributory introduction in the field. Morning Services in Jewish and Coptic repertoires are scrutinized through a textual comparison approach and by investigating various works of the Second Temple era.

Dedication and Acknowledgements

I dedicate this study to my mom Rose Mattar, who, before her departure to Christ in 1998 has always been my spiritual mentor and a zealous devotee to Coptic studies.

It is a pleasant duty to record my gratitude to my mentor, Dr. Wendy J. Porter, who supervised my study and made herself available for many hours of stimulating conversation on the themes of the thesis. Her humility in editing my manuscript and patiently helping me express my insights has been remarkable.

One more word of thanks, this time to Professor Stanley E. Porter, President and Dean of McMaster Divinity College, who despite his busy schedule, welcomed me to his office for long discussions bursting with invaluable advice and inspiration.

I am incredibly grateful to my wife, Eman Ghaly, who sparked the flame for me to complete my master's degree. Eman has shown considerable forbearance during the period of this research. I owe thanks to my son Philip, his wife Lindsay, and their beautiful daughters Grace Elizabeth and Magdalena Julie and Kiama, as well my cherished grandson Isaac for their prayers and love. Special thanks to my daughter Nada.

Also, a thank you note goes to my sister Catherine Tadros for her betokening warmth and generosity toward me during my visits to Egypt.

Special Thank you Note to Ruth Langer, PhD

Professor of Theology at Boston College and an expert on Jewish Liturgy and on Christian Jewish Relations

I cannot express enough gratitude to Prof Langer for how much time and effort she spent revising and appraising each statement in my research after obtaining my MA degree in 2015 at McMaster Divinity College, Ontario, Canada.

The invaluable insights and comments added by Prof. Langer were significant to avoid slipping into the abyss of anachronism or meagre evidence. While she meticulously revised my writing, she also showed her expertise in referring to the most updated scholarly views related to my topic. This is exceptional as I had never been one of her students at Boston College.

I simply cannot overstate how humbled I am to have known Prof. Langer and learned from her weighty publications.

I hope to remain in touch and continue learning from her wealth of knowledge in Jewish and early Christian liturgies, with which she is always so willing to offer help. She has furthered my drive towards becoming a better scholar in the new scholarship that I called "Judeo Coptic Studies". I appreciate it tremendously.

Table of Contents

History of this Book... 2
Introduction.. 9
1. Alexandrian Judaism—Backbone of the Early Egyptian Church? 9
2. The Writings of Hellenistic Judaism Reverberate in the Coptic Church.. 14
3. The Concept of "Judaism" and Some Coptic Observances.. 25
4. Conclusion: An Embryonic Stage for a New "Judeo-Copto" Scholarship 31
Chapter 1 Research History, Problems, and Possibilities 33
1. Historians Who Focus on the Early Alexandrian Papacy 36
2. Scholars Who Consider a Gnostic or Jewish Seed of the Coptic Church... 42
3. The Authors of the Catechism Books 51
4. Problems with the Standard Theory 53
5. Present Possibilities... 54
Chapter 2 Research Method.. 57
1. Three Difficult Questions... 57
2. The Historical Literary Approach to Liturgy 60
3. The Textual Correspondence 66
4. Theological Content in Liturgical Texts 68
5. Conclusion 71
Chapter 3 Parallels of the Morning Service in the Jewish and Coptic Liturgies 72

1. Introduction 72
2. Primary and Secondary Resources 73
3. The Morning Service in Seder R. Amram Gaon and The Divine Liturgy 76
4. Uniqueness of the Coptic Morning Service 80
5. Locating Jewish Segments in the Coptic Morning Service (Texts and Rubrics) 81
   A. A Preparation to Meet God 82
   B. "Pseuque de Zimra," "Psalmodia," and Matins Psalms 85
   C. The Shema 89
   D. The Tefillah 90

Chapter 4 Thematic Interrelations in the Jewish and Coptic Cycle of Luminaries 112
1. Glimpses of the Biblical Foundations of Luminary Liturgies 115
2. Second Temple Period and the Perception of "Luminaries" 119
   A. The Resources of the Second Temple Era 120
   B. Seder Amram Gaon (1 SAG): The Shema and Its Blessing, Amidah 132
   C. Luminaries and Related Topics in the Coptic Liturgy 138
   D. Angelology and the Luminaries 152
3. Conclusion: Luminaries in Second Temple Writings and Future Coptic Interrelations 157

Chapter 5 159
Overall Conclusion and Possibilities for Future Research 159

1. Early Alexandrian Church Fathers on the Liturgy... 160
2. Could the Jewish Halakah Dissipate the Cloud over the Coptic Liturgy? 166
  A. Definition of Halakah... 166
  B. The Talmudic Liturgical Halakah 167
  C. Halakah for the Communal Nature of Prayer: Some Talmudic Principles 168
  D. The Blessings in Rabbinic Prayer 169
  E. Specific Liturgical Principles 170
  F. Model of a non Halakic Dictum Related to the Morning Coptic Service 172
3. Possibilities for Further Research............................ 174
  A. The Embryonic Stage of a New "Judeo-Coptic" Scholarship... 174
  B. Network of Scholars for the New Scholarship 175
  C. Academic Projects... 175
4. Conclusion 182
Related Essay I Art Scholars: The Matter the Jewish and Coptic Art in Egypt... 184
Related Essay II The Jewish-Egyptian Heritage and its Impact on Coptic Church Architecture........................ 191
Jewish-Coptic Common Rituals and layouts................ 192
  A. The Altar الهَيكَل (alhaŷkal) and the Torah Shrine in the Synagogue 195
  B. The Sherkiah الشَرقية (alsh̲ar̊qīã) 198
  C. The Veil or الحِجاب (alḥijāb) 200
  D. Tamid תָּמִיד قَنديل الشَرقية (qandyl alsh̲ar̊qīãta) 204
elated Essay III 'Cosmic Music' (or 'Praise') from Greek Philosophy to Church Fathers:................................... 205

A Potential source towards Singing with a Melismatic Style? 205
Part I – Observations and Dictums from Greek Philosophers 208
　1. The Concept of Cosmic Music in the Ancient Greek Philosophy 208
Part II – Psalms Recognition of Cosmic Praise 218
　1. Biblical Tradition and Cosmic Praise 218
　2. Order in Universe and Human life in Hymns 220
　3. The Victory of God over Destructive forces in Kingship Psalms 222
　4. The Coming of the Judge: A Cosmic Joy for Divine Restoration 225
　5. Global focus on God's deeds in Creation and History 227
　6. Blessings for the Nations and the "Cosmic Scale" . 227
Part III – Philo of Alexandria 233
Part IV - Vowel alphabets: Gnostic legacy 238
Part V – Utterances of the Church Fathers on 'cosmic music' 239
　1. Athenagoras 241
　2. Clement of Alexandria 242
　3. Athanasius of Alexandria 249
　4. Serapion of Thumis 252
Part VI – Cosmic Music Concepts: Lyrics and Performance 253
　1. Liturgical Extracts 254
　2. Grapheme and Comments of the Way of Singing .. 255
Conclusion: From an Aesthetic to the Worship Ritual . 259

Related Essay IV 261
Documenting Oral Torah Tradition in Coptic Church and its Liturgy: Methodology and Anthology 261
What Is The 'Oral Torah'? 261
The Oral Torah and the Early Church Codes (see figure 1) 264
Methodology Dealing with Jewish Sources 270
   Questions 277
   B. Blessings: The Structural Framework of Rabbinic Prayer 284
Bibliography 291

List of Abbreviations

DL= Al Massoudy, Abdel Massih Saleb Al Baramoussy *Al-Khulaji* [*The Holy Euchologion*]. Cairo: Al Baramous Monastery, No publication year. (Coptic-Arabic).

DL = *The Divine Liturgy, The Anaphoras of Saints Basil, Gregory, and Cyril*. No city: Coptic Orthodox Diocese of Southern United States, 2007. (Coptic-Arabic-English).

1 SAG = Hedegård, David. *Seder R. Amram Gaon, Hebrew Text with Critical Apparatus Translation with Notes and Introduction* (Part I). Lund: Lundstedts Universitets, 1951. (English).

2 SAG = Kronheim, Tryggve. Seder R. Amram Gaon (Part II). Lund/Sweden: CWK Gleerup, 1974.

HPA = *The Holy Psalmody [Al Abssalmodieh Al Mokadessa]*. No publisher, no city, no year (rare book). (Coptic-Arabic).

HPE = *The Holy Psalmody*. Edited by Saint Mary and Saint Antonios Coptic Orthodox Church. New York: no publisher, no year. (Coptic-Arabic-English).

CE = *Coptic Encyclopedia*. Ed. by Aziz Suryal Atiya, Macmillan Publishers, 1991.

JE = *Jewish Encyclopedia*. Ed. by Joseph Jacobs and Isidore Singer. by KTAV Publishing House. NY 1960.

DALC = *Dictionnaire d'Archéologie et de Liturgie Chretienne*. Ed. by Fernand Carol. Paris Letouzey et Ané, 1907.

JSGRP: Goodenough, Erwin Ramsdell. *Jewish Symbols in the Greco-Roman Period. Pantheon Books,* 1953.

History of this Book

Back in Egypt, before immigrating to Canada in 2001, while I was a Ph.D. student in the Institute of Coptic Studies in Cairo (1996–2001) under the supervision of the late Dr. Ragheb Muftah,[1] I was consistently passionate about the origin of many of the old Liturgical songs. The outcome was limited due to an enormous lack of bibliographical sources in the Coptic institutes in general: most books were editioned some 40 years ago, many stakes were empty, and the carder was a pell-mell! However, I published a booklet in Arabic, reconnoitering the singing practice with long vocalisms and its roots in ancient Greek and early Christian beliefs. I was nominated in 1973 an *Anaghnostos*[2] at the Coptic church by the late Bishop Hedra, eparchy of Aswan, in Saint Georges Coptic Church (Sporting) in Alexandria: I can safely declare that I have a lifelong practical liturgical knowledge of the Egyptian Church. From 1997–2000, I enjoyed being an active speaker in the annual Arabic-Christian Heritage conferences[3] searching Arabic early medieval sources for

---

[1] Dr. Ragheb Moftah (1898–2001) was an Egyptian musicologist and scholar of the Coptic music heritage. He co-authored the article on "Coptic Music" for the *Coptic Encyclopedia*. He spent much of his life studying the recording and notation of Coptic liturgical texts.

[2] Anaghnostos (the 'Reader'). The word comes from the Greek for 'one who reads'.

[3] Some of my papers: "Advent Hymns (Khiak) Among the Egyptian Folklore and the Arab Patrimony" (2001); "The System of the 'Octoechos' in *Musbah El Zulma fi Idah El khedma*, by Ibn Kabar (2000)"; "Sim'ān ibn Kalil ibn Maqarah 1145–1235 and his theological work *Roudah El Farid* (1996)."

any insight into the Coptic liturgy as perceived by the Arabic speakers' intellectuals of this period. The outcomes were fascinating but did not obviously belong to the first centuries of Christianity in Egypt.

I had hoped to find in the Egyptian monasteries and the Papal Library content to satiate my hunger about my pressing topic; I was disenchanted as I was unable to find any relevant manuscripts. Instead, I pursued my research through other institutes, my favorite three libraries in Cairo: La Bibliothèque de l'IFAO[4] (Bab Al Luq), Le Collège de la Sainte Famille (Daher)[5] and the Franciscan Centre for Oriental Christian Studies (Musky).[6]

In 2013, when starting my Master's program at McMaster Divinity College in Ontario, I realized that many motives have driven my scholarship. My reasoning raises many questions. Many historians have traditionally believed that the Alexandrian Church originated with native Egyptians. The objective was to demonstrate that this was not the case, at least during the first three centuries.

Numerous fans of Coptic history deem that native Egyptians were the first followers of Jesus Christ. Following this path, they try to link every liturgical, theological, artistic and religious component in the Coptic

---

[4] Institut Français d'Archéologie Orientale, Cairo.

[5] Homage to father Maurice Martin SJ, well-known French scholars in Coptology who gave me the key of the Jesuits fathers' library (it was not open for the public) in order to go anytime there. Also, he was very helpful to prepare for me, each time I visited the library, many books related to my topic.

[6] Thanks to fathers Mansour Mistrih and Wadie Abu-Leif for their precious advice and help.

Church back to Egyptian civilisation. This assumption is offensive for Christian believers, but this bias blinded the eyes of many devoted historians. The reality is that when Egypt was evangelized, the country was under Greco-Roman culture. Unmistakably, the Hellenistic Jews lived in Alexandria, a cosmopolitan city which, from the time of Alexander the Great, was culturally and philosophically independent compared to other minor Egyptian cities. Initially, as per Jesus' instructions, missionaries targeted the "Children of Israel,"[7] the only people in the entire ancient world expecting the Messiah as prophesied in the Old Testament. The Jerusalem traditions of these missionaries would naturally have influenced the newly developing communities of Jesus' followers in the Diaspora.

The first book that I came across was The *Siddur of Saadia Gaon*.[8] It amazed me when I discovered many textual correspondences between the Jewish Morning Service prayers and its analog in the Coptic repertoire. I had not previously thought about a possible Jewish impact on early Christianity in general! I was never exposed to any Jewish study book in Egypt (before immigrating to Canada). Through writing my thesis in 2013, I devoted time and scientific attention to Coptic prayers holding a Jewish distinctiveness and employed by the church in the

---

[7] Matt 10:5; Matt. 15:24; Matt. 10:6: but go rather to the lost sheep of the house of Israel. ὁ δὲ ἀποκριθεὶς εἶπεν, Οὐκ ἀπεστάλην εἰ μὴ εἰς τὰ πρόβατα τὰ ἀπολωλότα οἴκου Ἰσραλυ.

[8] *The Seder* (or Siddur, prayerbook or order of prayers) of Rav Amram Gaon is the earliest surviving (Ninth Century CE) attempt to transcribe the weekly ritual of Jewish prayers for week-days, Sabbaths, and festivals.

core of the daily liturgy. This Jewish stamp means that these texts were probably well known to Jesus and the apostles as part of the traditional Jewish worship of their time.⁹ Similarities and differences in both traditions specifically in primary sources from late Judaism and early Christianity, brought me to an exciting field in academia that still requires many further explorations.

As I compared the Jewish and Coptic texts, I experienced both excitement and frustration. The parallelisms were enlightening but making the direct link from Jewish writings to Coptic liturgy from primary sources proved difficult. The task became even more difficult when delving into the reconstruction of the origins of the Alexandrian Church. Historical facts from early Christianity in Egypt are scarce, voiceless about the early Christian foundation in Egypt.¹⁰ Many of its early buildings were destroyed over the centuries and with no doubt its documents were burned.¹¹ Early church fathers of

---

⁹ In that sense, see Hedegård, David. *Seder R. Amram Gaon*, "Introduction," XIII–XVI.

¹⁰ See Introduction and Chapter 2.

¹¹ See Leclercq, "Egypte" vol. 4, 2476–2500 and "Archéologie d'Alexandrie," the Early Christian edifices and their Destiny: Church of Theonas, oratory which has been built by Theonas, was rebuilt and enlarged by the patriarch Athanathius (313–326). Archangel Michael or Church of Alexandria, destroyed in 969 CE. Κεςάρειον or Templeum Caesaris devoured by a fire in 912. St. Athanasius Church, converted to a Mosque after the Muslim conquest. The Apostle Mark Church Βουκόλια: Entirely Scorched by the occupation of the city of Alexandria (640?) St. Cyr and John Sanctuary, unknown cause Loss (survived until 620). St Menas (Mina) Sanctuary, Mareotis Lac, also unknown cause of loss. From all these edifices: no liturgical fragments

Alexandria barely discuss their contemporary liturgical practices.[12] On the other hand, when the Christianity movement started in the second half of the first century, the Second Temple writings were already massive, and some of them were added to the Septuagint, the Greek translation of the Old Testament that was used in Alexandria. Though, at the beginning of Christianity, some Jewish prayers, such as the Shema[13] and the Amidah[14] were already recognised in daily spiritual endeavors. Similar texts in both traditions, reinforced my questions on how these prayers and supplications came into the Alexandrian Church.[15] It was a challenge to determine the best methodology to locate an urtext within the late Second Temple and the Qumranic literature.[16]

As I faced these challenges, I was always bearing in mind what contribution my research will bring to the table in turn to challenge current thinking. It is obvious that Jesus was a Jew, the apostles were Jews, the first Christians were Jews. What is less evident, however, is the assertion that Christianity evolved from pagan Egyptian roots. In the contemporary scholarly context, there is a general consensus that the early Christian movement represented a significant departure from the tenets of Judaism. This shift

---

survived after its destruction (see same author "Archéologie d'Alexandrie," note 3, p.1114).

[12] See chapter 5.

[13] "Amidah" see Chapter 3.

[14] "Shema": see also Chapter 3, *for* both prayers pre-Christianity *see* S. Reef, *Problems with Prayers*, 7.

[15] See chapter 2.

[16] Jörg Frey, *Qumran and Christian Origins*.

was initiated by Jesus's disciples, who, in their role as perpetuators of their "Halakha"[17] (or "customs of their ancestors"), played a pivotal role in the preservation of their religious practices. In later years, these Jewish adherents were designated "Christians."[18]

From a personal standpoint, the composition of this book has been a cathartic endeavour, driven by the aspiration to establish a scientific commemoration of the contributions of the late Ragheb Muftah. Muftah devoted a significant portion of his career to the undertaking of his liturgical Coptic songs project, which entailed the transcription of vocal compositions into musical notation. A notable aspect of this project was his invitation of numerous European scholars of that era to Egypt, with the aim of fostering a deeper comprehension of the melodic origins of these compositions. Muftah observed a Jewish seed in the origin of some early laudatory texts.[19] However, during his time, the prevailing cultural tendency was to "Egyptianize" the heritage of the Alexandrian Church (as will be demonstrated subsequently in this book); this occurred in spite of Christ's instructions regarding evangelisation in Israel and the diaspora, as well as certain notable historical events as recorded in the book of Acts.[20]

---

[17] "Halakah" see Chapter 5.

[18] Acts 11: 26.

[19] Muftah, et al., "Coptic Music," 1715–47.

[20] Paul's mission was targeting the gentiles as per Jesus' marvellous plan.

Such "Egyptianity"[21] was and is still established in the mind of many individuals who are not aware of the history of their faith. It is due to a trend that was initiated mainly during the epochs of the Bonaparte's French campaign (1781–1801) and later by British occupation (1882–1956). During this time, numerous Orientalists and Egyptologists were infatuated with their topical pharaonic discoveries and somehow linked it to the origin of Egyptian Christianity. When Christianity emerged in Greco-Roman Egypt, the first believers followed Jesus by faith and by examining the Old Testament (Septuagint) prophecies, not by reading through pharaonic engravings to find a statement that a Messiah should come aimed at a divine salvation. Unfortunately, the conclusions of these archeologists obscured many Egyptian minds from recognizing the natural Jewish-apostolic seeds in the foundation of the early church in Egypt:[22] A furtherance of the Book of Acts.

It is noteworthy to add, after Nasser's revolution in 1952 and the expulsion of the Jews from Egypt in 1956: Jewish studies publications were confiscated from synagogues and library museums; and the Egyptian-Jewish heritage disappeared from the Egyptian mind and literature.

---

[21] Referring to the scholarly behaviour, described by the adjective 'Egyptian' to stress on rooting the Coptic liturgy to the ancient Egyptian civilization.

[22] See Chapter 1.

Introduction

1. Alexandrian Judaism—Backbone of the Early Egyptian Church?

Ivan Pavlov, Nobel Prize winner, states: "Don't become a mere recorder of facts but try to penetrate the mystery of their origin."[23] Indeed, the origin of the Coptic Orthodox Church is still a mystery for many historians.[24] The lack of documents regarding the early centuries of Coptic Church life causes confusion and many contradicting opinions, especially for Coptic worshippers. Many Copts would claim certainty about the Egyptian roots of the Coptic Church, but these would be more believable during the third century CE when the Coptic language flourished. Seeing an absolute "Egyptianity" in ritual, art, and the Church Fathers' apothegms in the first two centuries are unjustified. By the time of the advent of Christianity, even though Egypt was a Roman colony, Greek prestige was reigning overall. Egyptian Temples remained open for native Egyptians but with less influence on society, where the diversity of different ethnic groups was significant. Attempts to tie the early days of the Alexandrian Church primarily to ancient Egyptian culture impose false assertions. For example, how could one observe the early prayers of the Coptic Church, which display a massive quantity of direct quotations from

---

[23] Ivan Pavlov, *Bequest of Pavlov to the Academic Youth of His Country*, Nature 137, no. 3461 (1936): 572. https://doi.org/10.1038/137572a0

[23] Chapter 2 deals with the issue.

Scripture and include many Mosaic Law practices, yet still contend that the Church was derived from a pagan faith such as the Ancient Egyptian religion?

My research is about a new orientation towards understanding the origins of Coptic liturgy. It attempts to open a new door that may lead to deciphering some of the mysterious sources of the Coptic Church, not through documents that try to lay out its history (which provide limited information) but through its liturgy. My argument aims to shed light on the mutual interaction between Jewish and Coptic traditions as seen in the Coptic liturgy and, particularly in the Morning Service ritual. This investigation will explore possible influences of the Jewish liturgies, prayers, and writings of the late Second Temple era (200 BCE–70 CE) on the origins of some fundamental Coptic rituals.

Before I begin to lay out some of my findings that strengthen the likelihood of a Jewish seed in the Coptic Church, I want to emphasize a simple fact that is usually ignored and could impact the accuracy of finding elements that have Jewish roots in the Alexandrian liturgy. It is articulated here by R. T. Beckwith:

> At its origin, Christianity was a Jewish religion. Jesus Christ was a Jew, and his first followers were Jews. The Judaism of the first century, especially in the dispersion but also in Palestine, had been considerably influenced by Greek thought, culture, and language, but its roots were still in the Old Testament, and its basic languages were still Hebrew and Aramaic. The teaching of Jesus had, of course, great originality, but whatever in it was

traditional it owed to Judaism rather than to any other source. Moreover, in their practice, Jesus and his first followers conformed primarily to Jewish customs. When, therefore, the question is asked against what background Christian worship arose, the only answer that can be given is Jewish worship. Such Greek influences on Christian worship as had not first affected Jewish worship are mainly of later date. From the outset, the originality of Christianity is seen in its worship, but so is the traditional Jewish character of Christianity.[25]

How is this important statement revealed in the paradigm of the early Coptic Church? What counts as evidence? Is the large Jewish community that is known to have existed in Alexandria during the first century at the heart of this church? Does Scripture indicate any apostolic mission in Egypt? To what extent did Jewish beliefs shape Christian worship in the diasporic community of Egypt, where the Greek world of thought was widespread? Answering these questions requires one to look deeper into the many hidden aspects of the Coptic Church, particularly its liturgy.

While Beckwith's perspective is not wrong, it ignores the quick turn to Greek culture in the emerging church, even in the land of Israel. There is also a fallacy here in turning only to the worship life of Jews in the land of Israel, which was Hebrew and perhaps Aramaic based at this time. The contemporaneous Hellenistic and Greek-speaking Jewish community of Alexandria should also be considered. Though it is vital to focus on first-century

---

[25] Beckwith, "The Jewish Background to Christian Worship," 68.

Jewish communities in Egypt for studying the liturgy of Alexandria at its early stage, these are distinct cultural worlds in significant ways. The case of Egyptian Jews during the early centuries of our common era will be published shortly. Nevertheless, this book will focus only on the liturgical similarities between Jews and early Christian believers in Egypt. Based on the study conclusions, the reader may reflect on a reconstruction of the early times of the Coptic Church.

Intrinsically, the reasoning of Beckwith makes fair sense when we consider many of the primary factors related to the birth of Christianity in Egypt. When Christ commissioned his disciples to preach the Gospel, he commanded them to prioritize the "lost sheep of the house of Israel," [26] and this became an apostolic "custom."[27] Thus, priority was given to the Jews of Israel and of the diaspora when the early mission started. Also, on the day of Pentecost, Cyrene and Alexandria were broadly introduced in the first predictions of the apostles. Their citizens were stupefied when they witnessed the gift of tongues given to the apostles.[28] The episode of Apollos in Acts 18:24–28 narrates the story of a first-century Alexandrian Christian Jew, a contemporary of Paul. He is mentioned several times in the New Testament[29] and played an important role in the church in Ephesus and in Corinth. The Lukan account, however, does not relate to any mission activity by Apollos in Egypt. Schnabel locates

---

[26] Matt 10:5–6.

[27] Acts 17:1–2.

[28] Acts 2:10, 12.

[29] Acts 18:24, 19:1; 1 Cor 1:12, 3:4–6, 3:22, 4:6, 16:12; Titus 3:13.

early evangelism in Egypt and identifies some critical facts, including that Egypt was a Roman province since 30 BCE.[30] The Egyptian temples and priests were allowed to retain most of their privileges. Still, they had to accept the dissemination of the imperial cult. Jews were settled in Egypt during the time of Alexander the Great to escape the political upheavals in Syria. During around 311 BCE, under the rule of Ptolemy I Soter, thousands of prisoner Jews were brought to Egypt. The inscriptions attest to the existence of many synagogues in the time of Ptolemy III Euergetes (246–221 BCE).[31] Schnabel attests that "The Jewish communities of Alexandria, Rome, and Babylon were the largest outside of Palestine. As Alexandria was certainly a major community, the Jews of this city would have been a natural destination for the Christian missionaries."[32] A significant portion of Alexandria's total population was Jewish. They were Jews with Hellenistic education and culture who served as the transmitters of Philo's works and the Septuagint Bible.

These primary facts provide awareness about the importance of the Jewish community in Egypt during the early age of the Egyptian Church. Many years ago, this recognition encouraged me to start a serious and exciting exploration into the Jewish and Coptic traditions to find parallels in their liturgies. In the following pages of this chapter, I will refer to some Jewish liturgical

---

[30] Schnabel, *Early Christian Mission*, 852.

[31] Horbury and Noy, *Jewish Inscriptions of Greco-Roman Egypt*, 1–33.

[32] Schnabel, *Early Christian Mission*, 854. This perceptive might be considered as urban of scholars are not putting in consideration the Jews of Galilee and the rest of Judea.

reverberations that find their source in the writings of the late Second Temple era and still exist in the Coptic tradition. I will also show two slightly tangential Coptic observances that clearly come from the Mosaic Law and are steadily promulgated in both Jewish and Coptic rules as examples that undeniably link them together.

2. *The Writings of Hellenistic Judaism Reverberate in the Coptic Church*

In the field of Coptic studies, scholars have not made a great effort to explore and study the massive Jewish liturgy and some other literal sources of the late Second Temple era with the establishment of the Alexandrian Church and its liturgy during the first centuries. If Schnabel's statement cited above is accurate (with some reservation),[33] the Jewish communities in the diaspora, specifically Alexandrian Judaism with its multicultural heritage, should be considered significant historical liturgical sources of this unknown stage of the earliest history of the Alexandrian Church. Eventually, Alexandrian and Hellenistic Judaism developed extensive

---

[33] Blouin, *Le Conflit Judéo–Alexandrin de 38–41,* 15. Blouin believes the Alexandrian Jewish community to be the most important one after that of Jerusalem: "Si la majorité des habitants de l'Alexandrie des Lagides était d'origine grecque, la communauté juive y devint en peu de temps la plus importante du monde méditerranéen après celle de Jérusalem." (My translation: If the majority of the inhabitants of Lagides' Alexandria were of Greek origin, the Jewish community became in a short time the most important one in the Mediterranean world after the one of Jerusalem). This perceptive might be considered as urban of scholars are not putting in consideration the Jews of Galilee and the rest of Judea.

literature, some of which can be traced in the Coptic tradition in other forms of liturgy, hagiography, and the sayings of the Early Fathers. In this chapter, however, I will focus on several specific features and worship practices of Jewish liturgy and their possible—even likely transmission into the early Coptic tradition.

Second Temple era writings and the Dead Sea Scrolls[34] classify extensive collections of writings from the Jewish nation that scholars agree on impacting early Christianity.[35] Their sources include biblical, apocryphal, pseudepigraphic, and sectarian and non-sectarian Qumran texts. Some of these texts were circulated within Hellenistic Judaism communities (including Egypt). From this, a huge Jewish corpus (pre-Christianity) was translated to Coptic, primarily in Sahidic dialect.[36] Upon investigating some of these Jewish sources, I have found many elements appear to find parallels in Coptic church liturgical minutiae. In various sections from these

---

[34] Feldman, Louis H., et al. *Outside the Bible: Ancient Jewish Writings Related to Scripture.*; Stone et al., *Jewish Writings of the Second Temple Period.* Schiffman, *Texts and Traditions*, the author collects the most frequent sources cherished by the Jews of the Second Temple era. For Qumranic texts and Early Christianity, see: Jörg Frey, *Qumran and Christian Origins.* Jean-Sébastien Rey. "The Dead Sea Scrolls as Background to Postbiblical Judaism and Early Christianity," 296–98. For a collection of ancient texts: see Barnstone, Willis. *The Other Bible: Jewish Pseudepigrapha, Christian Apocrypha, Gnostic Scriptures, Kabbalah, Dead Sea Scrolls.*

[35] Frey, Jörg, et al. *Qumran and Christian Origins.* Anderson, Gary A., et al. *New Approaches to the Study of Biblical Interpretation in Judaism of the Second Temple Period and in Early Christianity.*

[36] Kulik, Alexander and others (eds), *A Guide to Early Jewish Texts and Traditions in Christian Transmission.*

categories, the list of similarities is lengthy and highly interwoven.

Biblical and apocryphal texts (from the late Second Temple era)[37] seemingly were shared by early Christians in Egypt, inherited textually from Hellenistic Judaism. To summarize: The chapters of Exodus 12–15 was a cherished inherited theme during the late Second Temple era, as they were also later in the Coptic liturgy. The story of the splitting of the Red Sea holds a long tradition in the Jewish ritual of the night preceding the Pesach feast.[38] The

---

[37] "Apocrypha" from Greek apokryptein, means "to hide away," in biblical literature, the history of the term's usage indicates that it referred to a body of esoteric writings that were at first prized, later tolerated, and finally excluded by the Protestants. However, some of these texts are included as canonic in the Vulgate and the Septuagint.

[38] It is noteworthy to emphasise on scholars' views. On Saturday night of the Jewish Passover, the retelling of the story of Exodus 12–15 is an important part of the Seder (the order of prayers) of that night. This part in the Seder is called "Maggid." The earliest documentation of this practice is mentioned in Exodus 13:8: "On that day tell your son, I do this because of what the Lord did for me when I came out of Egypt." The seder would have taken place on the eve of the 15th of Nisan, which is only on a fixed night of the week in the solar calendar that we know from Jubilees and some other Qumran sectarian texts. On the Jewish calendar, see Stern, Sacha. *Calendars in Antiquity Empires, States, and Societies*. Author argues the fact that there is no evidence for the seder as we know it until after the destruction of the Temple, and the "Maggid" itself seems to be a layer that emerges in the 3rd c. CE (maybe) but does not appear as we know it in the late first millennium manuscripts from the Cairo Geniza. The rabbinic seder eventually organizes its telling around Dt. 26's encapsulation of the story. However, the seder's focus is on the narrative of Exodus 1–12, to the point of the actual leaving of Egypt. The crossing of the sea is a week

salvation of God of the Children of Israel with the eloquence of Moses Song was already in Jewish liturgical practice before Christianity. Reif notices:

> By the time that Talmudic rabbis of the early Christian centuries were debating the matter of inclusion of biblical verses and chapters in their standard prayers for daily, Sabbath and festival use, there number of these that were well established by popular tradition with liturgical concept.[39]

Reif indicates that the more common and major examples are: a. The Shema[40] (we will focus on it in Chapter 4), b. The decalogue, c. The Hallel,[41] d. The Passover

---

later and is consequently the focus of the seventh day of Passover – at least by several centuries into the rabbinic period. The dynamic of telling one's children becomes important to the seder. The problematic is in understanding how this tradition came into Coptic repertoire is not documented this early, when Christianity was emerging. Indeed, the earliest descriptions of the rabbinic seder focus on learning the laws of the paschal sacrifice to take the place of its offering.

[39] Reif, Stefan C. *Problems with Prayers: Studies in the Textual History of Early Rabbinic Liturgy*, 7.

[40] "Shema: "The Jewish declaration of faith, 'Hear [Shema] O Israel, the Lord our God, the Lord is one (Deut 6:4).

[41] "Hallel:" Jewish liturgy holds two types of Hallel. A. "Egyptian Hallel" is the text of Pss.113–118 as read in synagogues on festive occasions. In ancient times Jews recited this hymn on the three Pilgrim Festivals, when they offered their required sacrifices in the Temple of Jerusalem. The Psalms expressed faith in, and gratitude for, Divine Providence. B. The "Great Hallel," Psalm 136, which is used in the morning service on the Sabbath festivals, and during the Passover seder. This Hallel survived in the Midnight Psalmody known as Hos (Ode) 2.

Haggadah,[42] e. The Song of the Sea,[43] f. The priestly Benediction,[44] g. The Trisagion.[45]

Similarly, the First Ode[46] (*Hos* in Coptic), which is the same biblical text as Exodus 12–15, is sung on the night before Coptic Bright Saturday, the Coptic Easter Eve.[47] It is also part of the Coptic Midnight Praise on Saturdays.[48] From the Greek additions to the *Book of Daniel*,[49] the "Prayer of Azariah" and the "Hymn of the Three Young

---

[42] "Haggadah:" 'The telling', the book containing the passages dealing with the theme of Exodus, recited at Passover Seder. The reading of the Haggadah is based on the verse: 'You shall tell your son on that day: it is because of what the Lord did for me when I came forth out of Egypt (Exodus 13:8).

[43] Exodus 15.

[44] Num. 6 :24–26.

[45] Isa 6:3.

[46] Muftah, et al., "Coptic Music," 1715–47. Authors explain the *Hos* (Odes) as a part in the Service of Psalmody and actually agree on a synagogal origin for these Odes. *Hos* ϩⲱⲥ Coptic derives from Egyptian h–s–j, "to sing, to praise." Burmester refers to them as odes. They are *Hos* One, Song of Moses (Ex. 15:1–21); *Hos* Two, Psalm 136 with an Alleluia refrain in each strophe; *Hos* Three, the Song of the Three Young Men (The Prayer of Azariah and the Song of the Three Holy Children is a lengthy passage that appears after Daniel 3:23 in the Septuagint); and *Hos* Four, Pss 148, 149, and 150. A fragment of papyrus, brought from the Fayyum, and published by W. E. Crum (*Catalogue of the Coptic Manuscripts* 51, 103), contains portions of *Hos* One and Three. Further, part of the Greek text of *Hos* Three has been found on an ostracon dating probably from the fifth century.

[47] Azmy, *Book of Holy Pascha,* 521–24.

[48] *The Holy Psalmody,* 15.

[49] Stone, *Jewish Writings,* 552–53.

Men,"[50] is drawn the Third Ode, which is also sung on the night that precedes "Bright Saturday" and Midnight Praise on Saturdays.[51] The Coptic text is derived from Greek Jewish texts,[52] and the Coptic and Greek forms have similar features.[53] Nickelsburg observes that the two texts, the "Prayer of Azariah" and the "Hymn of the Three Young Men," are in accordance with the Hellenistic Jewish prayers of the late Second Temple era.[54] Common features are that they appear to be antiphonal, have a repetitive refrain, and imitate the repetitive refrain of Psalm 136, which is the Second Ode or *Hos* that precedes this Danielic Hymn in the Coptic *Holy Psalmody*.[55]

---

[50] The additions to the *Book of Daniel* are preserved in the Septuagint and in the Greek version ascribed to Theodotion. The first to quote these songs is Justin Martyr (died 165 CE) in *Apologia* 1:46. See Flusser, "Psalms, Hymns and Prayers," 553.

[51] For "Bright Saturday," see Azmy, *Book of Holy Pascha*, 539–43; for every Saturday Midnight Praise, see *The Holy Psalmody*, 32–39.

[52] Biblical texts as the case of Exodus 15 and the Greek additions (Dn 3:52a–Dn 3:88b) are translated from the Septuagint to particularly the Coptic Sahidic. Depuydt, *Catalogue of Coptic Manuscripts in the Pierpont Morgan Library*, 113.

[53] For the Greek text, see Horst and Newman, *Early Jewish Prayers in Greek*, 181–215; Oegema "Reception of the Book of Daniel in the Early Church," 243–52.

[54] Nickelsburg, "The Bible Rewritten and Expanded," 149–52.

[55] *The Holy Psalmody*, 554. There has been significant work done on the characteristics of Second Temple-era liturgical language, part of the heritage of both Greek and Hebrew speaking Jews, and hence the church as well. See the work of those involved in the SBL project that published the 3 volumes: Boda, Mark J., et al. *Seeking the Favor of God*. Society of Biblical Literature, 2006.

A quick survey of the category of sacrifice and Law also shows the interconnection between Jewish and Coptic practices: the laws of purity for priests, as described in Leviticus 21, are still in effect today in the Coptic priesthood customs. Although the concept of purification is related to many biblical texts, but it is particularly prominent in the Coptic Church. Furthermore, when considered alongside the Pseudepigrapha of the *Testament of Levi*, which states: "Before you enter the sanctuary, bathe; while you are sacrificing, wash; and again, when sacrifice is concluded, wash."[56] it is clear why the Coptic priest still rigorously follows this liturgical requirement during Mass.[57]

It is significant that some reminiscences from the *Letter of Aristeas*,[58] a letter believed to be a composition of an Alexandrian Jew from between 170 and 100 BCE, concerning the translation of the Torah from Hebrew to Greek, are found in the *Coptic Synaxarium*.[59] In the *Synaxarium*, a liturgical reading under the eighth day of the

---

[56] Schiffman, *Texts and Traditions*, 353.

[57] Coptic priests wash their feet before the Morning Service (old tradition) and wash their hands before, during, and at the washing of the vessels at the end of the mass.

[58] Thackeray, ed., *The Letter of Aristeas*. The first major section of the *Letter* recounts the events surrounding Ptolemy's request for a translation of the Law. See Nickelsburg, "Stories of Biblical and Early Post-Biblical Times," 75–80.

[59] The *Synaxarium*, also called *Synaxarion*, is a compilation of hagiographies of saints and martyrs, a Coptic liturgical book, which according to the day, is read just before the Gospel during the mass. For more details on the legacy of the Synaxarium, see Atiya, "Copto–Arabic Synaxarion," 2171–90.

Coptic month of Amshir,[60] shows a combination of the translation event with the feast of "Presenting the Lord Christ in the Temple." Simeon the Elder (as portrayed in Luke 2:29–32) is believed to be one of the 70 elders who translated the Old Testament from Hebrew to Greek. The Coptic narrative seems to extend the story of the Septuagint to emphasize the virginity of Mary, the mother of Jesus. The *Synaxarium* states that Ptolemy Soter, in the year 296 BCE:

> Put every two of them [the Torah translators] in an isolated place so they would not agree on one translation and to ensure a correct text after comparing all of the translations. Simeon the elder was one of them. When Simeon was translating the verse from Isaiah 7:14, Behold, the virgin shall conceive and bear a Son, and shall call His name Immanuel, he was afraid to translate that a virgin would conceive, because the King would mock him. He wanted to translate the virgin as a young lady. He was disturbed because of this inaccurate translation, and God revealed to him in a vision that he would not die before he would see Christ the Lord born of a virgin.[61]

Locating an apocryphal or pseudepigraphal text of the Old Testament in the Coptic literature as seen previously in the case of *Hos* 3 (Daniel Greek addition) or the Egyptian *Synaxarium*, or one such as the *Letter of Aristeas*, should not be a surprise. Hellenistic Jewish writings were also quoted by some early Church Fathers,

---

[60] Amshir (Meshir, Coptic) is the sixth month of the Coptic calendar.
[61] *Coptic Synaxarium*, 1, 273–74.

as they perceived them to be reliable. For instance, by the first century, the Greek version of *1 Enoch*[62] was already a popular story in Alexandrian Jewish circles.[63] Pearson finds that Origen, well-known scholar, and early Alexandrian theologian (184–254 CE), while he was still in Alexandria, quotes *1 Enoch* 21.1 and 19 in his treatise, *On First Principles.* Origen introduces his quotations with the words, "Enoch speaks thus in his book" and "in the same book, Enoch himself being the speaker."[64] In his *Commentary on John*, Origen adds, "Jared was born to Maleleel, as it is written from the Book of Enoch…"[65] It

---

[62] The earliest books of 1 *Enoch* (known as *Ethiopic Apocalypse of Enoch*) are the *Book of the Watchers* and the *Astronomical Book*, which date to the third century BCE. The latest book of *1 Enoch* is the *Similitudes,* which dates to the first century BCE/CE. The book of *2 Enoch (*known as *Slavonic Apocalypse of Enoch)* survived in a number of Slavonic manuscripts, which date from the fourteenth to the eighteenth centuries CE. Some Coptic fragments were discovered in Qasr Ibrim (Nubia, Egypt). For more details, see Knibb, "Ethiopic Apocalypse of Enoch," 585–87; also, Orlov, "Slavonic Apocalypse of Enoch," 587–90. The *Enoch* books occupy an important place in the Coptic tradition. Both books (*1* and *2 Enoch*) need a detailed investigation. See Schiffman, *Texts and Tradition*, 336–52; Bautch, *Geography of 1 Enoch 17–19*; Vanbeek, "1 Enoch Among Jews and Christians,*"* 93–116. For the alleged priesthood of Enoch, see Bow, "Melchizedek's Birth Narrative in 2 Enoch," 33–42.

[63] Pearson, "Enoch in Egypt," 217.

[64] Pearson, "Enoch in Egypt," 219.

[65] Pearson, "Enoch in Egypt," 219. Here the author quotes Origen's saying from *Anti–Nicene Fathers* 10.371.

was only later, when Origen moved to Caesarea, that he started to doubt the authenticity of Enoch's Books.[66]

Apparently, late Second Temple writings already were being entrenched in the Alexandrian Church by the first Jewish-Christians believers during the first century. The next generation of Alexandrian Church leaders systematically ignored such things as Origen's statement about the apocryphal and pseudepigraphal biblical additions. Thus, it is hardly surprising that Athanasius, the bishop of Alexandria (296–373), in an abjuratory discourse in his Paschal Letter of 367, writes: "Who has made the simple folk believe that those books belong to Enoch even though no Scriptures existed before Moses?"[67]

This preliminary investigation into literary interactions between Jewish sources and Coptic tradition has led to the formulation of a hypothesis that asserts the instrumental role of Alexandrian Judaism in the comprehension of both the New Testament and the Pauline Epistles, as well as the Jewish roots of the early Alexandrian Church. The juxtaposition of these fragments offers a potential avenue for the reconstruction of the origins of the early Egyptian church, whilst concomitantly unveiling the Jewish origins of its primary liturgical texts, namely the Coptic Midnight Praise, Morning and Evening Services, and the Eucharist. This ambitious statement

---

[66] In his treatise *Against Celsus*, Origen states: "the books entitled Enoch are not generally held to be divine by the churches." Here Pearson, "Enoch in Egypt," 219, quotes Chadwick (trans.), *Origen: Contra Celsum,* 306.

[67] Pearson, "Enoch in Egypt," 219, quotes Brakke, *Athanasius and Politics of Asceticism*, 330.

should be considered with a degree of caution. With regard to Judaism, there is still no evidence that this can extend back into the Second Temple period from what emerges after the Temple's destruction. The paucity of extant information regarding the emergence of phenomena in the period under discussion, in the geographical area of the Land of Israel, outside of rabbinic circles, remains a significant lacuna in the field. The influence of rabbinic circles in Egypt is a topic that requires dedicated research to fully explore and comprehend.[68]

Both Jewish and Coptic liturgical practices are highly conservative in order to protect the faith tradition, the liturgical practices, and the customs against any forfeiture, manipulation, or modification. It is because of this conservation in that there is potential to find significant parallels. Likewise, while the Oral Torah[69] targets the

---

[68] This important advice is owed to R. Langer.

[69] Ancient rabbis grounded legal innovation in their claim to possess an Oral Torah (*Torah she-ba'al peh*) first revealed to Moses on Sinai alongside the Written Torah (*Torah she-bich'tav*) that it seeks to elucidate. The Oral Torah was passed down as oral tradition (hence the name) until the destruction of the Second Temple (70 CE), when fear of it being lost forever led to it being committed to writing for the first time. Traditionally, Oral Torah refers to the later works of the rabbinic period i.e., Mishnah and the Gemara: jointly known as Talmud. For Jewish oral tradition, see Elman and Gershoni, *Transmitting Jewish Traditions*; Gerhardsson, *Memory and Manuscript*; Neusner, *The Oral Torah* (Gerhardsson' work was debated later by Jaffee "How much Orality in the oral Torah?" and Smith, "A Comparison of Early Christian and Early Rabbinic Tradition;" Schimmel, *The Oral Law*. Many scholars argue that it is better to understand the Oral Torah to be fewer specific teachings than the methods of interpreting and applying

protection of unwritten Moses' teachings as he heard it from the mouth of God, the oral tradition in the Coptic Church resembles the sanctuary where the inherited elements of Hellenistic Judaism were kept virtually intact.

3. The Concept of "Judaism" and Some Coptic Observances

The term 'Judaism' is generally regarded as an abstract noun, denoting the culture of the people of Judah, which was the name of the country during the Second Temple period. However, given that the focus of this section pertains to Coptic observances that bear a potential Jewish lineage, the application of the concept of Halakhah (Hebrew, commonly translated in the LXX as nomos) appears more pertinent. This concept will be further elaborated upon in the subsequent sections, wherein the terms "tradition of their fathers" and "way of life" are employed. Jews aimed by their strict customs to thoroughly keep the "tradition of their fathers" as registered in New Testament.[70] Beyond question, in the Diaspora, this strict lifestyle marked the uniqueness of the Jewish society, especially when they lived or worked next to inhabitants who held very different beliefs. Their customs strictly complied with the Mosaic Law in various observances: e.g., circumcision, dietary patterns, keeping the Sabbath, and many others. At the beginning of the Hellenistic era

---

the written teachings to new circumstances. For Coptic oral tradition, see Malaty, *Tradition and Orthodoxy*; Awadalah, *Manaret El Akdas*, 6–16; Muftah, et al., "Coptic Music," 1715–47.

[70] Matt 15:2; Mark 7:3, 5.

(300 BCE), this lifestyle was already noticed and praised by the Greek historian, Hecataeus of Adbara. Despite the absence of substantiating evidence, the hypothesis that Judaism exhibited uniformity with regard to the observance of "tradition of their fathers" and "way of life" during the Second Temple era remains unsupported. The compendium of practices cited herein was indeed pervasive; however, it is improbable that it represented the totality of Judaism. It is evident that this "Judaism(s)" was one of the primary distinguishing features of Egyptian Jews, as well as in every region of the diaspora.

Diasporic Jews faced major challenges in maintaining their "ancestors' traditions", especially after Alexander the Great (356–323 BCE) overcame Darius III of Persia. Seeman observes that the accession of Alexander was met with "far-reaching consequences for Jews"[71] which had previously been the case with Babylonian and Persian cultures. Their encounter with a more expansive world, characterized by divergent dogmas from those delineated in the Old Testament, has been a pivotal aspect of their journey. During this formative period preceding the advent of Christianity, cities such as Rome, Alexandria, and Antioch experienced significant economic growth and attracted numerous Jews, who established thriving and vigorous communities branded by a sense of assurance in their conduct and distinctive identity. The Jews, however, did not perceive the commandments of the Old Testament as "restrictions"; rather, they were preserved as positive directions for "a way of life". [72]

---

[71] Seeman, "Jewish History from Alexander to Hadrian," 25.

[72] Gruen, "Judaism in the Diaspora," 81.

Many aspects of this Judaism, especially when observing it as a lifestyle, are still traceable in the Coptic tradition. The Coptic Church observes strict practices concerning circumcision, rituals surrounding menstruation, weekly two-days fasting,[73] ablution, and many other rituals. The reasons for discussing briefly topics like circumcision and a woman's menstruation in this section is because, although they do not directly influence the discussion of the Morning Service, they do occupy an important place in both Jewish and Coptic customs and give strong evidence of ties between the two in rituals and canons of both traditions. Their peculiar survival in the Coptic Church strengthens the evidence that Jewish influence on the Coptic Church bears significant further investigation. Although these practices are commanded in the Old Testament, this does not necessarily indicate that Judaism is the source. The key question is why the Coptic Church chose to implement these practises so vigorously, unlike other Christian denominations.

As I have mentioned, one example of the influence of Jewish regulations on Coptic practice can be seen in how the Copts strictly followed the practice of circumcision, at least until the mid-twentieth century in the main cities. It is still in effect in rural areas. On the eighth day after birth, the infant is circumcised.[74] On that day, family and friends gather to celebrate this event. Murqus Ibn Qanbar, a reformer of the late twelfth century, pleaded for the abolition of circumcision even though it was required

---

[73] In the Jewish tradition, the fasting is on Monday and Thursday; the Coptic days of fasting are Wednesday and Friday.

[74] Lev 12:2–3.

before infant baptism.[75] His petition included other items, such as confession to the priest and the administration of the Eucharist, but these were strongly opposed by the official defenders of Coptic morals and customs.[76] A historical view of this practice can be beneficial in understanding its inclusion in the Alexandrian Church. During the Hellenistic period, Greeks brought serious cultural and political pressure against the Jews who were strictly obeying the Mosaic Law in observing the act of circumcision.[77] Greeks detested the practice and considered it a barbaric mutilation of the human body. The book of *Maccabees* depicts this conflict in some daily challenges. Jews, who were eager to assimilate to the Greek culture, faced stigmas in participating at the athletic games in the Gymnasium.[78] To avoid such challenges, they performed "epispasm,"[79] a practice that reached a peak of popularity during the first century.[80] In a very informative article by David DeSilva,[81] the author mentions that in Alexandria, Philo (died circa 50 CE) defended the practice

---

[75] The male infant is baptized 40 days after his birth and the female 80 days after. See Georg Graf, *Eine Reforversuch innerhalb der Koptischen Kirche im Zwölften Jahrhundert*; Beaugé, "Un Réformateur copte au XIIe siècle," 5–34.

[76] Frederick, "Murqus Ibn Qanbar," 1699–1700; Basilios, "Baptism," 336–39.

[77] Gen 17:12, 14.

[78] 2 Macc 4:13–15.

[79] A surgical procedure, an operation that "corrected" a circumcised penis. Some might call it circumcision in reverse. See Hall, "Epispasm," 52–57.

[80] Hall, "Epispasm: Circumcision in Reverse," 52–57.

[81] deSilva, "Circumcision," 139–40.

of circumcision. He wrote about the hygienic benefits of being circumcised, the ritual purity, and fertility.[82] The ethical meaning of the practice, as expressed and promoted by Philo, reflects that this practice was strictly in effect, and that it was an issue within the Jewish community in Egypt. Therefore, this raises some questions: did this Jewish practice enter the Coptic ethical life through the first Judeo-Christians of Alexandria or just in fulfillment of the Mosaic Law? Why does the Coptic tradition cherish the rite of circumcision and link it to baptism (as was the case during Ibn Kanbar's time)? The mirroring of Jewish practice by Coptic Christians demands a closer inquiry of the pseudepigrapha and Dead Sea Scrolls, where this topic is treated at length.[83]

The second example of the influence of Jewish laws on Coptic practice can be seen in how the Coptic Church still watches over a woman's purification as stated in the Book of Leviticus, where God equates her uncleanness during her menstruation cycle with her impurity after giving birth to either a son or a daughter.[84] The language of the "Tohorot"[85] sections in different Jewish books, such

---

[82] deSilva, "Circumcision," 139, mentions the Philonic sources *Spec. Laws* 1.1.1–1.2.11.

[83] Bernat, "Circumcision," 471–74. It is difficult to clearly demonstrate that circumcision in the Coptic Church predates Islam or wasn't influenced by Arab circumcision. However, this could still be consistent with the practice of 'biblicizing' it by observing the eighth day.

[84] Lev 12:1–8; Lev 15:19–33.

[85] This is one of the six "orders" of the Mishnah and Tosefta (usually considered in that order). Within it is the "tractate" Niddah which is

as the Tosefta and the Mishna,[86] resounds also in the Coptic Canons. The church requires that the man abstain from sexual intercourse with his wife until her child is weaned. Concerning her fellowship with the congregation, the woman may enter the church, but she is forbidden to receive the Eucharist. The Coptic Church formulated the rules of a woman's purification as early as the third century. The Second Canon of Dionysius the archbishop of Alexandria (died circa 265 CE) states: "concerning the menstruating woman, whether they ought to enter the temple of God while in such a state, I think it superfluous even to put the question. For I opine, not even they themselves, being faithful and pious, would dare when in this state either to approach the Holy Table or to touch the body and blood of Christ."[87] Bishop Youssef notes that in this Canon, Dionysius conflates Christian altar with the Temple space.[88] It is surprising that he did not connect such early regulations with a potential influence of the Jewish community in Egypt. Despite many other Levitical ordinances, the question is why the woman's purification with its detailed regulations was still conveyed in the

---

specifically about menstrual impurity (which is somewhat different from childbirth impurity). Other tractates are also relevant.

[86] Neusner, *The Tosefta*, the section of "Niddah" deals with the woman's menstruation laws, 1779–1808; Danby, *Tractate Sanhedrin*, 745–57.

[87] Youssef, *Encyclopedia of Christian Q & A*, 699–701.

[88] Youssef, *Encyclopedia of Christian Q & A*, 701.

thirteen-century Church Canons as in *Misbah al-Zulmah* book of Ibn Kabar.[89]

4. Conclusion: An Embryonic Stage for a New "Judeo-Copto" Scholarship

In this introduction, I have depicted some of several Jewish signatures in the Coptic tradition that help to initiate a new direction in studying the origins of the Coptic Church liturgy and to contribute to its early historical reconstruction. As seen previously, the Jewish community in Egypt was an important target for the early Christian mission. Surely this is an important consideration in evaluating and probing the early stage of Egyptian Church history. Searching for similarities and digging into the late Second Temple era writings (200 BCE–70 CE), the early Jewish prayers, and rabbinic dictums, opens a wide door for locating the roots of some fundamental Coptic rituals and particularly the Coptic Morning Service, which forms the core of my thesis. This is an exciting study, because linking the two traditions wasn't feasible in the past. Judeo-Christian studies saw its momentum only during the last fifty years, while scholarship that perceives a possible Jewish core at the heart of the Egyptian Christianity has been on the rise only for the last twenty-five years.[90] This

---

[89] Ibn Kabar was a Coptic scholar, born at the end of the thirteenth century. He wrote an encyclopedia of Coptic ecclesiology in twenty-four sections, with numerous supplements, under the title of *Misbah al-Zulmah, Fi Idah al-Khidmah*. For his biography, see Atiya, "Ibn Kabar," 1267–68. For the canons in regard to the menstruation, see Ibn Kabar, *Misbah al-Zulmah*, 114, 138.

[90] In Chapter 2, I will discuss some of the history of the research and will highlight some of the recent scholarship.

thesis lays a foundation for a new Judeo-Coptic scholarship, which could advance Coptic liturgical studies significantly.

This book also targets an important lacuna in the spirituality of the contemporary Coptic worshipper. The mysteries and puzzles that surround many Coptic liturgical components prevent contemporary Coptic parishioners from praying with understanding (1 Cor. 14:15). The twenty-first century Copt needs a sort of "Halakah" guidance towards their worshipping practices.

The conclusion of this preliminary discourse demands a pivotal assertion: The investigation into the existence of numerous Jewish elements within the Coptic Church presented a considerable challenge. Despite the numerous significant similarities that will be demonstrated between the two liturgies, and the clear evidence of the deep embedding of Jewish traditions in the Coptic liturgical tradition, it is nearly impossible to prove precisely how the one was transferred to the other. An examination of historical documents pertaining to the early Egyptian Church reveals an absence of any explicit mention or reference to this matter. It is therefore important to be aware that an investigation of this nature is susceptible to anachronism. The socio-religious details of the community of the Jews of Egypt are of particular interest, as are their religious communal life as an integral part of the global Hellenistic Judaism, and their ties with the Jews of the Land of Israel.

Chapter 1
Research History, Problems, and Possibilities

My argument aims to demonstrate a clear Jewish impact on the early stage of the Alexandrian Church liturgy as seen in the Coptic Morning Service.[91] As I mentioned in the introduction, the primary historical facts of the Jewish legacy on some Coptic historical and liturgical facts; the notion of a Jewish impact on the Coptic Orthodox Church have not yet formed a dedicated team of Coptic liturgists or historians, to adhere to such academic path. However, tracing the Jewish influence on a crucial ritual such as the Coptic Morning Service has compelled me to enlarge my scope of understanding how primary sources describe the early days of the Church, how especially Coptic scholars picture its primitive seed, and how the Coptic Church perceives its origin. These stimulating avenues of scholarship represent the current research history of my argument.

Traditionally, most Coptic Church historians remain undecided to its origin. Some scholars observe a possible influence of Egyptian, Greek, or Jewish, without specifying which "influence" had the most impact on the

---

[91] The Ritual Raising of Incense occurs ideally twice daily in the evening and early morning after the Office of Midnight Praise and before the Holy Mass. This service entails the burning of incense, a thanksgiving prayer, numerous supplications (according to the appointed time: evening or morning) and finally the priestly blessing. For more details, please see Chapter 3.

church's beginning or exactly on which aspect, i.e., liturgy, practices, customs, art, liturgical cantillation, etc. The most common scholarly consensus is that Alexandria is considered the cradle of Christianity in Egypt because of its larger Jewish community in the diaspora. Alexandria was also an attractive target for early Christian missions. This important seaport city was a true melting pot "for many ethnic cultures, and the city itself was subject to a wide range of local developments, which created and formatted a distinct Alexandrian 'culture' as well as several distinct 'cultures.'"[92]

Depending on the scope of their research interests, some church historians perceive a mixture of cultures in the Coptic Church: This includes Egyptian, Greek, and Byzantine influences, which places the aura of the Church's origins in a gloomy sky. I would describe it as a broad-spectrum monograph about the Coptic Church, in which the authors lightly discuss the Church's origins. For example, a Professor of History at the University of Utah, Aziz Atiya, states in his book, *The Copts and Christian Civilization* (1979), "The origins of Coptic Christianity need no great elaboration. St. Mark the Evangelist is its recognized founder and first patriarch, in the fourth decade of the first century."[93] In other words, Atiya determines that no scholarly investigation is needed, and no other notions regarding the origins of the Coptic Church need to be considered. On the other hand, John Watson observes that worship in churches in Egypt reverberates different resonances with various cultural impacts. In *Among the*

---

[92] Hinge and Krasilnikoff, "Introduction," 9.

[93] Atiya, *The Copts and Christian Civilization*, 2.

Copts (2000), he writes, "the worship in Coptic churches conveys the sights and sounds of the mystical, Semitic and antique. From the moment when the Oriental Orthodox priest begins to sing the exquisite Arabic Melisma, the newcomer is beguiled."[94] Jill Kamil, on the other hand, in *Christianity in the Land of the Pharaohs* (2002),[95] bases her view of the Coptic Church ritual on personal observation during her stay in Egypt, although without any documented evidence. She is inclined towards a Pharaonic impact on the Copts in their social customs and church rituals.

In this chapter, I will group scholars interested in digging into the Coptic Church origins or the history of early Egyptian Christianity under different categories. The first group consists of historians who mainly attempt to find the origins of the Coptic Church through the early history of the Alexandrian papacy. The second category brings together scholars who do find some Jewish trace or seed in the origins of the Coptic Church. Their evidence and conclusions are vital for this dissertation to strengthen my case for a Jewish seed in the Coptic Church. Finally, the third category assesses the authors of the Coptic catechism books who study Church history and its liturgy.

---

[94] Watson, *Among the Copts*, 2.

[95] Kamil, *Christianity in the Land of the Pharaohs*. Instead of understanding the Philonic concept of the "Logos," the author tries to find its legacy in the Memphite doctrine, or cosmogony, which is regarded as a more sophisticated story of the creation than those of Heliopolis or Hermopolis. See p. 97. Also, she attempts to locate several biblical terms, such as in Genesis 1 and in John's Gospel, "the Creator spoke," within ancient Egyptian and gnostic literatures, see pp. 98, and 104–105.

Within this collection of writings, I will display how religious stories are considered an authoritative source in describing the early phases of the Church, regardless of their veracity.

After looking at these three groups, I will examine some problems with the existing hypotheses and theories to bring together evidence obtained from their findings that could be beneficial for a new scholarly orientation towards the origins of the Coptic Church, especially of its liturgy. When comparing these points of view with my search for evidence of a Jewish foundation in the Coptic liturgy, new criteria for evolving a fresh hypothesis will develop.

1. Historians Who Focus on the Early Alexandrian Papacy

The first group deals with historians who mainly attempt to study the early history of the Coptic Church through the biographies of the Alexandrian popes, highlighting the early traditions of St. Mark as the founder of the Alexandrian Church.

The *Church History* of Eusebius[96] (also known as *Historia Ecclesiastica*) is the first monograph, dating from the fourth century, that includes the evangelization of Egypt by St. Mark and his martyrdom in Alexandria. The

---

[96] Eusebius of Caesarea (c. 260–c. 340 CE) was a Roman historian of Greek descent. Eusebius' fame principally rests on his important book, *Historia Ecclesiastica*, which rightly earned for him the title "Father of Church History." When Caesarea became a center of persecution of Christians, he decided to flee to Tyre. From there he went to Egypt. In 313, he returned to Caesarea, where he was elected as its bishop in 315. See Atiya, "Eusebius of Caesarea," 1070–7.

Eusebius tradition wanted to present this apostolic figure as the founder of the Church of Alexandria after Mark's appointment of Anianus (the Greek name of Heb. Hananiah) as his successor in pastoring the followers of Christ in Egypt.[97] Starting from the fourth century; this tradition became the primary source of the apostolicity seed of the Coptic Church, which later entailed many traditions surrounding the ordination of the bishop of Alexandria (later called pope).[98] The Eusebius tradition heavily impacted the views of many following historians. Therefore, looking over the Coptic primary sources in this regard is worthwhile.

We find a monumental work from the tenth century called *Siyar al-Bi'ah al-Muqaddasah* ("*Biographies of the Holy Church*").[99] It was first translated and studied by Basil Evetts in 1904 when the Arabic title became the

---

[97] Eusebius, *Ecclesiastical History,* 2.24.1 (ed. E. Shwartz and T. Mommsen, 1903). Eusebius in the same book (2.15) also describes how Mark wrote his Gospel in Rome in response to several appeals from the Christians in Alexandria. In another book, also written by Eusebius, titled *Chronicles*, the author places Mark's arrival in Alexandria in 43 CE, the third year of Claudius' reign. In chapter 2:16, Eusebius tells us about Mark's mission in Alexandria and his establishment of churches (2.16.1–2). For book 2, chapters 15, 16 and 24, see Crusé, *The Ecclesiastical History*, 64–66 and 79–81.

[98] Traditions and liturgical symbols surrounding the ordination and the enthronement of the pope of Alexandria will be examined with the book of *Siyar al-Bi'ah al-Muqaddasah* attributed to Severus Ibn al-Mukaffa.

[99] Also known as *Tarikh Batarikat al-Kanisah al-Misriyah.*

History of the Patriarchs of Alexandria.[100] The *Siyar* was composed, in various epochs, by Coptic authors who recorded the history of the Church, and each one of them continued the work of his predecessor.[101] The consensus regarding the book's authorship is that it is attributed to Sawirus (Severus) ibn al-Mukaffa', who died in 987 CE.[102]

---

[100] The book of *Siyar al-Bi'ah al-Muqaddasah* preoccupied many scholars. Eusebe Rénaudot (1713) published the Latin translation known as *Historia Patriarcharum: Alexandrinorum Jacobitarum.* Evetts published and translated different parts from Severus' book between 1904 and 1910. See his work in *Patrologia Orientalis,* part 1 (1904), part 2 (1907), part 3 (1910).

[101] Den Heijer, "History of the Patriarchs of Alexandria," 1239–42. Heijer contests its attribution to Severus ibn al-Mukaffa as he considers him only a collector of popes' biographies from earliest sources. After Severus ibn al-Mukaffa, this tenth-century book was continued by Michael, bishop of Tinnis (11th century). He wrote in Coptic and covers the epoch between 880 to 1046 CE. Mawhub ibn Mansur ibn Mufarrig, deacon from Alexandria, and finally Pope Mark III, covers the epoch of 1131 to 1167.

[102] Severus is a well-known erudite on many subjects: first, on theological science, where he discussed all types of problems from the Coptic viewpoint. Second, he composed a number of items on Coptic traditions and liturgical practices. Third, he displayed an extraordinary knowledge of exegetical and biblical studies. A scholar like Atiya assumes that Severus must have memorized the whole Bible and that he was able to quote it freely in his disputation with Rabbi Moses in the presence of the Fatimid caliph al-Mu'izz in 975. Fourth, he proved himself to be the great champion of Coptic Christianity in works defending its doctrines against the intense attacks of the Melchite patriarch Eutychius (also known as Sa'id ibn Bitriq), a favorite of the Fatimid caliphs. In 950, Severus composed his book on the councils in reply to an abusive treatise by Eutychius. For his main works, see Atiya, "Sawirus Ibn Al-Muqaffa," 2100–103.

He was the bishop of al-Ashmunayn,[103] because of his erudition, he was highly venerated by contemporary patriarchs, respected by the Fatimid caliphs, and beloved and appreciated by noted figures of his day. The text of Severus regarding Mark's foundation of the Coptic Church demonstrates his dependence on Eusebius' opinions in his *Church History*.[104]

At the end of the nineteenth century, Edith Butcher, in *The Story of the Church of Egypt* (1897), mentions that St. Mark seems to have been accompanied by St. Peter to preach the Gospel in a city called Babylon in Egypt.[105] Montague Fowler, in *Christian Egypt: Past, Present and Future* (1902), also asserts that the Coptic Church's founder is St. Mark.[106] Although these are not scholarly books, they represent the current and common opinion among Copts, regarding the origins of the Coptic Church, and maintained throughout the twentieth century.

The early twenty-first century witnessed some remarkable work concerning the Coptic Church's history. In *Early Coptic Papacy*, Stephen Davis (2004) looks at the *History of Patriarchs* narrated by Severus and his predecessors with an eye of critique. In his first volume, he analyzes the development of the Egyptian papacy from its origins to the rise of Islam. In searching for the historical

---

[103] Al-Ashmunayn is the ancient Hermopolis Magna in the district of Antinopolis, new called El Sheikh Ibada, a small village in Upper Egypt.
[104] Seybold, "Severus: Historia Patriarcharum Alexandrinorum," 1, 2–3; 16–22.
[105] Butcher, *The Story of the Church of Egypt,* 19.
[106] Fowler, *Christian Egypt,* 2.

Mark, he finds that the New Testament writings do not connect the apostle with any Christian mission to Alexandria,[107] but rather to Pamphylia with Paul and Barnabas. The figure of Mark is also related to Peter. On this topic, Davis lists scholars[108] who question whether the Mark of 1 Peter[109] is the same person mentioned by Luke in Acts.[110] Early writings that connect Mark with Peter are inconsistent in providing clear information about Mark. Davis mentions that many early traditions surrounding the writings of the canonical Gospel of Mark were conjectured.

Most importantly, Davis observes the sources where Mark is portrayed as the founder of the Egyptian Church, including an essential quotation from Eusebius' book, the *History of the Church*, that must not be overlooked. Eusebius states: "Now they say that this Mark was the first to have set out to Egypt to preach the Gospel, which he had already written down for himself, and the first to have organized churches in Alexandria itself."[111] The language used by Eusebius shows that his knowledge about Mark's writing of his Gospel, and his organization of

---

[107] Davis, *The Early Coptic Papacy*, 2–4, sketches the figure of St. Mark through the New Testament. Mark is known as John Mark (Acts 12:12, 25), a companion of the early mission with Paul and Barnabas, who was Mark's cousin (Col 4:10), and known as a helper (13:5). He traveled with Paul and Barnabas to Pamphylia in Asia Minor where he left them and returned to Jerusalem (Acts 13:13). The consequence of his decision created a quarrel between Paul and Barnabas (Acts 15:39–40).

[108] For a list of scholars who debate this issue, see Davis, *Early Coptic Papacy,* 182 note 5.

[109] 1 Pet 5:13.

[110] Acts 12:12; 12:25; 13:5; 13:13; 15:37–39.

[111] Eusebius, *Historia Ecclesiastica* 2.16.1.

churches in Alexandria, is based on an oral tradition: "Now they say." Davis finds a controversial text attributed to Clement of Alexandria that refers to Mark's mission to Alexandria, where it states, he wrote his Gospel.[112] This document intrigues Davis as it corroborates John Chrysostom's saying about that.[113] But the authenticity of the text remains questionable. Davis also cites a lengthy quotation from Clement of Alexandria's letter, where he attests to the existence of Christians before Mark's arrival and the fact that he wrote his gospel for them.[114] The inaccuracies in the earliest information about Mark's activities and martyrdom in Alexandria "led to rise of oral traditions that tried to fill in the historical gaps."[115] A specific fourth-century text called 'Acts of Mark' — from which I believe the Coptic Synaxarium sourced Mark's biography — contains three significant accounts: Mark's establishment of the Church; his encounter with Anianus, the shoemaker (Mark's successor); and his martyrdom on the outskirts of Alexandria. The earliest of Mark's successors, as listed by Eusebius[116] includes a brief chronology, but according to Davis, there is almost nothing

---

[112] Davis, *Early Coptic Papacy*, 8. For the scholars who deal with Clement's attributed letter and the *Secret Gospel*, see 184 note 30.

[113] Davis quotes from John Chrysostom, *Homily on Matthew* 1.3 (*Patrologia Graeco)*, and from B.A. Pearson, "Earliest Christianity."

[114] For this lengthy quotation, see Davis, *Early Coptic Papacy*, 8–9.

[115] Davis, *Early Coptic Papacy*, 9.

[116] Eusebius, *Ecclesiastical History,* follows the successors of Mark chronologically: Anianus 2:29; Abilius 3:14; Primus 4:1; Justus 4:4; Eumenes 4:5; Mercianus 4:11; Celadion 4:11; Aggripinus 4:19; Julian 5:9; Demetrius 5:22.

about their lives and the leadership of the church during their time.

Despite many early documents dated from the second century examined by Davis, we find him quoting from Walter Bauer (whose work will be discussed later) that this lack of information about the Church's origin and the earliest of Mark's successors is "a mere echo and a puff of smoke."[117]

This longstanding Coptic tradition about St. Mark's mission, his gospel, his visit, and his martyrdom at Alexandria is repeated in countless monographs. Furthermore, we find that the relic of St. Mark also maintains an ongoing history, especially by Coptic scholars, for it continues to be tied to the liturgical ceremony of the new pope's ordination and enthronement even today. Otto Meinardus (2000) has been preoccupied with tracing its narrative from the earlier period to its "translation"[118] from Alexandria to Venice in the eighth century.[119]

2. *Scholars Who Consider a Gnostic or Jewish Seed of the Coptic Church*

This group of scholars ignores the Eusebian traditions about Mark as the founder of the Church and tries to find other evidence for the roots of Christianity in Egypt.

---

[117] Davis, *Early Coptic Papacy*, 14. Davis quotes Bauer, *Orthodoxy and Heresy*, 45.

[118] The "translation of relics" is the removal of the remains of the saint's body from one locality to another.

[119] Meinardus, *Two Thousand Years of Coptic Christianity*, 28–30.

Walter Bauer (1971) notes that the earliest predominant form of Christianity in Egypt was heretical, specifically Gnostic. He questions: "What reason could [churchmen] have had for being silent about the origins of Christianity in such an important center as Alexandria if there had been something favorable to report?"[120] Such a question encouraged Colin Roberts (1979) to investigate the issue of the obscurity of the early stage of the Church in the field of papyrology.[121] The importance of Roberts' survey is his finding of extant Christian manuscripts from the second century CE (there is no manuscript evidence from the first century).[122] He discovers in these literary sources a remarkable scribal feature: the "nomina sacra,"[123] which he

---

[120] Bauer, *Orthodoxy and Heresy*, 45. See also, Modrzejewski, *The Jews of Egypt*, 227. Bauer pursues the enigma of the silence of first-century documents. He sees that the reason for such silence is due to the annihilation of primitive Christianity along with the entire body in which it was immersed, i.e., the Jewish community. See also Pearson, *Gnosticism and Christianity*, 15.

[121] Roberts, *Manuscript, Society and Belief*. Prior to Roberts were Bell and Skeat, who, in *Fragments of an Unknown Gospel*, edited three different papyri from Egypt: an unknown gospel, where they found the tradition of using nomina sacra in scribal practices, two fragments belonging to 2 Chronicles 24: 17–27, and a leaf from a liturgical book that does not mention the name of Christ or Jesus.

[122] Some of Roberts' findings are: seven Old Testament, three New Testament, and four non-biblical gospels known as "Egerton Gospels," *Shepherd of Hermas*, *Gospel of Thomas* 26–28 (P. Oxy. 1), and *Irenaeus Adversus Haereses*. See Roberts, *Manuscript, Society and Belief*, 12–14; see also Pearson, "Earliest Christianity in Egypt," 101.

[123] The term "nomina sacra" (Latin) means "sacred names." It refers to customs of abbreviated writing of several frequently occurring

argues are of Jewish origin.[124] The penchant of scholars who follow Roberts is to continue to locate and investigate the earliest texts of the biblical manuscript and the Christian Church, which could offer further hope in locating the earliest foundations of the Egyptian Church.[125]

There is a noticeable gap in the scholarly assessments between those dismissive of a heretical origin and those open to the possibility of a Jewish Alexandrian seed. I will trace the studies that claim the potential of a Jewish origin by the chronology of their publications. In 1924, Idris Bell and Walter Crum tackled the theme of Alexandrian Judaism by focusing on translating the Greek *Letter of Claudius to the Alexandrines* (41 CE).[126] They also cite three other Coptic texts whose contents do not

---

divine names or titles in early Holy Scripture used in Greek, Latin, and Coptic manuscripts. Frequent nomina sacra include the words for God, Lord, Jesus, Christ, Son, Spirit, cross, Israel, Savior, Jerusalem, Man, and Heaven. Almost the same nomina sacra exist in the liturgical Coptic books. Concerning the nomina sacra in the Sahidic dialect, see Shisha-Halevy, "Sahidic," 194–202, and Hurtado, *The Earliest Christian Artifacts*, 95–110. The author mentions their provenance from Jewish as well as Coptic manuscripts. Kruger, *The Gospel of the Savior: An Analysis of P. Oxy. 840*, 57–60, traces many nomina sacra in this gospel.

[124] Roberts, *Manuscript, Society and Belief*, 26–34; see also Pearson, "Earliest Christianity in Egypt," 133.

[125] Bagnall, *Early Christian Books in Egypt*, 1–25, in predicting that the early Coptic history is "a puff of smoke," looks to papyrology to locate evidence against the view of a heretical origin of the Egyptian Church.

[126] Bell and Crum, *Jews and Christians in Egypt*. The other texts cited in this book are: the Meletian schism, the rights of the Alexandrines, and the correspondence of Paphnutius.

reflect the book title. In the book authored by Leslie Barnard, *The Apostolic Fathers and their Background* (1966), the author dedicates a chapter to Judaism in Egypt during the period of 70 to 135 CE, where he claims that the Epistle of Barnabas has been unnoticed by scholars, describing this epistle as a "piece of evidence for the understanding of Egyptian Judaism during this period."[127] He believes that the author is an Alexandrian rabbi who converted to Christianity,[128] for the author's division of the Epistle into Haggadah (Chapters 1–17) and Halakhah (Chapters 18–20) makes the text "strongly rabbinic," the Pesharim method adopted by the author in interpreting the Old Testament.[129] The Epistle also describes the religious life of the Jews of that period. Barnard argues as a conclusion to this Judeo-Christian book that the period of 70–135 CE witnessed the preparation for the triumph in Egypt of Pharisaic Judaism over Hellenistic and sectarian Judaism.[130]

Martiniano Roncaglia, in *Histoire de l'Église Copte* (1969), argues the possibility of a Jerusalemite origin of

---

[127] Barnard, *The Apostolic Fathers and their Background*, 46.

[128] Barnard, *The Apostolic Fathers and their Background*, 47.

[129] The word Hebrew word "pesharim" means "interpretation." It became known from one group of texts, numbering some hundreds, among the Dead Sea Scrolls. The "pesharim" give a theory of scriptural interpretation previously partly known, but now fully defined. The writers of "pesharim" believe that Scripture is written on two levels: the surface for ordinary readers with limited knowledge, the concealed one for specialists with higher knowledge. This is most clearly spelled out in the Habakkuk Pesher (1QpHab). See Brownlee, *The Midrash Pesher of Habakkuk*, 26.

[130] Barnard, *The Apostolic Fathers and their Background*, 47.

Egyptian Christianity. He ties the evangelization of Egypt to James who led the Church at its early stage.[131] In 1971, Robert Wilken emphasizes the importance of Judaism in Alexandria,[132] depicting the anti-Semitic attitude of pope Cyril (412–442 CE) towards the Alexandrian Jews.[133] In 1985, Aryeh Kasher outlines his thesis on Jews in Alexandria,[134] and provides details about the condition of the Jewish community in the Egyptian "Chora" and their organization.[135] He pursues two interesting topics: the Alexandrian Jewish community in the Talmud,[136] and the Alexandrian Jews in apocryphal literature.[137] In 1986, Birger Pearson and James Goehring edited a volume of different studies related to the roots of Egyptian

---

[131] Roncaglia, *Histoire de l'Eglise Copte*, 1, 53–62; see also, Pearson, *Gnosticism and Christianity*, 14.

[132] Wilken, *Judaism and the Early Christian Mind*; see his book chapters: "Judaism in Alexandria," 39–54, and "Cyril and the Jews," 54–68.

[133] The papacity period of Cyril (412–442 CE) is far later than the era of the Coptic Church's beginning.

[134] Kasher, *The Jews in Hellenistic and Roman Egypt*.

[135] "Chora" (Greek word) means "a city" ("small city," "a village") outside of a polis. Depicting the chora(s) where the Jews were established, Kasher discloses historical and geographical details that could support future study in examining the religious development (from Judaism to Christianity) of those choras from the late Second Temple era to the time of Cyril I. Scholarship that could help to collect relevant material includes: Amélineau, *La Géographie de l'Egypte Copte*; Viaud, *Les Pélérinages Coptes en Egypte*; Kerkeslager, "Jewish Pilgrimage and Jewish Identity," 99–122.

[136] Kasher, *The Jews in Hellenistic and Roman Egypt*, 346–56.

[137] Kasher, *The Jews in Hellenistic and Roman Egypt*, 208–33.

Christianity.¹³⁸ Contributions that are relevant to my survey include Pearson, "Earliest Christianity in Egypt," and Klijn, "Jewish Christianity in Egypt," where the authors emphasize the importance of the Jewish community at the birth of Christianity in Egypt.

For the last twenty-five years, curiosity about a possible Jewish core at the heart of Egyptian Christianity has been on the rise. The monographs published between 1990 and 2010 have focused on locating this potentiality by different means. Areas where there is a consensus include 1. the flight into Egypt (*Arabic Infancy Gospel* and *The Gospel of Pseudo Mathew*);*¹³⁹*

2. the historical demography of Jews in Alexandria;¹⁴⁰

3. the Christian missions started after the Pentecost feast (Acts 2), after which Jews have to return home with a motive of preaching the true Messiah;

---

[138] Pearson and Goehring (eds), *The Roots of Egyptian Christianity*; see Pearson's article, "Earliest Christianity in Egypt," 132–161, and Klijn's, "Jewish Christianity in Egypt," 161–78.

[139] In both apocryphal sources, the child Jesus is shown as a miracle worker. The *Gospel of Pseudo Mathew* contains not only stories of miracles performed by the child Jesus but also an account of the conversion of the whole city of Hermopolis (actually, town of El Ashmunein, in Al Minya governorate). Many apocryphal stories and legends are associated with the flight into Egypt.

[140] According to Josephus, *The Wars of Jews II* 385, the whole population of Egypt was 7,500,00 and the Jewish Egyptians represented eight percent of the whole population, which is thought to be a proof of Josephus' exaggeration. See, Josephus (trans. by Thackeray), *The Jewish War I–III*, 473–74.

4. the role of Apollos as an Alexandrian Jew in the Early Church as depicted in the New Testament;[141]

5. the uncertainty of who preached in Egypt: Peter[142] or Mark;[143] and

6. the important papyrological finding of C. Roberts,[144] which is regularly noted throughout subsequent scholarship.

Wilfred Griggs, in his book *Early Egyptian Christianity* (1990),[145] demonstrates the potential of Jewish influence for the Egyptian Church through an appraisal of the traditional elements (as mentioned above). Pearson, in *Gnosticism, Judaism, and Egyptian Christianity* (1990), after locating different Jewish elements in Gnosticism, finds that trying to identify the role of Gnosticism in the development of Christianity in Egypt involves a "very difficult problem of assessing just how important that role was." He adds, "The origins of Egyptian Christianity are shrouded in obscurity, owing to a dearth of reliable evidence."[146] Christian Cannuyer, a French scholar, discusses in his article, "L'Ancrage Juif de la

---

[141] Acts 18:24, 19:1; 1 Cor 1:12, 3:4–6, 3:22, 4:6, 16:12; Titus 3:13.

[142] 1 Peter 5:13 shows the probability that Peter wrote from the Babylon city (Old Cairo). Evidence is not compelling according to Griggs, *Early Egyptian Christianity*, 18.

[143] The tradition first claiming that the evangelizing of Egypt was by Mark originates in the Eusebius statement in *Ecclesiastical History* 2.16.1.

[144] Roberts, *Manuscript, Society and Belief.*

[145] Griggs, *Early Egyptian Christianity*, 4–34.

[146] Pearson, *Gnosticism, Judaism, and Egyptian Christianity*, 195.

Première Eglise d'Alexandrie,[147] the link between Alexandria and Jerusalem. At the conclusion of the article, the writer explains that Occidental Christians (the Catholic Church and the Protestant Church) have learned recently how to measure the importance of the Jewish foundation in their faith: "De nos jours, les chrétiens occidentaux apprennent à mesurer l'importance de l'enracinement juif de leur foi."[148] Joseph Modrzejewski, in his monograph *The Jews of Egypt*, wonders about the silence of Christian origins in Egypt and argues that it is due to the Trajan oppression of the Jewish rebellion. He states: "If primitive Christianity had not left any marks on Egyptian soil until the end of the second century, it was because it had annihilated along with the entire body in which it was immersed the Jewish community in Egypt."[149]

In 2004, Pearson, in *Gnosticism and Christianity in Roman and Coptic Egypt,* shows how the continuity of the Alexandrian Church tradition in choosing presbyters follows the model of the synagogue.[150] He details the use of references from the Enochic apocryphal books in the early Egyptian Church.[151] In 2007, his article, "Earliest Christianity in Egypt: Further Observations," summarizes the main ideas of his book *Gnosticism and Christianity*. Edwin Broadhead *Jewish Ways of Following Jesus* also lays out the two scholarly views about the origins of

---

[147] Cannuyer, "L'Ancrage Juif," 31–45.

[148] Cannuyer, "L'Ancrage Juif," 45.

[149] Modrzejewski, *The Jews of Egypt*, 227. See also Pearson, *Gnosticism and Christianity*, 14–15.

[150] Pearson, *Gnosticism and Christianity*, 18.

[151] Pearson, *Gnosticism and Christianity*, 132–42.

Egyptian Christianity, whether it is founded on Gnosticism or a messianic concept from the Jewish community of Egypt. He adds new elements, such as Origen's (185–254 CE) thesis about Jewish observances in fasting and circumcision, in *The Gospel of the Hebrews* as frequently quoted by Dydimus the Blind (313–398 CE).[152] He also adds a fourth-century witness from Oxyrhynchus (p. Oxy. 6.903), where the text appears to speak of visiting both church and synagogue.[153] James Paget, in *Jews, Christians and Jewish Christians in Antiquity* (2010), studies a vital new theme about the messianic hope in various Alexandrian apocryphal writings, both Christian and Jewish, such as the *Epistle of Barnabas* (probably Alexandrian), comparing it with *Church History* of Eusebius, especially book seven and the *Apocalypse of Elijah*.[154] Paget sees in the figure of Clement of Alexandria a Jewish influence that might be reflected in his making of Jewish literature and its presence in his extant works of Jewish opinion. This strengthens Paget's assumption that Clement has a viva voce with the Jews of Alexandria. Paget also supports the Jewish influence on Clement by mentioning a saying from Jerome, who states that Clement was one of those earlier Christian authors who often cited Jewish opinion when engaged in biblical interpretation.[155] He confirms that Clement states that he had a Jewish teacher from Palestine (*Strom* 1.11.2), probably

---

[152] Broadhead, *Jewish Ways of Following Jesus*, 117–19.
[153] Broadhead, *Jewish Ways of Following Jesus*, 119.
[154] Paget, *Jews, Christians and Jewish Christians in Antiquity*, 137–47.
[155] Paget, *Jews, Christians and Jewish Christians in Antiquity*, 92–93.

Pantaenus,[156] and asserts Clement's knowledge of Jewish sources in Greek.[157] This familiarity of Clement with the Jewish sources opens doors to further understanding of early Christian thinking in Alexandria and how the Jewish influences may have shaped the Coptic Church traditions.

3. The Authors of the Catechism Books

John Gee, in his article "Some Neglected Aspects" (2012), emphasizes the neglect of historical evidence in the mind of the Copts: "The want of historical verification does not seem to trouble Copts. If there is no evidence for the tradition, there is also no evidence against it: faith fills the gap."[158] The authors of the Coptic catechism books,[159] who

---

[156] This is the opinion of Eusebius, in his *Ecclesiastical History* 5.11.1.

[157] All the Jewish writings that Clement cites in his writings are in Paget, *Jews, Christians and Jewish Christians in Antiquity*, note 9, p. 93. Paget refers to Demetrius (*Strom* 1.141.1–2; 1.150.2); Aritobulus (*Strom* 1.72.4; 1:150:1;

5.97.7; 6.32.5); Aristeas (*Strom* 1.148.1–149.3); Artapanus (*Strom* 1.154.2); Pseudo-Hecataeus (*Strom* 5.113); Ezekiel the Tragedian (*Strom* 1.155.1–1.156.2); and *The Assumption of Moses* (*Strom* 6.132).

[158] Gee, "Some Neglected Aspects of Egypt's Conversion to Christianity," 43.

[159] See El Masry, *Story of the Copts*; Bishop Isizoros, *Al Kharida*; Menassa, *Tarikh Al Kenissa*, 9–10, where the author mentions the probability of the existence of Christianity in Alexandria, prior to St. Mark's mission. He includes four arguments for his idea: first, the location of Alexandria which is close to Palestine; second, in that city, there were different quarters belonging to Alexandrian Jews whose relationship with the Jews of Jerusalem was interconnected; third, St. Luke wrote his Gospel to Theophilus, an honorary person from Alexandria; fourth, some who believed in Christ after Peter's

explore the Church history and its liturgy, find in the homegrown religious stories a fruitful source for picturing the early stages of the Coptic Church, regardless of their legacy.[160] Coptic hagiographies recount episodes relevant to early apostolic missions to Egypt. For instance, even though the Coptic tradition credits Saint Mark with the evangelization of Egypt, we find in the *Synaxarium* that on the 9th of the Coptic month of Hator,[161] the Church commemorates St. Bartholomew, one of the Twelve Apostles, who also preached in Egypt in the oasis of Al-

---

preaching (Acts 2:10) were from Egypt and returned to their homeland with the new faith.

[160] The Coptic Church tradition asserts that the episode of the flight of Joseph, Mary and Jesus (Matt. 2:13–15) into Egypt is the starting point of evangelizing Egypt by Christ himself. The apocryphal narrative of the *Vision of Theophilus* (Patriarch of Alexandria 385–412 CE), recounts different miraculous stories that happened during their sojourn in many cities in Egypt. These so-called "heavenly visions" attest the primacy of the people of Egypt in the salvation process based on biblical quotations, such as Hos. 11:1, Isa 19:1, and Isa 19:25: "...Blessed be Egypt, my people..." See, *Vision of Theophilus*, transl. by Mingana; Malaty, *Introduction to the Coptic Orthodox Church*, 11–14. Crum, *Coptic Monuments*, while cataloguing Coptic manuscripts of the Cairo Egyptian Museum, mentions a parchment (# 8015) whose provenance is from Akhmin (South of Cairo) that recounts a story of Egyptian Jews who, after Christ's passion, attempted to decide on his divinity. The text is written in the Sahidic Coptic dialect.

[161] Bartholomew is commemorated on the first Thot. *Coptic Synaxarium*, 1, 1–2 states, "To this Apostle fell the lot to go [preach] to the oasis Al-Khargah."

Khargah.[162] The *Synaxarium* and almost all Egyptian monographs elude any perception of the evangelization of Jewish circles in Egypt during the early apostolic mission. However, the apostolic mission, whether through Mark, Bartholomew, or James, must be considered as a possible Jerusalemite impact on the founding of the early Egyptian Church.[163] The idea of any Jewishness in forming the early Coptic Church seems almost excluded from the modern Arabic-speaking Coptic authors' minds and certainly from their writings.

4. Problems with the Standard Theory

The first problem I found in exploring this research history was that the ongoing disagreement of scholars about the origin of the Alexandrian Church and its liturgy distorts the overall view. Secondly, most scholars who research the initiation of Jewish tradition in the development of Christianity in Egypt through specific historical facts fail to solve this enigmatic problem and end up repeating the same views. Thus, I believe that the potential for uncovering some of its origins could be brought about by focusing not on straightforward history (if history can even be considered as "straightforward") but by studying liturgies from both traditions to reach some conclusive facts. Thirdly, the consensus that the origins of Coptic Christianity need no investigation must be

---

[162] Al-Khargah Oasis is located in the Libyan Desert, about 200 km to the west of the Nile valley. It is the capital of New Valley Governorate. The oasis was known as the "Southern Oasis" to the Ancient Egyptians.

[163] Roncaglia, *Histoire de l'Eglise Copte*, 1, 53–62.

reassessed, as it is diverting scholars from seeing the existing conundrums. Fourthly, the major problem that could occur (at least for a Copt) when attempting to locate a Jewish seed in the Alexandrian Church is that this knowledge could be rejected outright by the Church leaders due to the fragile locality of the Coptic Church in a Muslim milieu that dislikes the perception of any Jewish role played in the past in any Egyptian institution.

5. *Present Possibilities*

However, I consider many rewarding possibilities. The potential to even begin to understand the first two centuries of the Coptic Church requires that scholars study the late Second Temple literature, Jewish liturgy, Jewish customs, and rabbinic dictums—without slipping into anachronism—to infer the ties between Hellenistic Judaism and the Coptic liturgy and its surrounding customs and traditions.

I believe that the lack of available information about the Coptic Church liturgy, especially in the West, prevents the progress of such scholarship. The Coptic liturgy is immense and is still not fully translated, annotated, commented on, or studied at an academic level comparable to scholarship about the Jewish liturgy and the Qumran texts. The real movement towards translating the massive Coptic liturgy—apart from the Euchologions—started only in the late 1960s when Copts began to emigrate from Egypt to different countries in Europe and North America. However, these translations are made for churchgoers, not for scholars. Fragments of the most valuable liturgical pieces are dispersed among many institutions worldwide; unfortunately, only the ones of lesser value remain available in Egyptian monasteries.

I summarize my ideas regarding future possibilities by following the order of the scholarship groups mentioned above:

1. the history of the *Siyar al-Bi'ah al-Muqaddasah* ("*Biographies of the Holy Church*") collected by Sawirus (Severus) ibn al-Mukaffa, tenth century, needs to be studied with recognition of the common conservatism of Arabic-Christian authors, like that of the Jewish late Second Temple writings.

2. Davis cites a lengthy quotation from Clement of Alexandria's letter, where his attestation of the existence of Christians before Mark's arrival needs more attention and updated research concerning this striking letter.[164]

3. The unknown biographies about the early papacy as described by Eusebius, *History of the Church,* following the successors of Mark chronologically—Anianus, Abilius, Primus, Justus, Eumenes, Mercianus, Celadion, Aggripinus, Julian, and Demetrius—need further investigation to determine if this enigmatic silence is due to the probability of their Jewishness origin, as it is assumed for the early bishops (patriarchs) of Jerusalem.[165]

---

[164] Davis, *Early Coptic Papacy,* 8–9.
[165] Kohler, "Easter," 5, 29. The author, while talking about the Easter celebration dates, states: "Under the first fifteen bishops of Jerusalem, who were all Jews, no difference occurred between the Jewish and the Christian dates."

4. The fact that scholars have overlooked or neglected the *Epistle of Barnabas* as a "piece of evidence for the understanding of Egyptian Judaism during this period" also needs more attention.

5. The insights of the early Fathers and their conservatism with the Jewish late Second Temple writings leaves us to consider how this impacted not only their narratives but also their shaping of the liturgy and customs that surrounded it.

Chapter 2
Research Method

Copts, as with many other Christians whose liturgical books encompass many early prayers, have hesitated to embark on a new approach to understanding their liturgy. Their explanation of the rituals does not go beyond personal meditations or pragmatic theories. The approach that I suggest and believe will be profitable in reconstructing the origins of the Coptic Church through its liturgy, is to move towards "liturgical non-isolation," or, better yet, liturgical collaboration. Dix discusses the problem of liturgical isolation and implicates it in his introduction to *The Shape of the Liturgy*. In contrast, he provides an academic invitation aiming to link and integrate the Christian liturgies to the "first formation of the semi-Jewish church of the apostolic age."[166] The common components in the Morning Service in both Jewish and Coptic traditions instilled in me the courage to build a case that may raise awareness that Coptic Church history might be reconstructed through its liturgy. Of course, this research requires a pertinent research technique.

1. Three Difficult Questions

At the outset of this chapter, I am confronted with three difficult questions: 1. As demonstrated in Chapter 1, many Jewish elements from the late Second Temple writings seem to echo throughout the Coptic tradition. Moreover, when examining the Morning Service in both

---

[166] Dix, *The Shape of the Liturgy*, 11.

traditions, striking textual, rubrical, and terminological similarities occur in this shared core daily ritual. Thus, my first main question is, how did such an impact occur, and when? Primary sources to answer this question are very scanty. I ponder the oral tradition and conservatism that were fundamental aspects and common practices in both Jewish and Coptic traditions in conserving faith and prayers. I wonder if this is how the interrelations happened. As seen in Chapter 1,[167] Jewish prayers were possibly transferred from generation to generation by a strict rule of oral tradition, and this practice continues throughout Coptic history.

As with many rabbinic sources, I am keen to explore their direct and indirect influence on the Coptic morning service. How were these sayings incorporated into the early Egyptian liturgy, and what role did they play? Did this only occur once the rabbis' sayings had been standardised in the second century CE in the book of the Mishna, or at a later date?[168] These theoretical views have not really been supported by new knowledge about Second

---

[167] See note 68.

[168] Heinemann, *Prayer in the Talmud*, 26; Bradshaw, *Search for the Origins*, 6–7; Hoffman, *The Canonization of the Synagogue Service*, 19. For the Coptic Church, studies focus more on the liturgical melodies than on liturgy prayers. Scholars investigate the reliability of oral tradition by comparing transcriptions of the same piece of music recorded decades apart by different scholars. These studies indicate that the simpler melodies may have remained intact for centuries. See Awadalah, *Manaret El Akdas*, 6–16; Muftah, et al., "Coptic Music," 1715–47.

Temple liturgy, especially from the Dead Sea Scrolls.[169] In addition, I suggest that we consider the Greek-speaking diaspora and the Hebrew-Aramaic world as two distinct entities. Particular attention should be paid to Judea in the Land of Israel, as it was here that Christianised Judaism, otherwise known as the "new way", emerged.[170]

2. Having identified striking similarities, such as those found in the Morning Service, the next key question is: what constitutes evidence? For example, how does one determine whether textual correspondence, rubrical commonality, and resemblance in terminology count as proof of the impact of the Jewish ethos on Coptic prayers?

3. The third main question is: what methodological approaches have scholars dealing with the origins of Christian worship adopted in their studies? Unfortunately,

---

[169] In a scholarly debate, new evidence from the Dead Sea Scrolls (DSS) has challenged older ideas about Second Temple prayer. These ideas had suggested either seamless continuity with later Rabbinic liturgy, or a focus on fixed prayers. Scholars such as Ezra Fleischer had argued for distinct Jewish traditions. However, the DSS reveal complex and diverse streams of prayer, such as apocalyptic and penitential prayers, which have surprising affinities with, but also differences from, later Judaism. This shows that the development was richer and less linear than was previously thought. Further insight can be gained from the work of Ruth Langer and Richard S. Sarason. "Re-examining the Early Evidence for Rabbinic Liturgy: How Fixed Were Its Prayer Texts?" (203–32); Langer "Revisiting Early Rabbinic Liturgy: The Recent Contributions of Ezra Fleischer." Prooftexts, vol. 19, no. 2, Johns Hopkins University Press, 1999, pp. 179–94.

[170] Bradshaw is sensitive to this in the 2nd ed. of his work, a correction from the 1st ed. See Bradshaw, *The Search for the Origins of Christian Worship*, 2002.

many scholars who emphasise tangible sources are quite vague about their actual research methods.

2. The Historical Literary Approach to Liturgy

This study will employ a historical literary approach to examine liturgy. Rather than focusing on social, political and economic factors, the main concern will be to explore the potential impact of religious ideas of Hellenistic Judaism, and more specifically Alexandrian Judaism, on the liturgical ritual of the Morning Service in the Alexandrian or Coptic Church.

The period of history most relevant to the research is the late Second Temple period (200 BCE–70 CE). Religious ideas are expressed through literary forms such as canonical texts, pseudepigrapha and dictums related to the "sages" and leaders of that time. These texts become particularly authoritative when used liturgically or in relation to rituals such as the Morning Service and other ceremonies in the Coptic Church.[171] Many biblical and non-biblical texts, as well as pseudepigraphal thematic concepts and liturgical practices, seem to have been inherited, sanctified and finally deposited in the laudatory repertoire of the Alexandrian Church. While these texts constitute the literary side of my research, the historical component encompasses the story of the Alexandrian Jews at the time of the Church's inception in Egypt. As Brian Stock states, the two cannot be separated:

---

[171] Some other Coptic rituals show striking similarities: the Evening Service, Baptism, the Palm Sunday procession (corresponding to the Sukkot Jewish ritual), and many others.

The historical is not isolated from the literary as fact and representation. The two aspects of the experience work together: the objectivity of the events spills over into the subjectivity of the records, perceptions, feelings, and observations. The transcribed experience also feeds back into the lived lives.[172]

As such, my research perspective will include that of a historian of liturgy or a church historian through its liturgy. In order to grasp how a textually Jewish-oriented community emerged in the early history of the Alexandrian Church, an evaluation of certain academic approaches to late Jewish and early Christian liturgy is required.

First, some understanding of the development of four major schools of thought, represented by four scholars, and as sketched by Paul Bradshaw, is required for my research.[173] Leopold Zunz (1794–1886) dealt with the evolution of the liturgy in the course of history. He focused on philological research in finding differences in the wording of prayers, as he compared different manuscripts. By comparing different forms and "peeling the layers," his goal was to recover the original "urtext." When the Cairo Genizah was discovered, Ismar Elbogen (1874–1943) used philological methods to analyze the history of the texts, viewing the original seed of the liturgy as having been gradually encapsulated in layers. Therefore, Louis Finkelstein (1895–1991), in studying the Amidah, emphasized the oral transmission of prayers. Finally,

---

[172] Stock, *Listening to the Text*, 29.

[173] Bradshaw, *Search for the Origins*, 1–26.

Joseph Heinemann[174] (1915–1977) suggested the possibility of locating the origin of individual Jewish liturgical texts based on the particular stylistic features.[175] Heinemann's methodology was later adopted by Lawrence Hoffmann,[176] Tzvee Zahavy, and Stefan Reif, who promote an integrated interdisciplinary approach, incorporating literary criticism, archaeology, history, etc.

When adopting such approaches, which I believe are applicable to my research, some other essential scholarly views are to be taken into consideration. In his studies on the importance of the social and cultural context

---

[174] Significant progress has been made since Heinemann's publication in 1964. The philological methods employed are no longer considered reliable, and flaws have been found in his form-critical theory. From 1990 onwards, Ezra Fleischer challenged both Heinemann's methods and conclusions. He argued that rabbinic prayer texts were not compiled before the destruction of the Temple in 70 CE, but by the rabbis shortly afterwards, when they made prayers mandatory for everyone. See Langer, 'Jewish Liturgy', 12, and her article. "Revisiting Early Rabbinic Liturgy: The Recent Contributions of Ezra Fleischer," 179–94.

[175] Texts addressed the congregation in the second person plural "you." He argues that there never was a single "urtext." He believes that the oral tradition creates a centralized authority that regulates worship practices.

[176] Bradshaw introduces Hoffman's article, "Reconstructing Ritual as Identity and Culture," in *The Making of Jewish and Christian Worship*, by mentioning that Hoffman advocates methodological principles in the application of the human sciences, particularly anthropology, to the interpretation of inherited texts, in order to reconstruct Jewish and Christian identity and culture (22).

for liturgy,[177] Geoffrey Wainwright wonders if the synagogue's liturgical impact on church narratives is more "rubrical"[178] or more "textual"[179] in character? Or both? I would add another impact to the "textual" and "the "rubrical": the *thematic* Jewish perceptions in the Coptic liturgy, as shown for instance, in the similarity of the concepts of angelology, luminaries, sacrifices (incense, offerings), and priestly purification, as shown in *Seder Amram Gaon* and the Coptic Morning Service. Wainwright raises an astute historical question about "liturgical continuities and discontinuities as the Church gradually defined itself over against Judaism. That question was not settled even by the close of the apostolic age."[180] Quoting from C. K. Barrett, he adds: "There was a continuing relation between Christianity and Judaism which involved both attraction and repulsion."[181]

---

[177] Wainwright, "The Periods of Liturgical History," 61–62. The author asks the same questions when investigating the sources of some liturgical practices mentioned in the New Testament, i.e., words spoken at Baptism (Matt 28:19; Acts 2:38; 8:16, 37; 10:48, 19:5; 22:16; Rom 10:9); and initiation including an anointing with oil (2 Cor 1:21; Eph 1:13; 4:30; 1 John 2:20, 27).

[178] These include the inaudible and audible prayers recited by the congregational leader, worshipper postures (to bow, to stand, to seat), the washing of feet in both *Seder Amram Gaon* and the Coptic Morning Service, and many others.

[179] These include the Berakhot and the supplications in both Jewish and Christian Morning Service, as well as the Priestly Blessing.

[180] Wainwright, "The Periods of Liturgical History," 62.

[181] Wainwright, "The Periods of Liturgical History," 62. He quotes Barrett, *The Gospel of John and Judaism*, 69.

Secondly, it is imperative to avoid the error of what Lawrence Hoffman calls falling into either "reductionism" or "expansionism."[182] When a scholar goes beyond textual and ritual reconstruction (which is the challenge of my study), he or she needs to determine the proper field of study, which is one thing for written text (e.g., liturgical), but another for cultural context (e.g., Hellenistic Judaism). Drawing on Arthur Koestler,[183] Hoffman states that in the past, systems theory faced a similar problem when trying to avoid "reductionism" on one hand and "expansionism" on the other hand. Reductionism is the error of reducing complex systems into their "atomistic bits," and, in doing that, destroying the system. The result is that one learns a lot about the bits but nothing about the system. Expansionism is the opposite error of keeping the interrelation of the "bits" within the system, and then of that system with other systems, and so forth endlessly, which at some point becomes an unachievable task. Hoffman suggests that the "solution is to recognize that the researcher has no option but to select an arbitrary subsystem somewhere between the two extremes."[184] For my study, the relevant subsystem is not to study the whole of Hellenistic Judaism with all its literary culture (expansionism) and its impact on the Alexandrian Church, but rather to focus on the society of the Egyptian Jews with its relationship to Alexandrian Judaism within the context of Hellenistic Judaism.

---

[182] Hoffman, "Reconstructing Ritual as Identity and Culture," 35.
[183] Hoffman takes the conception of "reductionism" and "expansionism" from Koestler, *The Ghost in the Machine,* 45–58.
[184] Hoffman, "Reconstructing Ritual as Identity and Culture," 35.

Thirdly, as his focus is on how to interpret early Christian liturgical evidence, several of the ten research principles outlined by Bradshaw in *The Making of Jewish and Christian Worship* are directly related to my study. Principle 1 reminds me to take into consideration that Jewish worship of the first century CE, from which Christian worship took its departure, was not fixed or uniform. Principle 5 asserts that when a variety of explanations are sophisticated for the origin of a liturgical custom, its true source has almost certainly been forgotten. Bradshaw gives the example of Theophilus, patriarch of Alexandria (fourth century), who apparently introduced baptismal chrism into Christian usage in response to the instruction of an angel to bring balsam trees from Jericho, plant them, and cook the spices.[185] Principle 6 cautions one about Christian ancient sources that are robed in "apostolic dress."[186] In this study, I will deal marginally with *The Apostolic Constitutions*, *The Egyptian Church Order,* and *The Alexandrian Synodus;* considered by the Coptic Church as a source of authoritative jurisprudence documents, containing directions for the conduct of worship as well as the words of prayers and other formularies to be used in the ritual. These documents are, as Bradshaw describes it, "masquerading in apostolic dress to lend themselves added authority—a judgment that is still not always fully appreciated by all contemporary scholars."[187] Thus, studying early Coptic liturgical texts needs a new look.

---

[185] Bradshaw, "Ten Principles," 11–12.

[186] Bradshaw, "Ten Principles," 12–13.

[187] Bradshaw, "Ten Principles," 12–13.

Fourthly, a scholarly approach is essential when dealing with pseudepigraphal liturgical texts. Many explicit biblical quotations from the Septuagint, as well as many Apocryphal Lives of the Prophets, were translated into Sahidic Coptic. Examples of these can be found in early Alexandrian Coptic-Greek texts. This interweaving of sources was common during the Greco-Roman period. Frances Young describes this phenomenon: Early Christianity originated among the Jewish community. This must be taken into account when considering the nature and context of early Christian literature, as an examination of its 'intertextuality' reveals a profound familiarity with the literature of the Jewish community, particularly in Greek.[188]

3. *The Textual Correspondence*

The purpose of studying with this view to textual correspondence is to demonstrate the possibility that the early Alexandrian Church leaders, or the first converted Jews, took over or transferred the literature of the Jews, claimed it as their own, and subsequently built liturgical explanations for its existence in the Coptic Church liturgy. Appropriately, the methodological approach in investigating the Christian transmission of Greek Jewish Scriptures used by Robert Kraft asks scholars to be sure

---

[188] Young, "Introduction," 7. For instance The Prayer of Azariah (also the Prayer of Manasseh) exist textually in the Coptic Midnight Psalmody known as Ode 3 or the Third *Hos*. For the Greek text and its textual correspondence with the Coptic version, see Horst and Newman, *Early Jewish Prayers in Greek*, 181–215.

that they have "re-evaluated and reformulated."[189] He suggests studying why the Judeo-Christians were motivated to transmit them, embellish them, and reshape them in the Greco-Roman world into the new faith liturgy.

Also, comparing Jewish and early Coptic texts must draw on the work of Anton Baumstark[190] and Gregory Dix,[191] who do textual comparison of some early liturgical texts. Scholarly interest in comparative liturgies in early Christian literature remains as intense as ever in early Jewish and Christian writings, but it continues in fragmented forms,[192] and has not been applied methodically within a Jewish Coptic framework.

The undertaking of a textual comparison between the Jewish and Coptic Morning Services will emphasize

---

[189] Kraft, *Exploring the Scripturesque*, 81. The author devotes a full chapter to investigating the methodology in dealing with this transmission in early Christianity. He concludes that "it is easy to criticize the way things have been done (by other scholars), but difficult to propose satisfactory alternatives," chapter 3, pp. 61–82.

[190] Baumstark, *Comparative Liturgy*.

[191] Dix, *The Shape of the Liturgy*.

[192] For instance, Bouyer, *Eucharist*. He argues that the Eucharistic favoritism between the members of Christ is the basis of the past conflict between Byzantines and Latins. This leads him to state, "No one was any longer able to reread the ancient (liturgical) formularies in accordance with their co-ordinates." Targeting the main contradictory views, Bouyer extends his study to compare the Alexandrian Anaphoras with familiar (the Berokat) and unfamiliar Jewish material (Amram Gaon book). Eucharist is not an *ex-nihilo* Christian creation but it was born from the Jewish home and synagogue. Bouyer mentions in passing the tie between the Alexandrian Anaphoras with *Amram Gaon Seder Order of Sabbath Prayer* (ninth century CE).

the common ritual patterns, which, in the case of the Coptic liturgy, can be seen to emerge from the Jewish urtext. The advantages of such scrutiny are highlighted by Dix, whose appreciation of the analysis of the ritual pattern is worth quoting here:

> The analysis of such a [liturgical] pattern and the tracing of its evolution open for the historian and the sociologist the most direct way to the sympathetic understanding "from within" of the mind of those who practice that religion, and so to a right appreciation of the genius of their belief and the value of their ideas and ideals of the human life.[193]

4. *Theological Content in Liturgical Texts*

Stephan Wahle describes some important reflections on the exploration of Jewish and Christian liturgies where he mainly focuses on a systematic theology of liturgy.[194] This methodology, in observing theological dimensions in the field of Judeo-Christian prayers, needs some attention while I am discussing different research methods. I will summarize the most relevant remarks to my research. The scrutiny of considering certain theological proportions in these prayers of the Jewish Morning Service could be of great help in understanding the relevant

---

[193] Dix, *The Shape of the Liturgy*, 9.

[194] In general, systematic theology draws on (but is not limited to) the foundational sacred text of Christianity, while simultaneously investigating the development of Christian doctrine over the course of history, particularly through philosophy, science, and ethics.

Halachic knowledge for similar prayers in the two repertoires.

Wahle sees that the main likenesses of Jewish-Christian liturgy are the research in concepts regarding the origin, the development, the influence, and the differences between the liturgies. He recommends that with these, the "theological" relevance must be considered as an "important supplement to 'historical' liturgical studies of the interrelations between Jewish Christian liturgies."[195]

He also considers Christian liturgy as neither a "prayed dogma" nor an obvious source of revelation. His view is that "the linguistic and the symbolic acts within the liturgy only lead directly to 'theo-logy' when other theological, philosophical, and cultural disciplines are included."[196] Wahle shares the definition of the task and the self-conception of systematic theology, which according to him (quoting from Helmut Hoping and Jan-Heiner Tück):

> It is determined by the Scriptures, the Apostolic Creed, its teaching and the place of liturgy in which the "Symbolum" originates.[197] Its purpose is the hermeneutic development of the tradition of faith, which depends on the historical

---

[195] Wahle, "Reflections on the Exploration," 169.

[196] Wahle, "Reflections on the Exploration," 170.

[197] Symbolum Apostolorum is the Apostles' Creed, which first appeared in the sixth century in the writings of Caesarius of Arles and in Ruffenus Rufinus' Commentary on the Apostle's Creed (407 CE) and in Pope Julius I (340 CE).

reconstruction of respective evidence without restricting itself to this aspect.[198]

Indeed, as Wahle sees, in Judaism, liturgical-theological reflections often hold a philosophical feature.[199] This philosophy implicates the large number of Second Temple writings belonging to the Jewish liturgy. Thus, the dilemma is not to locate a theology beyond the Morning Jewish Service prayers and assimilate it to the Coptic Morning Service to understand the Halakhah, but how to understand a Jewish theological core of meaning within the liturgical Coptic text. For example, are the rabbinical dictums concerning the eighteen Berakah evident in the actual form of the supplications of the Coptic Morning Service? To some degree, I will consider the rabbinical literature, which is often based on the Old Testament, as a coherent halakha for the contemporary Coptic worshipper to help elucidate many enigmas. Wahle writes, "My theory is that without ascertaining the theological 'content' of the developed forms of Jewish liturgy, one cannot reach the liturgical-theological goal of understanding the theological core of meaning of the Christian liturgy."[200]

An illustrative example of theological content in the Morning Service is worth mentioning. According to Wahle, the core of Jewish theology comprises the doctrine of God the Creator, his revelation to humankind (as

---

[198] Wahle, "Reflections on the Exploration," 170. The author quotes from Hoping and Tück, "Thesen zur inhaltlichen Bestmmtheit des Glaubens," 26.

[199] Wahle, "Reflections on the Exploration," 171.

[200] Wahle, "Reflections on the Exploration," 171.

recounted in the Book of Exodus, including the giving of the Torah), and the covenant he made with humanity. Wahle refers[201] to Jacob Petuchowski, who points out that the relative image of God (in creation, in revelation, and in redemption) "is the basis of the Jewish liturgy as a theological content." Petuchowski indicates that these images of God are reflected in the "theological structure of the Shema Yisra'el and its benedictions"[202] within the daily morning prayer. Therefore, it is unsurprising that these divine truths are also evident in the Coptic liturgy, notably in the Morning Service.[203]

5. Conclusion

The majority of scholars, including Dix,[204] Baumstark[205] and even Bradshaw,[206] focus more on discussing ancient sources that could help us understand the origin of the liturgy, and the works of other scholars in the field, than they do on delineating the methods that they have adopted. It seems that researchers studying the Jewish Christian liturgy have not yet defined the most appropriate methods. Therefore, as this current Judeo-Coptic study progresses and others join the field, it is hoped that further studies will contribute to the development of effective research methods.

---

[201] Wahle, "Reflections on the Exploration," 178.
[202] Wahle, "Reflections on the Exploration," 178.
[203] See Chapter 4.
[204] Dix, *The Shape of the Liturgy*.
[205] Baumstark, *Comparative Liturgy*.
[206] Bradshaw, *Search for the Origins*.

Chapter 3
Parallels of the Morning Service in the Jewish and Coptic Liturgies

1. Introduction

The fact that Alexandrian Judaism existed for at least two centuries before the common era, combined with innumerable late Second Temple writings that deal with Jewish worship, would suggest that the potential of finding a Jewish impact on the early stage of the Alexandrian Church would be ipso facto. However, as mentioned above, many Coptic scholars who have pursued the roots of the Egyptian Church through historical facts or literary evidence have not equally pursued its Jewish origin. In the present and following chapter (Chapters 3 and 4), I will examine a substantial common ritual existing in both Jewish and Coptic liturgies: the Morning Service (Heb. שַׁחֲרִית "*Schacharit*"; Coptic Ⲡⲧⲁⲗⲟ Ⲙⲡⲓⲥⲑⲟⲓⲛⲟⲩϥⲓ ⲛ̀ⲧⲉ ϨⲁⲚⲁⲦⲞⲞⲒ.[207] In both Jewish and Coptic traditions, the Morning Service holds nearly identical texts and order of prayers. In this chapter, after describing the unique features of the Morning Service in the Coptic Church, I will focus on the textual similarities, the common rubrics, and the familiar terminology in both Jewish and Coptic traditions. In Chapter 4, I will deal with the major thematic interrelations existing in different prayers in the Coptic

---

[207] "Raising incense at dawn." Known in arabic as "Raf Bukhur Baker."

Morning Service and their potential source from the Second Temple writings.

2. Primary and Secondary Resources

The aim of this section is to highlight the shared elements between the Jewish ritual and the Coptic Service for Morning Prayer. To emphasize the textual correspondence of the two rituals and the main liturgical practices that occur during this daily service, an accurate and reliable investigation is necessary. Similarities are noteworthy on several levels: the order of the prayers is almost the same, the biblical concepts are alike, and the meticulous details in the rubrics correspond to each other.[208] The primary texts, which will be examined from both perspectives, have credibility and legacy in both traditions. The book is known by his name, Seder R. Amram Gaon.[209] It was published by D. Hedegård after

---

[208] Remarkably these sources offer information on customary postures, such as kneeling and standing, as well as the positioning of the left and right feet.

[209] This book will henceforth be referred to as SAG. Amram Gaon was Head of the Sura Academy; he died about 875. He was a pupil of Naṭronai II, Gaon of Sura, and was exceptionally honored with the title of Gaon within the lifetime of his teacher. Upon Naṭronai's death, about 857, the full title and dignities of the gaonate were conferred upon Amram, and he held them until his death. He is the author of about 120 responsa touching almost every department of Jewish jurisprudence. But the most important work of Amram, which marks him as one of the most prominent of the geonim before Saadia, is his "Prayer-Book," the so-called "Seder (or Siddur) Rav Amram." Amram was the first to arrange a complete liturgy for use in synagogue and home. See, Ginzberg, "Amram Ben Sheshna," 536–37. For recent studies related

having been translated from the Hebrew text and is dated from the ninth century CE.[210]

From the Coptic tradition, I will base my study on *The Holy Euchologion*,[211] which was compiled by the scholar Hegemon Abdel Massih Saleb Al Massoudy Al

---

to R. Amran Gaon, See Brody, *The Geonim of Babylonia and the Shaping of Medieval Jewish Culture*. Following the discovery of the Cairo Genizah, widely regarded as the most important source for establishing the immense variety of details in liturgical practices, it has been suggested that the differences in Jewish prayers for the same rite may reflect a coherent argument against the liturgical tradition being conservative. The challenge is that even though Amram's book is the earliest complete prayer book, it does not reflect a tradition that would be familiar to Hellenistic Jews in Alexandria. However, there are textual similarities with the Coptic Morning Service that require further investigation in order to determine the liturgical origins of early Judeo-Christians in Egypt.

[210] Hedegård, *Seder R. Amram Gaon,* Part 1. See the previous note for details of the debate surrounding this date.

[211] The texts and rubrics belonging to the Offering of Incense Morning and Evening Services as well as for the three liturgies are found in the *Euchologion* (Arabic: *al-khulaji*), which prescribes the order of the various prayers, hymns, lections, versicles, petitions, and responses. These are sung in Greek, Coptic and Arabic today. The texts are written in the Bohairic dialect, though the Sahidic dialect may be heard in Upper Egypt. They are accompanied by a line-by-line Arabic translation, and all the rubrics are in Arabic. The last section of the *Euchologion* contains the texts of many chants and hymns proper to the various liturgical seasons. For more details on the *Euchologion*, see Ragheb Muftah, et al., "The Coptic Music," 1715–45; A. Basilios, "Euchologion," 1066–67.

Baramoussy.[212] Before he published the *Holy Euchologion* at the beginning of the twentieth century, he studied many manuscripts while he was librarian of the Coptic papal library for many years.[213] Also important to this study is Al Makary's book, *Salwat Raf' Al Bokhour fi Asheya wa' Baker (Office of Evening and Morning Incense)*, which investigates many manuscripts[214] in order to examine ritual discrepancies occurring in different versions. An important Coptic–Arabic manuscript, *Al Tartib Al Taksi*,[215] compiled by the Pope Gabriel V Ibn Turaik,[216] is also invaluable for its meticulousness in describing the Morning Service rubrics.

It would be premature to conclude that significant modifications in both liturgies must have been made because the Seder R. Amram Gaon and Coptic manuscripts containing the Morning Service are dated between the

---

[212] He was born in 1848 in a city called "Tahta" in the Sohag Governorate at Upper Egypt. He was known for his multilingual erudition (English, French, Hebrew, Amharic and Greek) and added to his proficiency in Arabic and Coptic. He was the librarian of the papal library for about thirty years. He wrote a massive monograph in Arabic *Al Tohfa Al Baramousseya* [*The Masterwork of Al Baramous*], the *Holy Euchologion* (which I refer to in this dissertation as "Massoudy,") and hundreds of articles in different periodicals. He died in 1935 after spending more than 60 years in the ascetic life. See *Massoudy*, 11. When using the same Euchologion in its English version, I will refer to it as "DL," *The Divine Liturgy* (Cairo, 2007).

[213] See the introduction of the *Holy Euchologion, Massoudy*, 3.

[214] For the list of manuscripts, see Al Makary, *Salwat,* 586–88.

[215] Abdallah, *L'Ordinamento Liturgico by Gabriel V* [*Al Tartib Al Taksi*].

[216] For Gabriel V's life and works, see Khalil, "Gabriel V," 1130–33.

ninth and fourteenth centuries. As discussed above, both faiths preserved meticulously the inherited tradition in different forms: the word of God, the Oral Torah,[217] and hypothetically prayers, rubrics, and customs. The faith itself was transferred as a trust from the Apostles to the neophytes.[218] Paul, in different epistles, outlines the importance of the tradition.[219] Both institutions admit that the conservatism of those who inherited and passed on the liturgy created a strong and largely unchanging oral tradition, not only in the spoken liturgy, but also in the singing that accompanies it. There is no reason to assume that any element in the Morning Service ritual in either faith was an innovation or an addition before the time of Ibn Al-Muquaffa[220] or Ibn Siba'.[221]

3. The Morning Service in Seder R. Amram Gaon and The Divine Liturgy

Apart from the Benedictions, the Siddur (SAG) is somewhat abridged, but Hedegård's footnotes provide

---

[217] See Related Essay IV.

[218] 2 Tim 2:2.

[219] 2 Thess 2:15; 2 Thess 3:6; Phil 4:9; 1 Cor 11:7.

[220] Ibn Al-Muquaffa' was bishop of Ashmunayn, well known for his colossal work *Tarikh Baṯarikat al-Iskandariyyah al-Quibt*, the History of Patriarchs of Alexandria, the Copts. For more information about the author, see Kanawaty, *Christianity and the Arabic Civilization*, 255–58; also see Atiya, "Copto-Arabic Literature," 1460–67.

[221] Ibn Siba' was a scholar, well known by his book printed in Cairo 1902, Latin version *Pretiosa Margarita de scientiis ecclesiasticis*, translated by Vincent Mistrih, Cairo, 1966. For more information about the author, see Kanawaty, *Christianity and the Arabic Civilization*, 255–58; also see Atiya, "Copto-Arabic Literature," 1460–67.

further insights into each section of the service, and the publication of this Hebrew text comes with rubrics, explanations, and multiple rabbinical dicta. The section on "what is said [to] prepare to meet [thy] God," involves a form of physical purification, with the hands, feet and face being washed before prayer begins. The following is the sequence of prayers:[222] 'Pseuqe de Zimra' ('Passage Songs'),[223] 'Shema' (Deuteronomy 6:4–9; 11:13–21; Numbers 15:37–41),[224] 'Tefillah' ('Prayers') [225] and finally 'Birkat Kohanim' ('The Priestly Blessing').[226]

In the Coptic tradition, there is a pre-Morning Service ritual amassed in two different books: the *Book of*

---

[222] For a description of the Jewish Morning Service as a daily public liturgy, see Idelsohn, *Jewish Liturgy and Its Development*, 73–122. See also a detailed description of the ritual of the Coptic Morning Service in Burmester, *The Egyptian or Coptic Church*.

[223] Passages from the Book of Psalms, 1 SAG, 26–3. This part of the liturgy definitely takes its form in the second half of the first millennium as the Talmud does not mention it in any detail. The question is whether this part of the liturgy is a creation or an adaptation by the Copts.

[224] 1 SAG, 36–69.

[225] 1 SAG, 70–121. The "Tefillah" consists of 18 (19) prayers, called "Blessings" or "Berakhot." Only the intermediate 12/13 benedictions are petitionary; the others are supplicatory. On weekdays, supplicatory prayer follows in a more formal form than it had in the period of the Seder Amram Gaon, though he still prescribes it. It is known also as 'Amidah'.

[226] 1 SAG, 122–37 (this is part of the repetition of the Tefillah, not separate from it].

Canonical Hours[227] and the *Holy Psalmody.*[228] Thus, the order of the morning Service in the Coptic tradition starts with Psalms of the First Hour,[229] then the *Doxology Adam Baker*, First Hour,[230] "The Prayer of Thanksgiving,"[231] "The Verses of Cymbals,"[232] "Litanies" (petition prayers, Coptic ⲉⲩⲭⲏ[233] for "Departed," "Sick," "Travelers," Sacrifices (Qurban),[234] followed by "Let Us Praise with the

---

[227] *Book of Seven Canonical Hours* (Arabic: *Ajbiyah*) is a book containing the offices for the seven canonical hours. It includes all the prayers, Psalms, Gospel readings, and petitions to be said at the various hours by day and night. This book counts seven canonical hours to be recited daily. The pre-Morning Service hour is the Prayer of the First Hour, also called morning or dawn prayer, to be recited just before the beginning of daylight. See, Basilios, "Book of Canonical Hours," 446–49.

[228] *The Holy Psalmody* (Arabic: *al-absalmudiyyah* or *al-tasbihah*) is a choral service that is performed immediately before the Evening Offering of Incense, at the conclusion of the Prayers of the Midnight Hour, and between the Office of Morning Prayer and the Morning Offering of Incense. Muftah, et al., "Coptic Music," 1715–45.

[229] *Book of Seven Canonical Hours*, 6–40

[230] *Holy Psalmody Arabic*, 267–82.

[231] DL, 3–7. Daily Doxology (Arabic, "tamjid"), a species of Coptic ecclesiastical hymnic compositions, in stanzas, usually addressed to the Virgin, to the angels, to individual saints, or to a particular category of saints. See Cody, "Doxology," 923–24.

[232] DL, 7–19.

[233] Daoud, *Dictionary of Coptic Language*, 845. This a Greek word frequently used by the Coptic scribes.

[234] DL, 19–28.

Angels,"[235] the "Trisagion,"[236] "The Doxologies,"[237] "The Orthodox Creed,"[238] Litany for the Gospel, "[239] Then reading the Gospel. There are "Five Short Litanies"[240] (for "The Peace," "The Patriarch and Bishops," "The Place," "Three Seasons," "The Assemblies") to be recited, then comes "The Absolution,"[241] and finally, "The Short Blessing (The Priestly Blessing)."[242]

The similarity of the order of prayers is not immediately apparent, because the Jewish texts are dispersed throughout the different sections of prayers of the Coptic Morning Service. However, examination of the Jewish rabbinic dictums that are included in Amram's book regarding the reason behind the order of the prayers will make the setting of the Coptic Morning Service and its significance more transparent according to the Jewish tradition.

It is noteworthy here to mention that the frankincense burning in the Coptic Morning Service is a unique characteristic that accompanies the priestly prayers. This includes invocations for the Blessing of the

---

[235] DL, 32–33.
[236] DL, 33–34.
[237] DL, 36–51.
[238] DL, 58–60.
[239] DL, 60–63.
[240] DL, 70–84.
[241] DL, 86–88.
[242] DL, 89–91.

Incense,²⁴³ the inaudible Prayer of Incense, the Three Short and Long Litanies (ⲉⲩⲭⲏ), and the petition of the Gospel. This topic needs to be studied separately to cover the large quantity of material regarding the incense as a burnt sacrifice, which entails many theological and liturgical subjects.²⁴⁴

4. Uniqueness of the Coptic Morning Service

Muftah and the other contributors to the article "Coptic Music" indicate the uniqueness of the Evening and Morning Service. They call them: "two special services unique to the Coptic Church."²⁴⁵ Al Makary²⁴⁶ confirms the historical legacy of the Morning and Evening Services by listing several decrees from the Coptic version of the *Canons of Hippolytus*,²⁴⁷ where the regulations of these

---

²⁴³ The incensing follows different rubrics regarding the blessing of incense, a specific protocol if other priests are partaking the service with him or higher clergy rank. For more details, see Burmester, *The Egyptian or Coptic Church*, 36–37.

²⁴⁴ The study of the incense in both Jewish and Coptic traditions is considered as one my future research projects. See Chapter 5.

²⁴⁵ Muftah, "Coptic Music," 1715–47.

²⁴⁶ Al Makary, *Salawat*, 66–68, lists the Hippolytus' canons 21:1–3, 26:1, 27:1. See also, Mettaous, *Rouhaniet Taks Al Kodass* [*The Spirituality of the Mass*], 30–81.

²⁴⁷ The *Canons of Hippolytus* is a Christian text composed of 38 decrees known as canons. The work has been dated to between 336 and 340 CE. Egypt is regarded as the place of origin. The author is unknown, though the work is a pseudo-Hippolytus, bishop of Rome, written "according to the instructions of the Apostles." See also, Bradshaw, *The Search of the Origins of Christian Worship*, 90–91.

daily services are strictly promulgated. He also sees that their origins (as both services hold almost identical texts) are concealed in the role of the incense burning and their related processions during those services. Al Makary states: "The practice of burning incense in the morning and evening dates back to when it was first used in the Tabernacle, God's meeting place with his people, and in the Jerusalemite Temple. This practice formed the core of the early Church."[248]

The church archives do not show the actual practice that the Morning Service is often incorporated into the liturgy of the mass.[249] This ritual was performed daily as a congregational prayer at the church.

5. *Locating Jewish Segments in the Coptic Morning Service (Texts and Rubrics)*

In this section, I will survey Jewish ritual prayers, and identify their parallels in the Coptic liturgy, as well as determining which extant Jewish texts exist in the Coptic Service.

Bradshaw sees the Canons of Hippolytus, a part of the corpus of the ancient church orders, as an enigma in offering apostolic prescriptions in liturgical practice. See also, Coquin, "Les Canons d'Hippolyte," 273–443.

[248] Al Makary, *Salawat*, 20.

[249] Examples of Arabic manuscripts regarding Morning and Evening Services that do not indicate their inclusion in the liturgy of the mass are noted in Macomber, *Catalogue of Christian Arabic Manuscripts of the Franciscan Center* (in Cairo): manuscripts 179 (1); 221 (1) evening only; 243 (147a); 298 (31). See also the overall inventory of Crum in, *Coptic Manuscripts in the British Museum*.

A. A Preparation to Meet God

Amram Gaon in 1 SAG did not start his Siddur with the "Pseuque de Zimra." Rather, he highlights the legacy and the necessity of the daily ablution: an "obligation," a "preparation before meeting thy God."[250] His prelude is to understand the common Jewish and Coptic concept of this segment of prayers, blessings that are said during the washing procedure prior to the Morning Service ritual. This preparation holds many interwoven themes that reach their momentous significance during the ritual itself (The Shema and the Tefillah). They correlate the fixed time (early morning) with the cock crowing time as the time to pray the early Berakot, which is recited in connection with the ablution. The correlation connects the resurrection of the "neshama" (the soul) after being dead (during the sleep) with blessing and thanksgiving prayers to the "Lord of all souls,"[251] who is the Creator and "the king of the universe."[252] All is interlaced with the theme of the order of nature (as God provides light),[253] which also is well interlocked with "the law and light" as referred to in Psalm 119.[254] These interwoven liturgical themes in this segment of the prayers prior to the start of the Jewish Morning Service clearly exist in the Coptic Morning Service liturgy. The subsequent focus will be on the requirement of individual purity and how important it before encountering God in the synagogue or the church.

---

[250] Amos 4:12.

[251] 1 SAG, 9.

[252] 1 SAG, 9.

[253] 1 SAG, 47–49.

[254] 1 SAG, 50–51.

The Requirement of Cleansing

Amram pictures the washing of the body, and specifically the hands, face, and feet, as an important preparation step to "prepare to meet thy God [of] Israel." The priests were commanded by God to wash their hands and feet before entering the tent of meeting.[255] In the Jewish liturgy, this stage is obligatory prior to the start of the reciting of the *Berakoth*. The ablutions before prayer are mentioned in the pseudepigraphical writings. Hedegård includes examples, such as[256] Judith, who performs her absolution before reciting her prayers,[257] and the Letter of Aristeas, which states that it is the custom of all Jews to wash their hands to prove that they have done no evil.[258]

The Coptic bishop Ibn Al Muquaffa' says: "About the order of the office (Morning Service) which compels the priest, (and the deacon) holders of the Service... he is urged to wash his feet before ascending the altar (called in Arabic *Heikal*) because it is the place of the dwelling of the Holy Spirit, the place of the body of the Son of God and his blood, and the place where angels reside."[259] Furthermore, like Amram,[260] he provides obvious reasons for purification, citing the region's dusty and dirty conditions and the wearing of sandals. Following Exodus 30:17–21, Ibn Al Muquaffa' requires that priests wash their feet in a bronze basin. He incorporates the Jewish ritual of 'Prepare

---

[255] Exod 30:17.
[256] Hedegård, 1 SAG, note 6.
[257] Hedegård, 1 SAG, note 7 (Judith 12:7).
[258] Hedegård, 1 SAG, note 7 (Arist 306).
[259] Al Makary, *Salwat*, 202.
[260] 1 SAG, 6.

to meet thy God' throughout the Coptic liturgy, not only through washing, but also by reciting inaudible prayers during this process.

In Coptic tradition, both clergy and all worshippers must be concerned with their physical purity before entering the church and more specifically before receiving the communion. The holiness of the Church is traditionally tied scripturally with the Jerusalem Temple;[261] sexual intercourse is prohibited the night before communion. Such regulations are characteristic of the Coptic tradition and traceable in some Qumranic texts. Harrington notes that during the Second Temple era, the sanctity of the Temple was extended to embrace the entire city of Jerusalem as prescribed in the Dead Sea Scrolls 4Q399 (frg. 3, lines 10–13). Also, the *Temple Scroll* describes a three-day process with baths before the impure can enter the Temple city, and sexual intercourse is prohibited: 11Q 19 45:11–12; CD 12.1–2.[262] The rabbinic literature, the Tohorot section in the Mishna, details the laws that address ritual purity. Further study would be required to describe adequately in detail the importance of this ritual of physical readiness to celebrate a new day and to meet God, as illustrated through rabbinical dictums and the sayings of medieval Coptic liturgists.

---

[261] *The Book of Khedmat Al Shamas*, 11 (Guidelines no. 4, 5). The deacon is required to recite Psalm 83 once he arrives at the church portal and until he reaches the altar; kneeling then, he says, "But I, by your great mercy, will come into your house; in reverence will I bow down toward your holy temple," Ps 5:7.

[262] Harrington, "Purity and Impurity," 1122.

B. "Pseuque de Zimra," "Psalmodia," and Matins Psalms

In Jewish tradition, the "Pseuque de Zimra" is considered as an individual "warm up," a sort of spiritual readiness[263] before the beginning of praying the core of the Morning Service (the Tefillah and the Shema). This warmup consists of singing the Hallel and reciting different passages of selected psalms. It appears that this custom existed before the second century CE.[264] Hofmann cites a dictum from Yose bar Chalafta, who reports: "May my lot be among those who complete a Hallel every day."[265]

The Jewish liturgical tradition seems to be undecided about which psalms constitute the Hallel. Usually, the Jews recited the Psalms of the Egyptian Hallel (Pss. 113–118) and other passages (Ps 115:18; Ps 145:21) or specifically Psalms 145–150.[266] Therefore, Hoffman notes that the Talmud identifies the "Great Hallel" as

---

[263] The physical readiness is obtained by washing and the spiritual readiness is by singing the Hallel and reciting specific psalms. For the rabbinic dictums and Halachic importance of the sense of a spiritual readiness, see Hoffman, "Introduction to the Liturgy," 3–6.

[264] Hofmann mentions a Mishnaic quote (c. 200 CE): "the pious ones of old used to tarry an hour and then pray, so as to focus themselves on God." The rabbinic works prior to that date do not discuss anything called "Pseuque de Zimra;" see Hoffman, "Introduction to the Liturgy," 5

[265] Hoffman, "Introduction to the Liturgy," 7. Hedegård sees in this quotation that the practice "cannot have been a new one in the times of R. Jose (a distinguished disciple of R. Aqiba, a rabbi of the later part of the first century CE), it must have been known at least as early as in the first century CE." 1 SAG, 26, notes 9–14.

[266] Hedegård, 1 SAG, note 6.1 SAG, notes 9–14.

Psalm 136.[267] As in the Jewish tradition, the Coptic repertoire preserves the singing of two particular Hallel sets: Psalm 136 (Ode 2), and Psalms 148, 149, and 150 (grouped under Ode 4) as part of the midnight psalmody, which are usually sung before dawn and prior[268] to the Morning Service.[269]

Also, the reciting of different passages or selected Psalms exists in the Coptic tradition. I believe that the passages that have survived are in "The Morning Doxology[270] where we find excerpts from different psalms (136:6; 28:2; 133:1). Most likely, these are the psalms that constitute The First Hour (the Matins) prayer.[271] These sets of psalms thoroughly echo the interwoven praying elements in the segment of "Preparation to meet God." Several examples show the parallelism. In *Seder Amram Gaon*, the Berakah "My God"[272] emphasizes the soul and the relevant divine dynamic who "creates," "forms," "preserves," "takes" (from me), restores, and "one day will

---

[267] Hoffman, "Introduction to the Liturgy," 7.

[268] As part of the Psalmody book, for its place prior to the Morning Service, see Burmester, *The Egyptian or Coptic Church*, 108.

[269] HPE, for the Second Ode (called *Hos* in Coptic), 24–30; for the Fourth Ode, 66–73.

[270] HPE, 247–50.

[271] The psalms of the First Hour (Prime) are to be found in the *Book of Seven Hours* (known as Agpeya or Agbeya). The Psalms that belong to this hour are Pss 1, 2, 3, 4, 5, 6, 8, 12, 13, 15, 16, 19, 25, 27, 63, 67, 70, 113 and 143 (in total 19 psalms).

[272] This Berakah is a prayer for waking up that is moved into public prayer to make sure that people are reciting it.

take it."²⁷³ It is also a concept of the renewed life that one experiences upon waking.

Apparently, the theme holds a certain importance within the Jewish mindset concerning the pre-Morning Service as well in the Coptic tradition. The theme of "Neshamat" (soul) is displayed significantly in the selection of Psalms of the First Hour in the *Book of Seven Canonical Hours*. The reflection of tying the "soul" with the time of daybreak is implicit. In the selected psalms, the word "soul" (נֶפֶשׁ *nepeš*), LXX (ψυχή *psychē*) is repeated 20 times[274],[275] Pss 3 (1 time), 6 (2 times), 12 (1 time), 15 (1 time), 18, 24 (3 times), 26 (1 time), 62 (4 times), 69 (1 time), and 142 (5 times). Always in the Prime Hour, we read "From the night season my soul awakes early unto you, O my God, for your precepts are a light upon the earth."[276] In the "Hail of Saint Mary," the worshipper asks

---

[273] 1 SAG, 8–9.

[274] This prayer book does not indicate the number of verses.

[275] The psalms below are numbered according to the numerical sequence of the Book of the Seven Canonical Hours. The psalms are numbered differently in the *Agpeya*, according to the numbering used in the Septuagint (Greek manuscript). The Septuagint translation is considered by the Orthodox Churches to be the oldest and most reliable manuscript of the Holy Bible. The differences in numbering begin with Psalms 9 and 10 (NKJV) = Psalm 9 (Septuagint). Due to the similarity in theme and pattern, these psalms were considered to be one and the same text. Note also that at the ninth hour of the Agpeya, Psalms 114 and 115 = Psalm 116 (NKJV). At Compline (12th hour), Psalms 146 and 147 = Psalm 147 (NKJV). Psalms 148-150 are the same in the Hebrew and Septuagint translations. Psalm 151, which is not recognized in the New King James Version (NKJV), begins the prayers of Bright Saturday (the night of the Apocalypse) in the Coptic Orthodox Church.

[276] *Book of Seven Canonical Hours*, 27.

in her intercession that the Lord "may have mercy on our souls..."[277]

Ugo Zanetti attempts to identify the motivation behind selecting particular psalms for each canonical hour. After examining various manuscripts, he determined that the psalms assigned to each canonical hour in the Agpeya follow the Palestinian psalter, which originated in Jerusalem. However, he leaves room for future research.[278]

1. Commonalities

In Jewish tradition, the "Birkhot Hashashar" consists of morning prayers were originally said privately and individually upon arising[279] and before going to the synagogue and worship. In Coptic tradition, the notion of such Berakhot reverberates in *The Book of Khedmat Al Shamas* as a required procedure, for a spiritual readiness, before going to church.[280]

---

[277] *Book of Seven Canonical Hours*, 27.

[278] Zanetti, "La Distribution des Psaumes dans l'Horlogion Copte," 323–69.

[279] Hoffman, "Introduction to the Liturgy," 25.

[280] *The Book of Khedmat Al Shamas*, 11 (Guidelines no.1–3). First, upon arising and before going early to the church, the deacon has to pray privately as described in Matt 6:6. Second, after leaving home, he has to repeat the following: Psalms 122, verses 4 and 5 of Psalm 27, and verse 4 of Psalm 65. Guideline 3 commands the deacon that upon entering the church, he has to picture it as he is entering heaven in order to stand before the 'Most High' and with the angels and saints.

C. The Shema

The second part of the Service is the Shema. After reciting the "Kaddish,"[281] a long prayer is said by the *Sheliach Tzibbur*[282] (or everyone) echoing many thematic similarities that exist in the Coptic Morning Service. As there are many interrelations and Jewish literature holds various biblical notions and numerous pseudepigraphal late Second Temple writings (also Qumranic sources), I will elaborate on that in Chapter 4. The most striking are the significance of the following keywords in the Jewish Morning Service and their ties with the concept of the morning time and creation, as they are also reverberated in the Coptic Morning Service: King (Creator) of the universe,[283] the luminaries (created by God and through their cycles are fixed the times of prayer),[284] "the hosts and the holy beings (angels), and their heavenly worship" (glorifying the Creator for making the cosmos, an ordered

---

[281] 1 SAG, 44–45.

[282] Sheliah Zibbur as per the *Jewish Encyclopedia* "is a congregational messenger or deputy or agent. During the time of the late Second Temple, it was the priest who represented the congregation in offering the sacrifice, and who, before the close of the service, pronounced the priestly benediction." See, Landsberg, "Sheliah Zibbur," 261.

[283] 1 SAG, 46. This is part of the blessing formula found in all parts of rabbinic Jewish liturgy. See Reuven Kimelman's articles about when the theme of divine kingship was added.

[284] 1 SAG, 47. For "the King of Universe" and luminaries, which are two closely related subjects, I will discuss briefly the biblical backbone of liturgies based on "luminaries" and especially the Morning Service, the imageries of luminaries in Chapter 4. The study will target also the subject of cosmic praise in the late Second Temple Judaism period and its perception of "luminaries" in order to understand how this concept was kept in the ritual.

world),[285] and "the law and light" (Ps 119).[286] Those keywords lead us to visualize the patterns of the Jewish daily prayers during the late Second Temple period and especially at the beginning of the first century CE.[287]

D. The Tefillah[288]

After praying the Shema, the "Tefillah" must be said. As mentioned previously, the Tefillah consists of

---

[285] 1 SAG, 47–49. In order to understand how the theme of "angels" shapes the liturgical pattern in the daily Jewish prayers, I will examine a Qumran text (4Q503) and its resemblance in the Morning Service in the Coptic church, a few examples from the Morning Doxology: HPA [Arabic Holy Psalmody], 265 (HPE, 341) [English Holy Psalmody]; Hail to angels and other "holy beings," HPA, 267 (HPE, 244); the Verses of Cymbals, HPA, 284–85 (HPE, 260); The Praise of the Angels which preludes with "Let us sing with the angels," HPA, 296 (HPE, 280–81). See also the section of Doxologies, for archangels: Michael, HPA, 318–20 (HPE, 296–97), Raphael, HPA, 322–24, (HPE 299–301); Surial, HPA 324–325 (HPE, 301–302); for Four Creatures (of the Revelation Book), HPA 325–27 (HPE, 303–304); for the "Twenty-Four Presbyters" (Elders of the Book of Revelation), HPA, 327–28 (HPE, 304–305); for "All the Heavenly" (beings), HPA, 329–31 (HPE, 305–308). A worthwhile study of some late Second Temple hymns includes those that refer to worship of heavenly beings the "Merkabah Hymn" and "the Angelic Liturgy," which are studied by Stone et al., *Jewish Writings Second Temple Period*, 565.

[286] 1 SAG, 50–51. For the relation between law and light in the context of Psalm 19, where the psalmist states "the heavens which declare the glory of God; and the skies proclaim the work of his hands," I will examine it also through the reciting of Shema and its echoes in the Coptic Morning Service. It is mentioned in the last paragraph of the "Praise of the Angels," PHA, 298 (HPE, 282).

[287] Penner, *Patterns of Daily Prayer*.

[288] 1 SAG, 70.

supplicatory prayers Berakhot, Bouyer has a remarkable dictum that is important to my research. He notes:

> When investigating the origins of the Christian Eucharist, the element of the synagogal liturgy that immediately attracts our attention is the type of prayers called Berakoth in Hebrew, a term for which the Greek word ευχαριστια was the first translation. In English ευχαριστια is generally translated to thanksgiving, as is Berakah, although the Jewish usage would be to call the berakoth, blessing.[289]

Bouyer attempted to study the Berakoth through the three Alexandrian Church Anaphoras (Basil, Gregory, and Cyril), but apparently did not notice how the Berakhot holds a more direct similarity in many ways with the petition prayers of the Coptic Morning Service than the Blessings of the Anaphoras.[290] In this part, the similarities are conspicuous, and I consider them strong evidence that the Coptic Morning Service was derived from the Jewish liturgy as compiled by Amram Gaon. I will investigate a number of pieces of evidence.

In this important segment of the ritual, first, I will include the etymology of the Hebrew word "Beraka" and "ⲡⲣⲟⲥⲉ" and "ⲧⲱⲃϩ," for all three hold the same contextual meaning. Second, the examination of the Jewish features of the Berakah in the Coptic litanies may lead us

---

[289] Bouyer, *Eucharist and Spirituality*, 11.

[290] The word "Anaphora" is normally used in the Coptic Church for the three Eucharistic liturgies: Liturgy of St. Basil, Liturgy of St. Gregory, and Liturgy of St. Cyril.

to understand the reason why the Coptic litanies (as called in the *Holy Euchologion*) are shaped in a similar form. Third, the number of Berakhot in both liturgies is significant, and fourth, there is a striking textual correspondence between both forms of petitions.

1. Etymology of Hebrew "Beraka" and Coptic "Ⲡⲣⲟⲥⲉ"

In both Jewish and Coptic Morning Services, the ritual consists of a group of supplicatory prayers, varying in the topic of the supplication. In the Jewish ritual, the prayer of supplication is recited after the Shema; and in the Coptic ritual, it follows the incensing of the Altar.

The word Tefillah means "supplication," known in Aramaic as "selota." The Greek equivalent to this word is ευχαι.[291] Hedegård noted that as early "as in the LXX, the verb 'Hitpallel' is regularly translated to προσευχεσθαι and Tefillah is frequently translated by προσευχη."[292] Furthermore, he mentions a significant comment from Luke 11:1: the disciples of Christ the disciples of Christ were not asking for a prayer in general but for a προσευχεσθαι, a Tefillah.

Remarkably, all the supplications and responses by the deacon during the Coptic Morning Service are grouped under a title in Arabic called *Iprosat al Shammas*, which is a translation of the Greek word προσευχη. This word was naturalized in the Coptic language with many others and became ⲡⲣⲟⲥⲉⲩⲭⲏ. In the Coptic Morning and Evening

---

[291] The Greek word ευχαι (the same word in Coptic) means a wish, expressed as a petition to God, or in votive obligation: a prayer or a vow.

[292] Hedegård, 1 SAG, note 7.

Incense Service, the deacon frequently recites this word when he calls the congregation to pray, or to beseech the Lord for the supplication subject. It comes in different forms, such as ⲡⲣⲟⲥⲉⲩⲝⲁⲥⲑⲉ (let us pray), [293] or ⲧⲱⲃϩ (Coptic, ask for).[294] Waheeb Girgis states that some Greek religious terms entered the Egyptian language via the Jews in Egypt:[295]

> Whose religious expressions must have been known centuries before the Coptic translation of the Bible took place. The Septuagint itself was made in the third century before Christ. Therefore, the Jewish religious terms must have found some hospitality among the Egyptian words, at least by way of comparison, accord, or contrast, between the Jewish and the Egyptian religions. This hospitality was warmly extended when the Old Testament became in Christian Egypt a constituent part of the Holy Scriptures i.e., ἄγγελος, angel; ἀμήν, amen; θυσία, offering; θυσιαστήριον, altar; and many others.[296]

2. Jewish Features of Berakah in Coptic Litanies

The features are, as given by Hedegård in his introduction in the Seder Amram book: a. The narrative structure of the Beraka is to follow a fixed norm. The

---

[293] *The Book of Khedmat Al Shamas*, 3–13.

[294] In Arabic طلبة (*Telbah*) means "ask for." However, the majority of the new euchologions translate the Coptic word "to pray" and not "to ask."

[295] Jews who lived in Egypt during the late Second Temple era.

[296] Girgis, *Greek Words in Coptic Usage*, 18. See also, Mallon, *La grammaire Copte*, 4–5; Daoud, *The Dictionary of the Coptic Language* (Coptic-Arabic), 829–87.

beraka should begin with "Blessed be thou, JHWH, our God, King of the Universe."[297] Hedegård notes that it is not always the case that the exact word, "King of the Universe," is used in all the eighteen Berakhot. It appears this formula aims to praise God as the sovereign of the world. This narrative rule, which reflects the concept of the dominant God (who is in control) over the world, occurs also in many Coptic litanies.[298] b. The Beraka is to end with a benediction known as "sealing a prayer,"[299] stating: "blessed be thou."[300] Likewise, the rule of the closing prayer or sealing prayer is respected in many Coptic litanies.[301] c. There are both "Short" and "Long" formulas

---

[297] 1 SAG, introduction, 33. According to the Talmud, this is formalized only in the 3rd c. CE. There is a shortened form, without the reference to God's sovereignty, which concludes "long" Berakhot. The only exception in opening formulae is in the Amidah, where the language is that of God in Exodus 3:15.

[298] Litanies for "The Departed" (DL, 19), for "The Sick" (DL, 23), for "The Peace" (DL, 70), and, for "The Assemblies" (DL, 79). They all start with the same formula: "Let us ask God the 'Pantocrator' (ⲡⲓⲡⲁⲛⲧⲟⲕⲣⲁⲧⲱⲣ), the Father of our Lord, God, and Savior Jesus Christ."

[299] 1 SAG, introduction, 33.

[300] 1 SAG, introduction, 33.

[301] The concept of "sealing a prayer" occurs also in the same litanies mentioned above. It occurs once after these petitions (litanies) and after the Thanksgiving Prayer, which precedes the petitions. The sealing prayer is unvarying: "[Stanza 1] Through the grace, compassion, and love of mankind of your only begotten Son, our Lord, God and Savior Jesus Christ. [Stanza 2] Through whom the glory, the honor, the dominion, and the worship are due unto you, with him and the Holy Spirit, the giver of life, who is of one essence with you. [Stanza 3] Now and all times and unto the age of all ages. Amen."

of Berakhot.[302] Both could be either praise to the name of God[303] or a petition.[304] In the Morning Service in Jewish and Coptic traditions, both formulas are categorized under "Long Litanies" and "Short Litanies."[305] d. The Beraka is

---

[302] Abu Dirham indicates two types of Berakhot regarding narrative length: "Those that are shaped according to the short formula and those which are shaped according to the long formula." David ben Josef ben David Abudirham (1340 CE) *Sefer Ḥibbur Perush ha-Berakhot we-ha-Tefillot* ("Commentary on the Blessings and Prayers") or known also as Sefer Abu Dirham, 2B, 3A, quoted by Hedegård, intro 1 SAG, 34. For the importance of the "blessing" in Jewish liturgy, see Millgram, *Jewish Worship*, 89, 94.

[303] Hedegård gives some examples, such as "Blessed be thou JHWH, our God King of Universe, who hast not made me a heathen" (1 SAG, 9–10). Three Berakhot are said when the priest puts a spoonful of incense into the censor: First spoonful: "Blessed be the Father, the Pantocrator. Amen." Second spoonful: "Blessed be his only-begotten son, Jesus Christ our Lord. Amen". The third and last: "Blessed be the Holy Spirit the Paraclete. Amen." (For the three blessings, see DL, 10 and *Massoudy,* 35). Many other examples exist from both traditions.

[304] In the Coptic tradition, in the Morning Service, additional litanies to the long ones are also short litanies, in a form of petition. They are also recited during the ritual. For all the short litanies, see DL, 70–81.

[305] See Table of Contents, DL, XIII. In the Coptic Morning Service, the litanies (petitions) are divided in two groups; the short litanies are for the Peace of Church, the Patriarch and Bishops, the Place (salvation of world and this city), the Three Seasons of the Year, and the Assemblies. The long ones are for the Departed, the Sick, the Travelers, and the Sacrifices. To put things in perspective: Not sure this is a real parallel. This is language which derives from the Mishnah's discussion of the blessings around Shema, but no one is quite sure what it refers to. See Langer, *To Worship God Properly*.

to express a congregational need and not an individual one.[306]

3. Number of Berakhot in Both Traditions

In the Jewish liturgical tradition, the number of Berakhot contained in the "Tefillah" varies between seventeen and nineteen [307] (this number is without the shortened forms for holidays. Hedegård displays the traditional rabbinic view in this regard by quoting from RaMBaM,[308] who explains that prior to Rabbi Gamaliel,[309]

---

[306] The Tefillah, with its eighteen (nineteen) Berakhot, is the principle supplicatory prayer of the Jewish liturgy. Seemingly it is also the case for the litanies of the Coptic liturgy, where all rituals repeat the petition that occur in the Morning Service. Both Berakhot and Coptic litanies "are formulated in the plural to be used by the congregation, and the petitions are requests which concern the need of the whole congregation" (1 SAG, intro 36). Hedegård observes that except for a couple petitions in the Tefillah that are "national," many others are for the good of the community of God (peace, rain, harvest). Likewise, the Coptic petitions (litanies) focus on the congregational needs, not on the individual requests. The Coptic liturgists strengthen such perception: see, for instance, Rafael, *Isnaou Hada L'Zikri*, 87.

Only with in the Amidah. There are other contexts, especially non-petitionary ones, where the function is individual.

[307] 1 SAG, 71, Hedegård's notes 30–60.

[308] Moses Ben Maimon known as RaMBaM, Talmudist, philosopher, astronomer, and physician; born at Cordova, March 30, 1135; died at Cairo, Dec. 13, 1204; known in Arabic literature as Abu 'Imran Musa ben Maimun ibn 'Abd Allah.

[309] Rabban Gamaliel II was a rabbi from the second generation of Tannaim. He was the first person to lead the Sanhedrin as nasi after the fall of the Second Temple in 70 CE. He was the son of Shimon ben Gamaliel, one of Jerusalem's foremost men in the war against the

the number was already eighteen and he is the one who added the nineteenth (Birkat ha-minim). Coptic liturgists also reckon that the number of litanies that belong to the Morning Service and the three known liturgies[310] are either between 17 or 18.[311] The striking annotation is that the liturgy of St. Cyril, which is considered the oldest in the Coptic repertoire, consists of seventeen counts and includes all the Coptic Morning Service litanies and many others.[312]

4. Textual Correspondence between Berakhot and Coptic Litanies

A brief introduction to each Berakah is necessary here before discussing the textual similarity. The first *Berakah* "Abot" (the Fathers), is about God's covenant

---

Romans, and grandson of Gamaliel (Died: 114 AD) The life period of Rabbi Gamaliel was par excellence the embryonic stage of shaping the Christian liturgy through the first converted Jews in Palestine and the diaspora. Believing also that Paul was a scholar in the Gamaliel School, Hedegård's statement holds a significant value that "At the time of Christ, then, the Eighteen Benedictions were recited in the synagogue service on weekdays and the seven Benedictions and Holy Days. But no regulations were made for the private recital of the Tefillah." Hedegård, note 72.

[310] Again, the three known liturgies in the Coptic Church are the Liturgy of St. Basil of Caesarea, the Liturgy of St. Gregory of Nazianzus, and the Liturgy of St. Cyril of Alexandria.

[311] Bishop Mettaous states that the litanies, in particular, in the Liturgy of St. Cyril, the oldest anaphora in the Egyptian church counts seventeen. See Mettaous, *Al Thalathat Kodassat*, 120. Rafael, *Isnaou Hada L'Zikri*, 86–87, counts eighteen litanies that are spread between the Morning Service and the Eucharist mass.

[312] *Massoudy*, 411–50.

with the Patriarchs (Abraham, Isaac, Jacob);[313] the second *Berakah* "Geburot," is about the mighty God, Lord of the Universe, who resurrects the dead and who causes the wind to blow and the rain to fall.[314] The third is "Quedushat Hashem" ("Sanctification of the Name"),[315] meaning all generations will give homage to the name of God.[316] Fourth, is the *Berakah Bina* "intelligence" called also *Berakah chokma* ("the Prayer of Wisdom"): the wisdom that distinguishes between holy and profane, and clean and unclean (but also includes the divine favoritism for man in getting knowledge from the Torah.[317] Fifth is known as *Berakah Teshuba* ("Return" [to God]), a petition for forgiveness via repentance.[318] The name of the sixth *Berakah* is "Selicha" ("Forgiveness"): God is always ready to receive the repentant sinner and forgive him.[319] The seventh is called *Berakah* "Guella" ("Redemption"). This petition holds eschatological ideas about the future Messiah.[320] Eighth is *Refua* ("Healing"), a petition for the healing of the sick. Ninth, this *Berakah* starts with "Bless this Year," called *birkat Ha-shanim* ("Prayer for the [Good] Year); it is a request for a divine blessing for rain and dew.[321] Tenth is the *Quibbus Galuijot* ("Gathering

---

[313] 1 SAG, 83.

[314] 1 SAG, 85.

[315] The Quedusha, the Thrice Holy, is recited during this Berakah, 1 SAG, 86.

[316] 1 SAG, 86.

[317] 1 SAG, 87.

[318] 1 SAG, 87–88.

[319] 1 SAG, 88.

[320] 1 SAG, 89.

[321] 1 SAG, 89–90.

Together of the Dispersed"), a petition for assembling the scattered Jews of the diaspora.[322] Eleventh, called *Berakah Mishpat* (Prayer for Justice), is a petition for the restoration of political autonomy holding also messianic visions.[323] Twelfth is *Berakah Ha-minim* ("Prayer against Heretics"), a petition targeting the separation of Christianity from Judaism, to suppress false teaching.[324] The thirteenth is *Berakah Saddiqin* ("Prayer for the Righteous"), a prayer for the proselytes, for a true convert to Israel.[325] The fourteenth petition is the *Berakah Jerusalem*, God's city, appealing for the building of the city and the continuance of the divine presence.[326] The fifteenth is *Berakah David* ("A Prayer for David"), petition that God may cause the Messiah of the house of David to come.[327] Sixteenth is called *Tefillah* ("A Prayer"): a petition that God may hear the entire prayer of his people Israel.[328] The seventeenth *Berakah* is called "Aboda" ("Service" or "Worship"), a prayer for God's graciousness to accept offerings and prayer; it was a prayer recited in the Temple of Jerusalem in connection with the daily sacrifices.[329] Eighteenth is *Berakah Hodaa* ("Give Thanks"), giving thanks to God for

---

[322] 1 SAG, 91–92.
[323] 1 SAG, 92–93.
[324] 1 SAG, 93.
[325] 1 SAG, 94–95.
[326] 1 SAG, 95.
[327] 1 SAG, 95–96.
[328] 1 SAG, 96.
[329] 1 SAG, 96–97.

his good deeds.³³⁰ The nineteenth is *Berakah Kohanim* ("Priestly Blessing"), praying God to grant his peace.³³¹

The reverberation of the subject of almost each *beraka* is echoed in the Coptic petitions. In this chapter, I can only outline the analogies in just a few *Berakhot*, leaving the others for a further survey. For instance, the eighth *Berakah Refua* ("Healing"), interrelates with the Coptic Litany of the Sick,³³² the ninth, "Bless this year" called "Berakah Ha-shanim", interconnects with the Coptic Three Seasons of the Year,³³³ and the twelfth, *Berakah Haminim* ("Prayer against Heretics") is indicated as a litany with no title, and is the ending part of the Coptic Litany of Assemblies.

The Jewish *Sheliah Zibbur* (the person who prays on behalf of the congregation) recites, "Heal us, JHWH and we shall be healed, save us and we shall be saved, and grant a perfect healing to our wounds; for thou God, are a merciful Physician. Blessed be thou, JHWH who heals the sick of the people of Israel."³³⁴ Meanwhile, the Coptic Litany for the Sick is more elaborate, but still holds the main obvious keywords like "grant us, with them, health and healing" (ⲙ̀ⲡⲓⲟⲩϫⲁⲓ ⲛⲉⲙ ⲡⲓⲧⲁⲗϭⲟ). The word "wounds" in the Coptic prayer may refer to more than a specific injury, but to a larger continuum, such as an emotional depression, or a moral humiliation. This is seen

---

³³⁰ 1 SAG, 97.
³³¹ 1 SAG, 98–99.
³³² DL, 23.
³³³ DL, 78.
³³⁴ 1 SAG, 89.

in the Coptic text:[335] "Those in prisons or dungeons, those in exile or captivity, or those held in bitter bondage, O Lord set them all free…" If the Hebrew text implores God for healing because Israel is God's people, the Coptic text shows the same concept of divine covenant: "…remember, O Lord, the sick among your people", Ⲡ϶ⲟⲓⲥ̀ ⲛⲛⲏⲉⲧϣⲱⲛⲓ̀ ⲛⲧⲉ ⲡⲉⲕⲗⲁⲟⲥ." Remarkably, both petitions implore the godly "Physician" who, according to the Coptic version, is "the true physician of our souls and bodies ⲡⲓⲥⲓⲛⲓ̀ ⲙⲙⲏⲓ̀ ⲛⲧⲉ ⲛⲉⲛ ⲯⲩⲭⲏ ⲛⲉⲙ ⲛⲉⲛⲥⲱⲙⲁ."

The Jewish *birkat Ha-shanim*[336] interconnects even more textually with the Coptic litany, "For Three Seasons of the Year."[337] The rubrics are common in the timing of reciting both petitions. In both calendars, the yearly cycle is divided into three seasons, with the liturgical texts changing accordingly. And the season is changed according to the Jewish settlement in the Diaspora. (No in the Land of Israel.). Hedegård emphasizes how local geographical factors impacted the prayer. He mentions,[338] for instance, "In Babylonia, the prayer for rain was inserted in the ninth paragraph (Berakah) of the Tefillah from the sixtieth day of the autumnal equinox, (the 3rd of December), but in Palestine it was inserted from the seventh of Marcheshvan."[339] Hedegård, apparently, finds

---

[335] DL, 23–25.

[336] 1 SAG, 89–91.

[337] DL, 74–77.

[338] Hedegård, 1 SAG, note 91.

[339] Marcheshvan is the only month of the Jewish year that has no special days, neither feast nor fast. An equivalent is Coptic month, the Nasie, ⲡⲓⲕⲟⲩϫⲓ ⲛⲁⲃⲟⲧ, known as "the Small Month."

solid rabbinic literature behind the recitation of the appropriate part of the Berakah, according to the proper season. Amram, based on the Palestinian calendar, lists the first of the three seasons as follows: Imploring God for dew and rain is from the sixtieth day after the autumnal day (after the autumnal equinox) until the afternoon Tefillah, including the eve of the first day of the Passover. For the other two seasons, Amram does not mention what Jews have to pray during the other two seasons; he is content in saying, "But from the afternoon Tefillah of the fourteenth of Nissan, i.e., the eve of the festival, one does not pray for dew and rain in the birkat ha-shanim until the sixtieth day after the autumnal equinox comes. And the sixtieth day itself one prays [for dew and rain]." [340] Evidently, he wanted to stay out of trouble from the other Jewish teachers of the Academy, by not deciding what to address the other two seasons of the year. There are functionally two seasons: summer and winter. The shift points are the first day of Passover and the day of assembly following Sukkot/Tabernacles. However, petitioning for rain is postponed allowing those who were in Jerusalem for Sukkot to get home, hence the two weeks following the festival in Israel itself, and the calculation according to the solar calendar for the Diaspora. This does not constitute a system that prays for rain according to local needs at all, as such prayers are only for rain in the land of Israel according to its rainy season.

In the Coptic liturgy, the priest says the appropriate prayer according to the season: the Litany of the Waters: Paoni 12 to Paapi 9 (June 19 to Oct. 19/20); Litany for the

---

[340] 1 SAG, 91.

Seeds: Paapi 10 to Tobi (Oct. 20/21 to Jan 18/19); and the Litany for the Fruits: Toibi 11 to Paoni 11 (Jan. 19/20 to June 18).[341]

The literary similarities are striking. Both texts express the main idea of the mighty God who controls the cosmic elements, such as rain, dew and winds. Thus, abundance will yield to prosperity, peace, and hope. Examples include SAG: "Give dew and rain for the blessing upon the face of the earth", DL: "Give joy to the face of the earth"; SAG: "Bless the year unto us", DL: "Bless the crown of the year with your goodness."

Birkat Ha-minim ("Prayer against Heretics") is found in a non-named litany, ending the Coptic Litany of Assemblies. It seems that in the past, DL 80–81, this litany was unconnected to the Litany of Assemblies. It focuses on asking God to grant the church assemblies a secure environment. God is graciously asked to demolish any "obstacle or hindrance" that may endanger the congregation. This interference is assumed to be the worship of idols, the power of Satan, and especially heretics, heresies, instigators, and dissensions. The priest asks the Lord to disperse their counsel as he dispersed the counsel of Ahithophel.[342] However, in the long historical background of *Berakah Ha-minim*,[343] the word "minim"

---

[341] For more information about the Coptic calendar, see Cody, "Coptic Calendar," 433–36.

[342] 2 Sam 17:1–23.

[343] This petition was targeting the separation of Jewish Christians from the synagogue. Later there was tension between the Jews and the Jewish Christians, such that the latter were called Christians.

stands for any kind of heretic. The rabbinic writings,[344] and equally the Coptic ritual, varied their types: atheist, the idol worshippers, and slanderers. Both liturgies beg the Lord for a harsh, quick reaction towards them, by using the same prayer words. It is noteworthy to display both texts. SAG: "And for the slanderers[345] let there be no hope, and let all the wicked perish in a moment and let all our enemies be speedily cut off, and the dominion of arrogance do thou speedily uproot and crush and humble in our days..." DL:

> Satan with all his evil powers, trample and humiliate under our feet speedily...the enemies of your holy church...strip their vanity, show them their weakness speedily ʻⲛⲭⲱⲗⲉⲙ. Bring to naught their intrigues, their madness, their wickedness, and their slanders, which they commit against us.[346]

5. Rubrics of the Tefillah

A "rubric" is a word or section of text that is traditionally written or printed in red ink for emphasis and is written for the benefit or instruction of the priest or presenter of the material, often including directions for the congregation or worshippers. The word derives from the Latin "rubrica" meaning "red ochre" or "chalk." In the language of liturgy, this technical term may refer to any liturgical actions customarily performed over the course of

---

[344] 1 SAG, 93.

[345] The dating of Birkat Ha-minim is a matter of debate regarding its ancient place in Jewish liturgy. See R. Langer's book *Cursing the Christians? A History of the Birkat HaMinim*.

[346] DL, 80–81.

a service. In Coptic manuscripts and Coptic printed liturgical books, usually the rubric is written in red. In the Jewish Morning service, numerous rubrics address physical position, posture, and attitude of the worshipper during the reciting of the "Tefillah," which include instructions, such as "to stand up in fear,"[347] "praying towards Jerusalem,"[348] "put the worshipper's feet in the right order."[349] Despite the numerous rubrics mentioned by Hedegård, my discussion must be limited to these three for now. In both traditions, the massive quantity of relevant literature is fascinating. It would require numerous pages to describe these rubrics properly.[350]

a. "To Stand Up in Fear" [351]

The Tefillah is recited [352]standing. Amram commands that "they stand up for the Tefillah. And, a person who prays the Tefillah must concentrate his mind because the rabbis taught: A person who prays must concentrate his heart."[353] Hedegård finds that to stand up is tied with the concentration of the mind, based on rabbinic dictums. For instance, he quotes from RaMBaM, *HT*, 4,15:

---

[347] 1 SAG, 73, 75, 79.

[348] 1 SAG, 81.

[349] 1 SAG, 82.

[350] These appear in Amram's text because it was written as a book of liturgical instruction for communities that badly needed it. However, until the modern era, most rites included minimal rubrics in their liturgical texts, so Amram's work is exceptional in this respect. Here, Amram is summarising and quoting Babylonian Talmudic traditions.

[351] 1 SAG 73, 75, 79.

[352] 1 SAG, 83, Hedegård's note.

[353] 1 SAG, 75–76.

"If one prayed the Tefillah without concentration of mind, he must recite it again with concentration."[354] Hedegård explains: "A man who prays the Tefillah should consider himself as if he stood before the Divine Presence, in accordance with that which is written: I have set JHWH always before me (Ps 16:8)."[355]

At the beginning of the Coptic Morning Service, after the priest says, "Let us pray," the deacon calls the congregation to "Stand up for praying."[356] This ⲉⲡⲓⲡⲣⲟⲥⲉⲩⲭⲏ ⲥⲧⲁⲑⲏⲧⲉ [357] is repeated five times during the ritual: once at the beginning and the others at the opening of the litanies.[358] The symbolism is clear, that every time a Jew or Copt prays the petitions, they should concentrate on each word, as they are standing in fear in God's presence. The formula of standing or bowing in the fear of God is common in the Coptic Service.[359] At the reading of the Gospel, the deacon commands the congregation to "Stand in fear and listen…" (DL 66, 67); and after the litanies, he says, "Let us attend in the fear of God." This liturgical

---

[354] Hedegård, note 75.

[355] Hedegård, note 75.

[356] DL, 2. In *Massoudy*, this command is based on Mark 11:25 and Ps 134:1. See p. 28, note 2.

[357] Al Makary notices that in the Euchologion this deacon's responsa is said in Greek and never translated to Coptic. He adds that the fact that the deacon calls the congregation to stand up prior to any liturgical prayer "is a unique case [compared to other liturgies], a special feature in the Coptic liturgy." Al Makary, *Salawat,* 346, 355.

[358] *Massoudy,* 28, 36, 38, 45, 79.

[359] DL, 85.

symbol leads us to the orientation of the worshipper while he stands in God's presence.

b. Praying towards Jerusalem, towards the East

Apparently, both Jewish and Coptic traditions from the early centuries CE were preoccupied with the orientation of the worshipper when praying the Jewish prayers or in the Christian Church. Amram, as he composed his siddur in Babylonia, required the worshipper of the Tefillah to turn westward.[360] Hedegård explains that the reason is because Jews living in that city should turn in the direction of Jerusalem when reciting the Tefillah.[361]

In the Euchologion, the red rubric commands the priest to face towards the East before reciting the litanies.[362] The Alexandrian Church favours the East, and this has been the custom in its communal and private prayers from the early centuries. Basilios originates the eastward orientation from the time of the *Apostolic Constitutions*, which prescribe: "All rise up with one consent and, looking toward the east . . . pray to God eastward."[363] The orientation of the synagogue towards the East (Only when west of Jerusalem...) and possible

---

[360] 1 SAG, 81.

[361] 1 SAG, 81, Hedegård's note.

[362] Massoudy, 46.

[363] Basilios, "Orientation towards the East," 1846. The Coptic Church evidence is based on Mal 4:2; Matt 24:27. The Basilios adds to his article an important quotation from Saint Ephraim the Syrian (306–373), "The Jews looked to Jerusalem in their prayers, for it was their holy country. As for us, the Paradise is our country, which was in the East. Therefore, we are ordered to look towards the East during our prayers."

correlations with the Coptic Church may also be an area for future reflection.[364]

c. The Obligation of Putting the Feet[365] "in Right Order"

It is prominent that in the Old Testament, the "right" and "left" hands or feet hold deep theological meanings.[366] But in a liturgical context, this looks uncommon. In SAG, the putting of the feet in the right position seems to have been important at the time of composing the siddur and appears to be an ancient peculiar duty during the Morning Service. In the Coptic Morning Service ritual, the rubric specifies that the Coptic priest, while going up to the altar, must place his right foot first, and when he goes down, he places his left foot first.[367] This exigency is better understood in a halachic context. Hedegård cites from two Amoraim (R. Levi and R. Simon) an unclear dictum, but it reverberates with the Coptic rubric:

> One of them says: As the angels. The other says: As the priests. He who says: As the

---

[364] The topic is also stimulating in regard to the common liturgical architectural concept of the synagogue and the Coptic Church. See Ryken et al., "East," 225–26; Levine, *The Ancient Synagogue*, 326–30; Malaty, *The Church: House of God*, 74–77 (Early Church Fathers and the Eastward orientation); Basilios, "Orientation towards the East," 1846.

[365] 1 SAG, 82.

[366] On the right as opposed to the left, see Gen 48:12–20; Exod 29:22; Lev 7:32. It symbolizes also strength and weakness: Exod 15:6, 12; Isa 62:8; Ps 17:7; 44:4.

[367] DL, 9. *Massoudy*, 43.

priests [emphasizes] that it is written: Thou shalt not go up unto my altar, that thy nakedness should not be discovered thereon, that [in walking] their heel touches the toe and the toe touches the heel. And who says: As the angels [emphasizes] that is written: And their feet were straight feet. [368]

In Amram's quotation, the "putting the feet in the right order" matters when the priest "goes up into [the Lord's] altar." Just to highlight the importance of the correct position of the worshipper's feet in the Jewish Morning Service, Jacobson also provides further clarification. He quotes from *Shibbole ha-Lekett*,[369] that the Geonim believe that the resting of the shekinah above the worshipper requires him to step back three spaces so that "the left foot is moved back first."[370] To conclude this part, the following quotation captures the importance of a liturgical rubric: "Obviously, symbolic sets are deeds which give concrete expression to some idea or emotions. At times, the power of a symbol [a rubric] is greater than pure verbal articulation."[371]

e. The Priestly Blessing

The Priestly Blessing, which is the last part in both Jewish[372] and Coptic Morning Services, manifests also a

---

[368] 1 SAG, 82.

[369] A halakhic work by Zedekiah ben Abraham Anav (1210–1280); Jacobson, *Meditations on the Siddur*, 111.

[370] Jacobson, *Meditations on the Siddur*, 111.

[371] Jacobson, *Meditations on the Siddur*, 105. On this sort of discussion, see Uri Ehrlich's book on Nonverbal elements of prayer.

[372] 1 SAG, 122–26.

textual and scriptural analogy.³⁷³ In both traditions, the "Priestly Blessing" is a mix of a petition asking God to provide peace and bestow blessings upon the community through the priest. This Blessing is according to Num 6:22–27. A priestly blessing in a synagogue seems odd, but in Amram it is clearly stated that a priest, or one claiming priestly descent, has the legitimacy to recite this blessing over the congregation. According to Hedegård, it is at an early date that the Priestly Blessing was transferred to the synagogue, as the Mishna presupposes it to be an integral part of the synagogue service (Ber. V, 4; Meg. IV, 3, 5, 6, 7, 10). He also notes that "Since the Mishna speaks of the priestly blessing as an integral part of the synagogue service, it seems very probable that this blessing belonged to the synagogue service at the time of Christ."³⁷⁴

Amram also indicates that if no priests are present, the Seliach sibbur says an alternative blessing that also contains "JHWH make his face shine upon thee and be gracious unto thee: JHWH turn his face unto thee, and give thee peace…"³⁷⁵ Remarkably, the Coptic liturgy preserves the same blessing in its Morning Service but in two parts. The first part is called "The Canon:"³⁷⁶ "May God have

---

³⁷³ DL, 89. The "Short Blessing" starts with "May God have compassion upon us." DL, 92, where the priest says the last part of his blessing, it begins: "O king of peace, grant us your peace, establish for us your peace, and forgive our sins…" *Massoudy*, 112.

³⁷⁴ 1 SAG, 122, Hedegård's note. Except that there is no evidence for it until the rabbinic period. It does seem to be an element of Temple liturgy that was transferred to the synagogue, in slightly altered form, but still performed by men of the priestly families.

³⁷⁵ 1 SAG, 126.

³⁷⁶ *Massoudy*, 108 (the title).

compassion upon us, manifest His face upon us, and have mercy upon us.³⁷⁷ O Lord save Your people, bless your inheritance, shepherd them, and raise them up forever."³⁷⁸ The second part is called "First Baraka:"³⁷⁹ ("Blessing" in Arabic is بركة) "O King of peace,³⁸⁰ Grant us your peace, establish for us your peace, and forgive us our sins,"³⁸¹ which resounds with Amram's saying that the Seliach sibbur should conclude the blessing with the words, "who makest peace."

---

[377] Ps 67:1; Lev 6: 22–27.
[378] DL, 89; Ps 28:9.
[379] *Massoudy*, 112 (the title).
[380] Isa 9: 6–7.
[381] DL, 92.

Chapter 4
Thematic Interrelations in the Jewish and Coptic Cycle of Luminaries

The Coptic Morning Service appears to hold many Jewish signatures. These, I believe, are an inheritance of the Temple, and the Jewish liturgies and prayers of the first century. This worship originates in Jewish Scripture and somehow interconnects with certain late Second Temple writings that have influenced the Coptic Church. The evidence of textual correspondences between the two traditions, as seen in Chapter 3, calls for a thematic analysis. Such scrutiny might help to clarify the Jewish influence on the arrangement of prayers in the Coptic Morning Service, as well as its connection with the whole corpus of the Coptic liturgy. One particularly important shared theme, which can be seen as a network that holds many shared Judeo-Coptic topics, is the Jewish conceptualization of the cycle of luminaries (sun, moon, stars, and seasons). Topics that are shared originate in Scripture, are well-expressed in the texts of the prayers, and even have an impact on the worship melodies, as we will see throughout this chapter.

To probe this conceptualization of the cycle of the luminaries and its origin in both traditions, I compare various writings. The Old Testament passages, which I include in this chapter, hold a foundational role in understanding the potential Jewish impact of the theme of luminaries on the Coptic liturgy. The episode of Creation in Genesis is the first seed that grew into a massive tree displaying numerous branches of liturgical forms. Also, the book of Psalms frequently demonstrates how the luminaries are an integral part of all creation, where cosmic praise is offered to God, the Creator, and the "King of the Universe."

My selection of texts from the literature of Qumran shows a development of the theme of luminaries in the Qumran prayers and praises. What shows in that literature is a new understanding of structuring a corpus of liturgy based on the cycles of the moon and the sun. Apparently, different significant elements were added to this corpus, such as angels, archangels, light, and many other concepts, which illustrate an inherent perception of a tie between heaven and earth in praising the Creator. Thus, the Jewish Morning Service shows a bond between the Old Testament and Qumran texts, and sheds some light on the Coptic Morning Service, where the concept of luminary cycles and cosmic elements are integral.

Despite the voluminous literature that exists regarding the conception of the account of the Creation, which entails the notion of "luminaries" and "cycles,"[382] it is necessary to outline the main topics that I have chosen to demonstrate a multifaceted thematic interrelation between the Jewish and Coptic Morning Services. The impressive array of topics that are based on the account of Creation (in the Coptic Morning and Evening Service) make a multilayered world of liturgical texts and practices. Even if these acquire new aspects with the new perceptions of early Christianity, the Jewish theme of luminaries survives distinctively through many centuries in the Alexandrian tradition. To complete this study, it is necessary to follow

---

[382] Cycles also refer to time as the year, 24 hours of a day, which hold the morning and evening time of prayers.

a certain chronological order to outline how the Coptic conservatism has retained the Jewish view of luminaries. First, the starting point is to find biblical foundations of luminary liturgies, including how the daily prayer is based on the luminary cycles of the heaven. Secondly, it is important to gather some facts regarding the perception of luminaries during the late Second Temple era drawing on a selection of Dead Sea Scrolls and Qumranic texts. Thirdly, it is instructive to look for the connection between late Second Temple writings and the texts regarding "luminaries" in *Seder Amram Gaon* (1 SAG). Fourthly, the chronology then points towards uncovering which of those inherited Jewish concepts, in Scripture and in late Second Temple writings, are reflected in the Coptic liturgy, and especially where the Jewish reverberation is obvious in many aspects. Finally, I will conclude with my concern about the importance of further studies that draws on the Jewish concept of luminaries in an extensive investigation to decipher more accurately the basis for many Coptic liturgical practices.[383]

---

[383] This approach looks at the development of liturgical language and concepts in the Second Temple period. Further investigation should focus on evidence from the Temple period, not rabbinic liturgy. Parallels will exist as both traditions draw on how liturgy was constructed and developed in the earlier period.

1. Glimpses of the Biblical Foundations of Luminary Liturgies

The meaning of the word "luminary" is based on the Latin *luminarium* or *lumen*, signifying "light."[384] The Bible is enveloped with the imagery of light, both literally and figuratively. In Genesis 1, light was the first thing created by God.[385] As the source of light, God the Creator ordered the three main luminaries: the sun, the moon, and the stars to come into existence: "And God said, 'Let there be light, and there was light. And God saw that the light was good."[386] While the luminaries are vital elements for life, they are just a part of the universal creation of God. The "six-day realms"[387] reflect the grandeur of this "King of the Universe" who transformed the "chaos" into "cosmos."[388]

---

[384] אוֹר '(*owr, ore*) means (Gen 1:3): illumination or (concrete) luminary (in every sense, including lightning, happiness, etc.): bright, clear, daylight, morning, sun. LXX provides for the same Heb. word φῶς (*phōs*), which is the root of φωστήρ (*phōstēr*) meaning also a cause of light, illuminator; a light, a luminary, a star, Phil. 2:15; radiance, or, luminary, Rev. 21:11.

[385] Gen 1:3–4.

[386] Gen 1:3–4 RSV.

[387] Day 1 - realms of light and dark, Day 2 - realms of waters and sky, Day 3 - realm of dry land, Day 4 - realms filled with heavenly lights (sun and moon/stars), Day 5 - realms filled with fish and birds, Day 6 - realm filled with animals and humans.

[388] The luminaries, by regulating day and night, the seasonal rotation, and the agrarian system, demonstrate the wisdom of God through his Creation (Pss 104:24, 136:5; Prov 3:19, 8:22, 8:27–28). Their role in the universe reflects the notion of "order as a result of God" that is

From the earliest time, the triad of the sun, moon and stars "etched the minds of the Bible readers through the centuries,"[389] and, ad hoc, were implemented into their liturgical texts. These three luminaries rule the sky and mark the borderline between darkness and light. Always perceived as a daily supernatural phenomenon, pagans worshipped the supremacy of this triad. However, the Israelites[390] were distinguished from them by blessing the transcendent Creator who brought them into existence[391] and established their daily cycle.[392] Multiple biblical references and specifically those in the Book of Psalms[393]

---

necessary for natural stability. Thus, the Greek word "cosmos" is crucial for this study. In the Septuagint, the Greek verb κοσμεω (*kosmeo*) means: to put in proper order, to decorate (literally or figuratively), to adorn, garnish, or trim (2 Chr 3:6; Esth 1:6; Jdt 12:15; 2 Macc 9:16; 3 Macc 3:5, 5:45; 3 Macc 6:1; Eccl 7:13; Sir 16:27; 29:26; 38:28; 42:21; 45:12; 47:10; 50:9; 50:14; Mic 6:9; Jer 4:30; Bar 6:10; Ezek 16:11, 13; 23:40). This definition is also evident throughout the New Testament writings. The New Testament Greek Lexicon states that κοσμος (kosmos) is an apt and harmonious arrangement or constitution, order, decoration, adornment, e.g., the arrangement of the stars, "the heavenly hosts," as the ornament of the heavens as in 1 Peter 3:3: an adorning world.

[389] Ryken et al., *Dictionary of Biblical Imagery*, 10.
[390] Moses warned the Israelites not to worship the sun, moon, and stars. See Deut 4:19.
[391] Gen 1:16–18.
[392] The daily cycle is well described in Eccl 1:5; 19:6; and Prov 7:23.
[393] The Psalms of praise (i.e. Pss 8; 19; 33; 103; 104; 145–150) celebrate and revere the worthiness of God through his creation not only for his making but also for establishing the "cosmos" as an orderly created universe in place of chaos, which is figuratively seen in the image of a formless, desolate, empty earth, as well as the darkness that was covering the deep water (Gen 1:2).

that are related to this cosmic triad, and their involvements, in different accounts, influenced Jewish theology, which in turn was foundational to the development of their distinguished liturgy and worship.[394] This laudatory repertoire holds interplanetary and cosmic elements that aim to glorify God for his magnificent creation.

The question that must be asked is whether the daily prayer of early Hebrew people is based on the luminary cycles of the heavens? The biblical theology described above seems not to be the only main source for a liturgy that holds cosmic proportions. The theme of luminaries embraces manifold topics. The rational relationship between the cycles of the heavenly luminaries and the time of prayers was surely already in the mindset of the people of the ancient Mediterranean and the Near Eastern world. In Egypt, the evidence is obvious. Hundreds of laudatory texts attest to how the sun is revered at sunrise. The jubilance expressed by the worshippers and their symbolic metaphors about ☉ 𓁛 Ra, the Sun-God, mainly focused on its light and heat, is overwhelming. The prayer time and related ritual are meticulously described in these

---

[394] Psalms, which express the purpose of praising God, are often called hymns of praise and often "praise God for the orderliness of his creation" (see Futato, *Interpreting the Psalms*, 146). One example, Psalm 148, summons all heavenly creatures (vv. 1–6) as well as earthly creatures (vv. 7–14) to offer a hymn of praise. The psalmist starts with the spiritual beings (angels, his heavenly host), followed by the luminaries (sun, moon, shining stars), and finally the clouds (water above the skies). Amazingly, other parts of creation are called to join this universal choir: lightning, clouds, winds, hail, snow and clouds, stormy winds, wild animals, even cattle, small creatures, and flying birds.

Egyptian laudatory texts. Sun, moon, and stars and their effects on the daily Egyptian life were constantly a source for a vast leitmotif for praising gods.[395] The Egyptian myth of the luminaries was also expressed in the Babylonian and later in the early Hebrew ceremonies in some festivals. W. O. E. Oesterley observes multiple parallels between the Spring Feast of Unleavened Bread and the Babylonian Feast of Shamas, the Sun-God. The Midsummer Feast of the Weeks was also connected with sun worship. The New Year Festival of the Tabernacles was celebrated in honor of Yahweh the King, Creator, and giver of the fruits of the earth. Oesterley (for the Jewish culture),[396] Barucq (for the Egyptian culture),[397] and Castellino (for the Babylonian culture),[398] find interesting parallels between pagan hymns and Jewish psalms when dealing with rituals related to the luminaries. They note that the themes of creation, light, jubilance, death (symbol of night), and resurrection (twilight), repeatedly were inserted ad hoc into the morning or evening rituals. Penner asserts that the relationship between the cycles of the heavens and the time of prayers is "ubiquitous" in both the pagan world and within the community of the Jews.[399] In the Old Testament, God commands the Israelite priests to offer sacrifices of animals

---

[395] Barucq, *L'Expression de la Louange Divine*, 201–19. The contextual similarity between the Pharaonic texts and Psalms is stunning.

[396] Oesterley, *Myth and Ritual*, 111–46.

[397] Barucq, *L'Expression de la Louange Divine*.

[398] Castellino, *Le Lamentazioni Individuali*.

[399] Penner, *Patterns of Daily Prayer*, 101.

in the morning and evening, which are considered the time of transition from light to darkness.⁴⁰⁰

2. Second Temple Period and the Perception of "Luminaries"

Penner and many other scholars observe that prayer at the exchange of luminaries becomes a popular practice in the late Second Temple period.⁴⁰¹ The significance of this epoch is that Judaism had further developed and the transition from the Judaism of the Hebrew Bible to Talmudic or Rabbinic Judaism was complete.⁴⁰² Also, Jewish writings in various dispersed communities (Alexandria, Dead Sea, Palestine, Syria) were growing and resulted in an important corpus of literature shaping specific concepts related to biblical stories, wisdom literature, and Qumran literature. These communities even produced new extra-biblical Psalms, hymns, and prayers. In these writings, there is a growing popularity of prayer focused on the exchange of the luminaries, especially related to the morning prayers, and the impact of these Jewish writings, both directly and indirectly on the Alexandrian Church liturgy is significant.

The texts explored below will help to reassess the origin of the liturgy of the Egyptian Church. The common characteristics of these texts help to determine to what

---

⁴⁰⁰ Exod 29:38–39.
⁴⁰¹ Penner, *Patterns of Daily Prayer*, 101; Falk, *Daily, Sabbath and Festival Prayers*, 47–49; Chazon, "When Did They Pray," 73–75.
⁴⁰² Schiffman, *Understanding Second Temple and Rabbinic Judaism*, 3–14.

degree the early Jews of Alexandria may have transferred their cherished praying and worshipping patterns to the new faith community of Christians. Clearly, one of the transferred patterns focuses on luminaries and their associated themes.

To discover similarities in the domain of luminaries, this study requires a close look at the resources of the designated period, some examination of how the rudiments of the Old Testament were combined with late Second Temple era insights, some attempt to identify and reconstruct the liturgical function of luminaries, and, finally, a textual and thematic comparison between both Jewish and Christian liturgies.

A. The Resources of the Second Temple Era

1. The Dead Sea Scrolls

The Dead Sea Scrolls count more than two hundred prayers, including several liturgical texts that explicitly state the time of prayers to be used on a daily or weekly basis. Penner observes that the trend of the interrelation between daily prayer and the luminary cycles was a countercultural occurrence during the late Second Temple era.[403] He attributes this popularity to the abundance of Jewish writings related to the subject. He studies two corpuses of texts from the Dead Sea Scrolls corpus, *Daily Prayers* (4Q503) and the *Apocryphon of Moses* (4Q408). The importance of his study clarifies some interrelation between luminaries and other topics. This also sheds some

---

[403] Penner, *Patterns of Daily Prayer*, 101.

light on the implications for their introduction into the Egyptian Church liturgy.

Both corpuses' texts (*Daily Prayers* and the *Apocryphon of Moses*) exemplify possible reasons for the practice of praying in coordination with the luminary cycle. The seed is embedded in the episode of creation in Genesis 1. Verses 14–18 state that God made the two great lights. The greater light (the sun) is to rule the day, and the lesser light (the moon and stars) are to rule the night. Penner writes: "The fact that the luminaries moved with such regularity and that these movements were set according to divine law made the celestial lights ideal markers for those looking to establish a scheduled pattern of daily prayer."[404] This establishes the connection between luminaries and creation.

Later, we see that some apocalyptic writings, such as *1 Enoch*,[405] describe the heavenly angels singing praises to God at certain times of the day,[406] and that human beings should simultaneously coordinate their time of prayers with celestial praise. In the same book of Enoch, the author adds an additional insight: the stars and angels coalesced.

---

[404] Penner, *Patterns of Daily Prayer*, 101. See also the inscriptions of Beni Hassan as described by Fillion, *La Bible Commentée d'après la Vulgate*, 6.

[405] 1 En 18:35; 21:16; 82:9–20; 86:1–4; 90:24. The text of *1 Enoch* was circulated widely in Egypt in a Greek version. It continued in use in many of Egypt's monasteries, both in Greek and Coptic, long after it was proscribed by Athanasius in his famous paschal letter of 367. For more details, see Pearson, "Enoch in Egypt," 216–31.

[406] Job 38:7 reflects a similar idea: "while the morning stars sang together, and all the angels shouted for joy?"

This coalescence is due not only to its existence in the texts of the late Second Temple era, but, I believe, is due to an etymological issue in the Greek of the Septuagint. When the word "host" is mentioned, the Greek uses various terms, and these terms invite this idea of coalescence. Several verses help to clarify this issue. For instance, in Exodus 14:41, and 14:28, the word δύναμις (*dunamis*) ("host") means "miraculous power," usually attributed to God ἡ δύναμις κυρίου "all the hosts of the LORD." In 1 Sam. 1:3, the Greek the word is σαβαωθ (*Sabaoth*), a Hebrew word צְבָאוֹת (*tsaba'*) adopted by the Greek Septuagint, which means "armies," a military epithet of God. In other passages, such as 1 Kings 22:19, the word στρατιὰ (*stratia*) designates both the angels and the celestial luminaries. Furthermore, the meaning is ambiguous between "army of angels," "stars," and "mighty power." The notion that angels and stars are connected may find its derivation in the Septuagint translation of the word "host," which may be translated as "stars," "angels," or "powers."

Penner contends that this angelic praise that took place in the heavenly sanctuary provides a suitable template for the Jews of the late Second Temple era: "This sanctuary was conceived as a place of worship without the blood of sacrifices."[407] While the expression of a non-bloody sacrifice as an offering of lips is an Old Testament term,[408] the author of the book of Hebrews exhorts Christians to "offer continually to God a sacrifice of praise,

---

[407] Penner, *Patterns of Daily Prayer*, 102.
[408] Lev 7:12.

the fruit of lips that confess his name."[409] Here, another connection between luminaries and their fixed time of worship for both angels and humans becomes apparent: angels are offering God praise without a sacrifice of blood. Does a connection exist between this kind of sacrifice and angels? Can it be traced in Alexandrian Church tradition?

The Qumran texts studied by Penner are a subject of debate, as to whether praying according to the cycle of the luminaries is a Qumran sectarian phenomenon or a common practice during the late Second Temple writings. Falk argues that this practice was non-sectarian, as different groups of Jews were praying according to fixed hours.[410] Also, Penner strongly suggests that different scribes copied some Qumran writings, and especially the book of *Words of Luminaries* during different eras.

2. 4Q503, Daily Prayer

4Q503, *Daily Prayer*, contains communal blessings to be recited in the evening and at sunrise each day for one month of the year. The main liturgical feature is the antiphonally-arranged component of each prayer that is marked by abrupt but regular changes of pronouns. The third person is used in the opening directive of each prayer prior to every blessing: "And [they] shall bless, answer, and say."[411] In the prayer text, God is addressed in the second person singular (you): "And, we the sons of your covenant will praise your name." In the closing blessing of

---

[409] Heb 13:15; Jer. 33:11; Pss 50:14, 23; 54:6; 107:22.
[410] Falk, *Daily, Sabbath and Festival Prayers*, 14–15.
[411] Penner, *Patterns of Daily Prayer*, 108.

the prayer, Israel is always addressed in the second person: "Peace be upon you, Israel."

In 4Q503, the daily prayers are regulated according to the 364-day solar calendar. Penner notes that since this text lost its beginning and its end, he assumes that 4Q503 could include additional months of the year. He notes that the basic evidence of this fragmentary text, aside from its liturgical purpose, is to establish a calendar of prayer that is coordinated with the cycles of the sun and moon.

In the *Daily Prayers*, some technical terms are frequently used, such as "divisions of light" and "divisions of night."[412] They reflect the required exactitude in times of prayer. This pattern follows the concept of the "order" in the cosmos, the rotation between sun and moon in fixing the hourly order of prayers. Esther Chazon argues that in some cases, as mentioned in fragments 7–9, and 3–4, "the sons of your covenant shall praise … with all the divisions of light," indicates metaphorically that the angelic host praising God is associated with the luminaries.[413] Angels are shining stars or, simply, they are light.

Another important feature in 4Q503 is the phenomenon of "praying with angels." It is a very interesting style of worship, not only in that it was exceptionally connected to the divinely established order of the cosmos, but also because "it allowed the community to live in coordination with, and correspondence to, the praises of their angelic counterparts in the heaven

---

[412] Penner, *Patterns of Daily Prayer*, 113.
[413] Chazon, "The Function of the Qumran Prayer Texts," 223. Penner, *Patterns of Daily Prayer*, 114.

above."[414] Within this idea, 4Q503 mentions frequently that the earthly congregation is regularly to be "praising" and "witnessing" together with angels (11, 4; 37–38, 21; 64, 5; 65, 3; 66, 1; 78, 2; 98, 1).[415] Remarkably, this sharing of praise between worshippers and angels is found in these morning prayers, because it is also central to the Coptic Morning Service. The angels are referred to as "witnesses," "holy ones," and "heavenly hosts or troop of lights."

It appears that a liturgical phenomenon is recognized in the Second Temple era: on the schedule of the luminaries, angelic praise and human praise mirror each ot. This is clearly reflected as in early Alexandrian Christian texts.[416]

3. 4Q408, Apocryphon of Moses

The *Apocryphon of Moses* is a short prayer. It is not meant to be a daily invocation. As it is concise, the full text can be quoted here:

> 5 when the ornaments of His Glory shine out from the holy abode [will answer all.]
>
> 6 Israel Blessed is YHWH be you, O Lord, who are righteous in all your ways, who are strong in force, who are kind in your judgments, who are trustworthy

---

[414] Penner, *Patterns of Daily Prayer,* 118.

[415] Penner, *Patterns of Daily Prayer,* 118.

[416] The bibliography listed by Penner, 119, n. 54, is an excellent resource for further study on humans and angels participating in common worship. Multiple examples of the human-angelic praise are found in different resources from the late Second Temple era.

7 in all your perceptible precepts, who are wise with all insight, who are shaking off with all (?) strength, who guide, to cause to rise the [ ]

8 that you have created the morning as a sign, causing the appearance of the dominion of light for the area of the day at the firmament of the heavens at the beginning.

9 for their work to bless your holy name when they see that the light is good and when they recognized that in all [ ]

10 [] men that is [you] have created the evening as a sign causing the appearance of the dominion [of darkness for the area of the night]

11 after the work to bless [your holy name, when] they see that good are all the stars.[417]

Common features can easily be traced between the *Daily Prayers* and the *Apocryphon of Moses*. The description of the exchange of the heavenly lights precedes the body of the prayer and shows that at the appearance of the light, Israel will bless Yahweh. The theme of coordination of the prayer with the cycles of morning and evening of luminaries is well described. The Law ("divine precepts") is part of this cosmic prayer. The expression, "light is good," recalls the account of creation in Genesis 1. Chazon, in her article "When Did They Pray?"[418] examines various texts from the collection of the community of Qumran to perceive the times for prayer and the associated literature. She divides these Qumranic texts

---

[417] Penner, *Patterns of Daily Prayer*, 132.
[418] Chazon, "When Did They Pray," 43.

into two categories. First, category A, is the group of texts where prayer times are coordinated with the movements of heavenly lights (sunset and sunrise). In the second, category B, are prayers that follow the sacrificial time and are coordinated with the hours when the daily, Sabbath, and festival sacrifices were offered at the Temple.

Chazon demonstrates the prayer of category A by selecting a certain hymn that has no title. It is preserved in 1QS, 4QS, and in 1QH.[419] This hymn shows the commitment of the hymnist to praise God during the day, the course of the year, and according to the sabbatical cycles. The opening lines of the hymn include several examples:

> At the times ordained by Him: at the beginning of the dominion of light, and its coming round when it retires to its appointed place; at the beginning of the watches of darkness when He unlocks their storehouse and spreads them out, and at their coming round when they retire before the light.[420]

The cycle of the luminaries between night and day is easily recognized in this part of the hymn by the use of words "beginning," "coming round," and "retire." The hymn also emphasizes the divinely appointed time for prayers for evening and morning. Chazon illustrates the prayer of category B with a prose inset known as *David's Compositions*, which comes near the end of the large Psalms scroll from Cave 11 (11 QPS a XXVII, 4–8):

---

[419] Chazon, "When Did They Pray," 43.
[420] Chazon, "When Did They Pray," 44.

> And he [David] wrote 3,600 psalms; and songs to sing before the altar over the whole-burnt *tamid*[421] offering every day, for all the days of the year, 364; and for the *qorban* [offering] of the Sabbaths, 52 songs; and for the *qorban* [offering] of the New Moons and for all Solemn Assemblies for the Day of Atonement, 30 songs.[422]

In this inset, David is credited with having created a liturgical accompaniment to the Temple sacrifices. This quotation shows that there are a specific number of songs for each occasion (qorban of the Sabbath: 52 songs; for New Moons and other festivals: 30 songs). The diversity of the laudatory texts according to the daily offering and feasts suggests this might be the practice during the period in which it was composed. This inset reflects on 1 Chron 23:30–31 and Sir 50:18. The arrangement of specific songs related to a certain festival and even just for a weekday is a phenomenon that seems to be continued later in the Early Egyptian Church. This can be seen not only in the divergence of texts for each day's praise as they occur in the Coptic book of Psalmody,[423] but also in the changing

---

[421] Perpetual/daily (Sanctuary lamp).

[422] Chazon, "When Did They Pray," 47.

[423] The *Book of Psalmody* (known also as *The Holy Psalmody*) is the main book of hymns in the Coptic Church. It contains different forms of praise, such as "Hos" (Coptic: means praise), "Psali" (Greek: means singing), "Theotokion" (Greek, means to venerate the Theotokos, the mother of God), and "Doxology" (Greek: means to glorify). The hymns labeled "doxology" exalt God for his incarnation. Other doxologies are prescribed for use on the greater feasts, on Lenten

of melody for these same texts according to the seasons. David's Compositions invites the angels to praise God in the heavenly Temple. These angels are also described as angelic priests, who, by their singing, participate in the heavenly Temple.

As noted by David Flusser,[424] the importance of the *Songs of David* for the history of Jewish worship is undeniable. He adds that not only do they attest actual liturgical practices of circles close to the Essenes, but they also contain liturgical phrases that reappear in rabbinic prayers. He mentions that verses 2:20 and 4:11–12 are relevant for the history of *Kaddish*.

The liturgical terms used in *David's Compositions* occur in abundance in the Coptic liturgical books. The "whole-burnt *Tamid*" is still the lamp that exists in the altar of any Coptic church. It is also known as قَنديل الشَرقية (*Kandil al sharqiyyah*)[425] (the lamp of the Eastward).[426] The "altar" is known in Hebrew as מִזְבֵּחַ (*mizbeach*), but this is specifically a sacrificial altar in Jewish usage, which means that it applies only to the Temple. Christian usage

---

weekdays, on the Saturdays and Sundays of Lent, and in the Coptic month of Khiak. The *Book of Psalmody* is divided into two parts; the first part, the "Annual Psalmody," is to be sung during the whole liturgical year, except the month of Khiak, which precedes Christmas. The second part, the "Khiak Psalmody," is to be sung during the Advent month of Khiak. For more details about the *Book of Psalmody*, see Cody, "Doxology," 923–24; Muftah, "Coptic Music", 1715–47; Mettaous, *Rouhaniet Al Tasbeha*, 34–37.

[424] Flusser, "Psalms, Hymns, and Prayers," 569.

[425] Still used in Coptic monasteries, the lamps are lighted with oil.

[426] For more details about the Eastward and the lamp, see Malaty, *The Church House of God,* 74.

can be different because of the sacrificial understandings of the eucharist. Copts still designate the sanctuary with the same Hebrew word, and for Copts, the term still holds the Jewish concept of the place where sacrifices are slaughtered.[427] Concerning the word קָרְבָּן (*qorban*), this is also a frequent liturgical term in the Coptic liturgical books, and, again, it is the Hebrew word that is used, with the same Jewish concept of a sacrifice, oblation that is offered to God, whether bloody or bloodless.[428]

4. *The Book of Words of Luminaries, 4Q504, 4Q506*

In Cave 4 at Qumran, fragments of three copies of a collection of prayers were found. Scholars believe that this collection holds great importance for understanding the history of the Jewish liturgy. The oldest manuscript dates from the early Hasmonean period (about 150 BCE).[429] Falk and Chazon reject the idea that this book belonged to a sectarian community (Qumran), which suggests that the content of this book was sufficiently popular that it may have been known to the Jewish worshipper.

The Book of Words of Luminaries is a book of hymns that is intended not for personal use but as a collection of community prayers. Its liturgical features can be summarized by the following characteristics. First, each

---

[427] For more details about the altar, see Malaty, *The Church House of God*, 15; and Grossman, "Altar," 105–107.

[428] For more details about qorban, see Kohler, "Korban," 561; Hammond and Brightman, *Liturgies, Eastern and Western*, 569; Viaud, *Les Coptes d'Égypte*, 106.

[429] Flusser, "Psalms, Hymns and Prayers," 566–68.

prayer includes a superscription correlating to a specific day of the week. Second, the use of the third person plural as well as addressing God with second person demonstrates a communal recitation. Third, the content of each of the weekday petitions is thematically connected so that each prayer is integral to the whole of the liturgy, which in total communicates the history of God in dealing with Israel, by use of a portion from the Bible. Fourth, the themes that are recounted for each weekday are significant. Penner includes more information about specific days:[430] the prayer for Sunday begins with "Adam." Friday recounts Israel's exile and restoration; for the Sabbath, the hymns of praise replace the petitions, which include an invitation to join the praise of the angels. Each of these is distinctively mirrored by the Coptic liturgical directions for these same days.

The concept of each prayer, including a superscription correlating to a specific day of the week in *The Book of Words of Luminaries* echoes with the daily structure in the Coptic *Book of Psalmody*. Every Coptic liturgical day consists of a "Psali of the day," a "Theotokion of the day"[431] (known also as تذاكية *Tazakia*),[432] and a تفسير *Tafsir* of the day."[433] The Psali tend to repeat the Name of the Lord Jesus Christ in almost

---

[430] Penner, *Patterns of Daily Prayer*, 104.

[431] "Theotokion" is a hymn in praise of the Blessed Virgin, also known as "Theotokia" in the Coptic Church. For more details, see Ishaq, "Theotokion," 2254–55.

[432] I am not able to find a suitable English translation.

[433] "Tafsir" is known also as "Tarh." "Tarh" (pl. "turuhat") usually denotes a paraphrase used to explain a "Theotokion," or Gospel reading. See Muftah, "Coptic Music," 1728.

every quatrain. The Theotokian recounts the story of salvation from the Old Testament time with its prophecies to Christ's incarnation in the womb of Mary. The "Tafsir" paraphrases the main ideas mentioned in the ابصالية "Psali" and the الثاؤتوكية "Theotokion."

The liturgical feature of using the third person plural as well as addressing God with the second person in *The Book of Words of Luminaries* resounds also in the "Psali," the "Theotokion," and the "Tafsir" in the Coptic *Book of Psalmody*.

By examining this sample of late Second Temple writings, we see common features that tie the luminaries and the time of prayers together in two liturgies. Two further examples from the Jewish Morning Service also help to clarify this link.

B. Seder Amram Gaon (1 SAG): The Shema and Its Blessing, Amidah

In the liturgy of the Jewish Morning Service as described by Amram Gaon, it is easy to recall the Qumran concept of luminaries. Two main parts will help to clarify where the theme of luminaries directly and indirectly emerges: the Berakah, "My God,"[434] and the reciting of the Shema.

1. Berakah "My God": Luminaries, Soul, and Resurrection

> My God, the soul thou gavest me is pure, thou didst create it into me, thou didst form it into

---

[434] 1 SAG, 8–9.

me, thou preservest it within me, and thou hast taken it from me, thou hast restored it in me, and thou wilt one day take it from me, and thou will restore it in the time to come. And so long, as my soul is within me, I give thanks unto thee, JHWH, my God, Lord of souls. Blessed be thou, JHWH, who restores souls to the dead corpses.[435]

This short Berakah is said at the beginning of the Jewish Morning Service.[436] According to the Talmud, [437] "My God" should be recited when awakening in the morning, before a man has said or done anything. Here, in this prayer, the theme of creation is referenced by the "soul thou gavest to me." The description of the divine dynamics of the soul is significant: "create," "form," "preserve" (into me), "taken (from me)," "restore it (in me)," "one day will take it from me."

The "*neshama*," the soul, which is pure when given to the human, relates the text to Genesis 2:7, when "God breathed into his nostrils their breath of life, and the creature became a living being." But in the text quoted above, the journey of the soul that is gifted to the individual goes through different phases throughout the day. God preserves it for the continuance of life (symbolically during the day);[438] in sleep, God takes it from the person (at night); in the moment of death, "will one day take it;" and finally

---

[435] 1 SAG, 8–9.

[436] Only in the post-Talmudic period. It may have emerged in Babylonia as well as the Jerusalem Talmud has a very different prayer.

[437] 1 SAG, 8. Hedegård does not mention the Talmudic reference.

[438] Ps 97:10; 121:7.

in the resurrection, "will restore it" again. Thus, offering a thanksgiving prayer to God for his power as Creator, as "Lord of Souls," or "King of the Universe,"[439] is obviously attached to the creation of human beings.

As seen in Chapter 3, the theme of *"neshama"* occurs also in the Prime Hour prayer of the Coptic *Book of Hours*[440] where the prayed psalms reflect the theme of beseeching God to keep and restore the human soul against any dangerous circumstances. In various parts of this canonical hour, we find a tie between the "neshama," the night (death), and the daylight (life or creation).

2. *The Reciting of the Shema*[441]

The "liturgical Shema" in the Jewish Morning and the Evening Services consists of three portions: Deut. 6:4–9, 11:13–21, and Num. 15:39–41. Through a long narrative,[442] Amram outlines the importance of the exact time for praying the Shema in the morning, as debated by the rabbis and the sages. The same concern has been described previously when he mentions the Berakah, "My God." The rabbis have a rich literature concerning the time of reading the morning Shema. They specify that it should begin at daybreak, "when there is sufficient light to

---

[439] This term is the beginning of the Berakah, 1 SAG, 9.

[440] The Arabic word اجبية (*Agpeya*) has its roots in the Coptic morpheme ⲘⲠⲚⲀⲨⲚ, meaning 'at the time of' (i.e. the first, third, sixth hour etc.).

[441] It is worth noting that there is no unequivocal evidence of the recitation of the Shema during the Second Temple period. One might expect Philo or Josephus to have mentioned it, but they did not. There is also no evidence of it at Qumran.

[442] 1 SAG, 36–39.

distinguish between purple and white, or to recognize a person, after a short acquaintance, at a distance of four ells,[443] and to last until the sun's rays are seen."[444]

After reciting the Shema, we read many other prayers in 1 SAG, which offer key features. First, the creation episode is shown in the *chazzan* recitation of the *Kaddish*[445] ("Holy") and is linked to universal ascendant blessings, hymns, and praises to the throne of God, who is known within the Shema section as the King of the Universe:[446]

> Magnified and sanctified[447] and praised be his great name in the world which he has created according to his will... Praised and glorified and exalted and honored and magnified and lauded be the name of the Holy One, blessed be He. Amen. Thou be high above all blessings and hymns and praises and consolations which are uttered in the world...[448]

---

[443] Ell is a unit of measurement, originally a cubit, i.e., approximating the length of a man's arm.

[444] For literature on the time of reciting, see Eisenstein, "Shema," 286–87.

[445] The Kaddish (is not part of the Shema complex. It is functioning here as a punctuation mark within the service) – as it does in numerous other points.

[446] 1 SAG, 46.

[447] Kaddish text is based on Ezek 38.

[448] 1 SAG, 41–42.

After the *Kaddish*, the *Sheliach sibbur*[449] recites a blessing, which connects directly to the topic of this chapter. The full section is long,[450] but contains important perceptions relevant to the luminaries: i.e., creation, light, angels, and the angelic praise. I will cite some excerpts, and provide some comments:

> Blessed be thou, JHWH, our God, King of the Universe, who formest light created darkness, who makest peace and createst all things: Who in mercy givest light to the earth and to them that dwell thereon and, in his goodness, renewest the creation every day continually. How manifold are thy works, JHWH. In wisdom hast thou made them all… The blessed God, great in knowledge, prepared and formed the rays of the sun: it was a boon he produced as a glory to his name. He set the luminaries round his strength. The chiefs of his hosts are holy beings, they exalt the Almighty, continually declare the glory of God and his holiness… Creator of ministering spirit, and all his ministering spirits stand in the height of the universe, and with awe proclaim aloud in unison the words of the living God and everlasting King…

---

[449] Nowadays, a "celebrant in the synagogue." His rank is higher than the Chazzan, who is a singer. Everyone is obliged to recite this prayer, led by the Sheliach Tzibbur, for the benefit of those who do not know how. A chazzan is a professional Sheliach Tzibbur.

[450] 1 SAG, 46–51.

This is a eulogy describing the goodness of God in his creation, and, in his mercy, he gives light. Hedegård notes that starting with "the blessed God," the Hebrew text has an alphabetical arrangement, that is, an acrostic. Hymns of praise in Coptic tradition are frequently composed as acrostics. Creation is also linked to the "glory of his name." "The chiefs of his hosts" in this passage would be the archangels, especially Michael and Gabriel.[451] The celestial praise is ceaseless, which reflects a day and night cycle of worship.

After a striking description of the angels (the hosts), the text continues that "With holy melody they all respond in unison in fear, and say with awe: Holy, Holy, Holy is JHWH of hosts: the whole earth is full of his glory… Give thanks to him that makes the great lights for his grace endureth forever. Blessed be thou, JHWH, Creator of luminaries."[452] The "ministering spirits" is mentioned in the same portion of the text in which "they take upon themselves the yoke of the kingdom of heaven in chanting the "Quedusha."[453] Hedegård observes that they both—the

---

[451] 1 SAG, 47. A detailed study of the rabbinic sayings belonging to this subject would be beneficial in understanding the setting of the archangels as described in various liturgical texts.

[452] 1 SAG, 48–49.

[453] The "Quedusha" or "Kedushah" ("holiness") is the third blessing of the Amidah. The blessing's full appellation is *Kedushat ha-Shem* (Sanctification of the Name) to distinguish it from "Kedushat ha-Yom" ("Sanctification of the Day"), the central blessing of the Sabbath and festival. Popularly, however, the term *Kedushah* refers to the additions and responses recited by the cantor and congregation in the third benediction during the repetition of the *Amidah*. The word "kadosh" is the main theme of this doxology, hence the name "Kedushah."

angels and the Israelites—take upon them the yoke of praising with the "Quedusha." This doxology is based on Isaiah 6:3 and will be discussed in further detail below.

The purpose of this discourse is to place emphasis on the three blessings recited during the Jewish Morning Service. Collectively, these blessings pertain to the foundational principles of divine knowledge, encompassing creation, revelation, and redemption. This commonality serves as the unifying factor that binds them together.

C. Luminaries and Related Topics in the Coptic Liturgy

1. Links between "Mazkeerim" and "Ozkor" in the Coptic Morning Service

The Jewish tradition of reciting aloud some significant biblical themes is seen by Simcha Cohen as an opportunity to observe the biblical mitzvah,[454] and to remember the deeds and the wonders of God.[455] He emphasizes it with the reciting of the last portion of the Shema in a loud voice. The last phrases of the Shema contain the remembrance of God's deliverance of the children of Israel from the land of Egypt. Cohen recounts that the Talmud (in Berachot 12b) states that the target of this liturgical rubric is "Mazkeerim yetziat mitzrayim balaylot," which means: "We mention the Exodus in the

---

[454] Hebrew word means "commandment" of the Torah.
[455] Cohen, *Timely Jewish Questions: Timely Rabbinic Answers*, 192–93.

evening time." He notices that this "Mazkeerim" is different from the word "zochrim," which means that one should remember the Exodus. The Talmudic text states "mazkeerim," which means that one is obliged to make others recall the Exodus. Praying, singing, and or reciting are a means of awareness of the wonders of God.[456]

It is remarkable that this word "zochrim" or "mazker" is like the Arabic word "Ozkor," which means "remember," for it is ubiquitous in both prayers and worshipping (singing) texts in the Coptic liturgical books. This "remembrance" seems to have a deeper meaning within the Jewish liturgical texts. Future research may reveal to what extent the Copts understand this Jewish connotation and how it is implicated in their liturgy.[457] In the *Divine Liturgies*,[458] we find the word "Remember" (ⲁⲣⲓϥⲙⲉⲩⲓ) in all seven petitions that are recited during the Mass. This word occurs in the petition of the Church Peace,[459] of the Church Fathers,[460] of Church

---

[456] The context of this passage in the Talmud makes it clear that the dispute concerns whether the final section of the biblical passages should be included in evening prayers at all. (Berakhot 2a, specifically around 2a:8-9, Gemara).

[457] This has to do with both languages being Semitic and this being a cognate term.

[458] The *Divine Liturgy* is a book of the three liturgies (Saint Basil, Saint Gregory, and Saint Cyril). They are currently the only ones used by a Coptic priest.

[459] DL, 199.

[460] DL, 200.

Presbyters,[461] for the Mercy,[462] for the Place,[463] for the Seasons,[464] and for Oblations.[465]

Before examining the impact of the Jewish writings and the Amram's Morning Service liturgy, I will recapitulate the ubiquitous prayer patterns during the late Second Temple regarding the luminaries and associated subjects. This summary merely hints at the extent of their existence in the Alexandrian Church liturgy. Scripture is the backbone of liturgies that are based on the cycle of the luminaries. The concepts of the power of God in creating a cosmos, that is, order instead of chaos, the manifestation of his wisdom in governing the whole universe, and the stability of the universal system, all entail cosmic thanksgiving praise from all creatures.

The late Second Temple period formed patterns to the prayers. Some of these relate directly to the Alexandrian Church liturgy, particularly to the Morning Service and the hymnic texts included in the *Book of Psalmody*. Although the Septuagint is believed to provide the key to understanding the coalescence of angels, stars, and powers in the liturgical texts; though this topic deserves an extensive etymological survey of the massive Coptic liturgical corpus.

The Qumran texts discussed above show specific liturgical forms. In 4Q503, *Daily Prayers,* we examined

---

[461] DL, 201.
[462] DL, 202.
[463] DL, 202.
[464] DL, 203–207.
[465] DL, 208.

several features: blessings for evening time, blessings for sunrise, and the liturgical calendar of prayers that is coordinated with cycles of the sun and moon. The text mentions

"Divisions of lights," which are connected to the time of prayer during the day; it also expresses an idea of "praying with the angels" who "witness" the human praise while they are rising to God. In 4Q408, *Apocryphon of Moses*, the pattern of the coordination between the cycle of luminaries and the time of prayers is also perceived. Other Scriptural concepts added to the text include the Law with its precepts as the light. In 1QS, 4QS, and 1QH (untitled text), the hymnist shows commitment in praising God during the day, the year, and the sabbatical cycles. *David's Compositions*, 11QPS *a* XXVII, 4–8 suggests a liturgical arrangement of specific songs for festivals and weekdays.

In *The Book of Words of Luminaries*, each prayer includes a superscription to a specific day of the week. Also, there is a fast exchange of pronouns between the third person "they," when the community is designated, and "you," when addressing God.

In *Seder Amram Gaon* 1 SAG, the liturgy of Morning Service (specifically Tefillah) frequently mentions the expression, "King of the Universe." The term is used specifically when the text demonstrates the concept of thanking God for creating the "neshama," "the soul." In the section that includes reciting the Shema, we see again the angelic praise in two forms, the *Kiddush* and the

*Quedusha.*⁴⁶⁶ In the Jewish Morning Service, angels and archangels, "the chiefs of hosts," praise the Creator. Luminaries and light are two frequent themes in that Service. Each of these mentioned has a clear parallel in the Coptic liturgy and provides numerous threads that appear to clearly tie the two liturgies intrinsically together.

Similarities between the late Second Temple Jewish and Alexandrian liturgies are striking. In some cases, this analogy is seen through liturgical texts, such as parallelism in the Jewish and Coptic Morning Service. Sometimes the influence of the luminary cycles is shown, as in the Coptic *Book of Psalmody*, in an entire corpus of prayers, such as those labeled as "Psalis," "Theotokion," and "Tafsir" for each weekday or feast. The challenge to collect all the different liturgical pieces from both Jewish and Alexandrian liturgical books is overwhelming. However, I will examine some similarities of topics in several relevant Alexandrian and Jewish sources.

2. The Exchange of Luminaries and Types of Prayer

The luminaries move in a regular pattern by following the divine law. This makes the celestial lights the ideal marker for the divinely scheduled times of prayer.

---

[466] To circumvent any potential ambiguity, some terms related to *Kiddush* need to be defined. *Kiddush* is the sanctification of the day for Sabbaths and festivals. *Kedushah* (angelic liturgy); *Qedushat Hashem* (Sanctification of God) which can include the angelic liturgy); *Qedushat Hayom* (sanctification of the day, within the Amidah); *Kaddish* (Doxological praise of God) used mostly to separate the parts of the service).

These ideal markers are the basis of the Alexandrian liturgy.

In the Egyptian Morning Service, the notion of creation, lights, and angels and archangels are embedded in the "Doxologies" of this service.[467] The Evening Service deals with other themes related to the night, such as the sunset, sleep, and human death. The Evening Service also displays different invocations asking the Lord to grant his peace and his protection against committing sins during the night. These same themes are also recurrent in the Coptic *Agpeya*: the daily fixed-hours collection.

On a weekly arrangement, the *Book of Psalmody* contains fixed "Doxologies," Theotokions,"[468] and "Psalis"[469] for every weekday. On an annual scale, seasons and festivals have their fixed Doxologies and hymns. The striking point is not only that the laudatory texts change according to the praying time (night, day, weekday, or seasons), but the melodies also vary accordingly. Melody is *lahn* in Arabic.[470] The melody changes according to the

---

[467] Also known as "Doxologia" (Arabic, *Tamjid*). The Coptic Doxology is a type of hymnic composition, written in stanzas, and usually addressed to the Virgin, to the angels, to individual saints, or to a particular category of saints. For more details, see Cody, "Doxology," 923–24.

[468] Again "Theotokion" is a hymn in praise of the Blessed Virgin, plural "Theotokia." See Ishaq, "Theotokion," 2254–55.

[469] "Psali" is a hymn, usually consisting of twenty-four strophes. They are acrostics; each strophe begins with the successive letter of twenty-four letters of the Geek or Coptic alphabet. For more details, see Kuhn, "Poetry," 1985–86.

[470] For more details about the melodies, see Muftah, "Coptic Music," 1745–47.

weekdays, using two melodic tones, named "Adam" and "Batos." For seasons, the tones are multiple: tones *Lahn al-huzn*, "of grief" for Holy Week; *lahn al-farah*, "of Joy" for feasts"; *lahn al-ma'ruf*, "familiar", for non-feast seasons; *lahn Khiak*,[471] for the Advent; and *lahn-al-Sayam*, for the Lent period.

Thus, the rotation of sun and moon is the foundation of not only the establishment of a huge corpus of Coptic prayers and hymns but of their musical components as well. The Coptic calendar also specifies Scripture and non-Scriptural readings for every day, and for each season, as laid out in the Coptic lectionary.[472] Unsurprisingly, the solar calendar has a strong connection with the agriculture in Egypt and farmers are extremely dependent on it.

This liturgical system has numerous aspects that could reveal further Jewish influences. However, here I will focus on the two frequent melodies, named "Adam" and "Batos." Hymns labeled "Adam" are to be sung Sunday through Tuesday, and on certain specified festival days; while hymns labeled "Batos" are reserved for Wednesday through Saturday. The common explanation for these two labels is that the names of the two tunes are derived from the first word of two different "Theotokions."

---

[471] "Khiak" is a Coptic month; on the 29th of Khiak, the Copts celebrate Christmas.

[472] Werner, in his book, *The Sacred Bridge*, vol. 2, compares the lectionary of the synagogue and the Qumran lectionary. His findings are interesting, but also provide a possible model for comparison between Coptic and the synagogue lectionaries. For more details, see Basilios, "Lectionary," 1435–37.

"Adam" ⲁⲇⲁⲙ derives from Monday's "When Adam became of contrite spirit," and "Batos" ⲃⲁⲧⲟⲥ (bush) is from the Thursday's "Theotokion" for "the bush which Moses saw." "Batos" and "Adam" are distinct from each other in verse structure, length, and mood.

3. Creation and Sabbath Themes in the Coptic Liturgy

God's creation of the heavy luminaries on the fourth day of the creation provides for two main domains of prayers, day and night. His instigation of the Sabbath on the seventh day provides one of the foundational pieces of Christian liturgy. In the Coptic liturgy, in particular, creation is built into its very structure.

In *Seder Amram Gaon*, the episode of creation is related to the Morning Service.[473] The rabbinic sayings link the Sabbath to creation. They believe that "on the eve of the first Sabbath the creation of humans took place, and on Friday, on the sixth of the month, at the sixth hour of the day, Israel received the commandments."[474] From this Jewish conception, we see some corresponding elements in the context of the Alexandrian Church. The earliest Alexandrian Fathers maintained the relationship between creation and Sabbath, and to this day, the Fathers of the

---

[473] 1 SAG, 8–9.

[474] For this link between the creation account and the weekday liturgy, see Dugmore, *The Influence of the Synagogue*, 26–42. Creation of Adam on the sixth day derives from Genesis 1 directly. The Sinai revelation is dated by the rabbis to the 6th day of the third month – to the completion of the biblical Omer period and the feast of weeks.

Egyptian Church articulate a particular reverence for this connection.

a. Singing the Genesis 1 Account

Before I describe the relationship between creation and Sabbath as maintained by the earliest Alexandrian Fathers, I raise a question about whether early Jewish worship sustained the idea of singing Genesis 1. Frank Polak advocates a poetic reading of the Hebrew creation account in Genesis 1. He approaches this account not only to reveal its powerful image as poetry, but also as a hymn. He argues that "The purpose of hymnic poetry (in Gen. 1) is to praise and celebrate the mighty deeds of God. The creation account distinctively fulfills this function, since it presents the divine praise of the world as created by God."[475] Polak's statement implies that it is not surprising if both the Jewish community and the Early Church intended to praise God—and, possibly, musically—with the words of this first chapter of the Bible. The reason for mentioning Polak's advocacy is that if the Genesis text is not textually incorporated in the Coptic laudatory repertoire, it may still be seen in the *Psalmody Book* in its two main parts: The Morning بَاكِر (*Baker*) and the Midnight Praise نِصف الليل (*Nesf-al-leil*).[476]

In the Alexandrian Church's Morning and Midnight Praise تَسْبِحة (*Tasbeha*), one focus is on how the whole creation and specifically the cycle of the luminaries reveals and reflects the divine order by which they have been created. The Coptic Church seems to cherish the

---

[475] Polak, "Poetic Style and Parallelism in the Creation Account," 5.

[476] Some hints about the recitation of this text can be found in Mishnah Taanit, Chapter 3, which describes what the local Jews in the Land of Israel did when their priests took their turns to serve in Jerusalem. This practice ceased to exist after 70 CE.

biblical conception of this account in Genesis 1. The creatures reflect the glory of the Creator. The luminary cycles reflect the harmony in creation.[477] The ordered universe or cosmos reverberates the ultimate harmony eternally pre-existent in the Trinity: Father to Son to Holy Spirit. They live in perfect, united, eternal harmony with one another, from which all other "harmonies" gain their existence and to which all other harmonies reflect and find their purpose. This harmony creates the accord between all the cosmic creatures for praising their Creator. Clearly, the early Alexandrian Church cherished the concept of cosmic praise and inserted it at the heart of its liturgy.

In the *Psalmody Book*, this cosmic praise, which magnifies God as Creator and displays the reverential attitude of "all" creation to the "One," is sung during the Midnight Praise (*Nesf-al-leil*), which is daily between 4 A.M. and 7 A.M., followed by the Morning Praise, just before the Morning Offering Incense. The core of every nightly praise in the *Book of Psalmody*[478] is the chanting of the Four Praises (*Hos*, ϩⲱⲥ, in Coptic: praise, or ode). The First *Hos* is the Song of Moses (Exodus 15), where the Creator established a road in the Red Sea. The Second *Hos* is Psalm 136 [135], a *Todah* to God, for he created heaven and earth (sun, moon, stars) with intelligence and knowledge (v. 5). It is also a praise of deliverance of the Israelite from the yoke of the Egyptians (vv. 10–15). The Third *Hos* consists of the praise of the Three Hebrew Children after their divine deliverance from the furnace, taken from the Apocryphal Greek version of the book of

---

[477] Gen 1:26; John 1:3; Col. 1:15–17.

[478] See the *Book of the Holy Pascha*, 519–56.

Daniel. In each quatrain, the creatures are summoned to praise. This *Hos* is well-known as the Azariah Prayer, which was Second Temple praise. Some extracts are included here:

> Bless the Lord, all you powers (hosts) of the Lord, Praise Him and exalt Him above all forever.
>
> Bless the Lord, O Sun and Moon, Praise Him and exalt Him above all forever.
>
> Bless the Lord, all you Stars of heaven, Praise Him and exalt Him above all forever.[479]
>
> In the "Psali Batos" for "The Three Saintly Children," it also says:
>
> The heavens declare the glory of God until this day, O you angels whom He has made, Praise Him and exalt Him above all.
>
> Now you powers (hosts) of the Lord, bless His honored name, O sun and moon and the stars, Praise Him and exalt Him above all.[480]
>
> You also, O nights and days, light and darkness and lightning, glorify the Lover of mankind, Praise Him and exalt Him above all.[481]

The Fourth *Hos* is a joint doxological praise from Psalms 148, 149, and 150, centered by Psalm 148 where all creatures join the heavenly and the earthly choir. Moses warned the Israelites not to worship the sun, moon, and

---

[479] HPE, 33–34.
[480] HPE, 42.
[481] HPE, 43.

stars,[482] lest the people begin to believe that these luminaries are gods. However, the concept of singing in the Four *Hos* in the *Psalmody Book* is different: the luminaries are not getting worship from any worshipper, but they are the ones who worship and glorify their Creator.

b. The Sabbath: The Creation in the Alexandrian Liturgy

This section aims not to study the Sabbath and its impact on the Early Church,[483] nor to discuss the debate between Western and Eastern practices in observing it, but to briefly trace the episode of creation in the Alexandrian liturgy. Emile Ishaq's article, "Saturday," stresses how the Alexandrian Church observes this day: as the day of Creation. For instance, he draws on *The Apostolic Constitutions* (circa 375–380), which states:

> But keep the Sabbath and the Lord's Day festival, because the former is the memorial of the creation, and the latter of the resurrection. But there is one only Sabbath to be observed by you in the whole year, which is that of our Lord's burial, on which men ought to keep a fast… Not that the Sabbath-day is a day of fasting, being the rest from the creation, but because we ought to fast on this one Sabbath

---

[482] Deut 4:19.

[483] The universal church had to wait until the Council of Laodicea (343–381) to legislate in Canon 29 that "Christians must not Judaize by resting on the Sabbath, but must work on that day, rather honoring the Lord's Day, and if they can, resting then as Christians. But if any shall be found to be Judaizers, let them be anathema from Christ."

only, while on this day the Creator was under the earth.[484]

He also quotes from Pope Christodoulus (1046–1077 CE), displaying how the church continued to follow the same rule of *The Apostolic Constitutions*: "And it is not allowed to any of the faithful to fast on a Saturday, except on one Saturday in the whole year, and this is the Great Saturday which is the end of the fast."[485] This impacts the liturgical rubrics concerning Saturday. It should be noted here that the Coptic Church nowadays observes Saturday as a festal day, and prostrations are prohibited all year-round. The exception is for Holy Saturday, on which fasting is to be observed because Christ was still in the tomb. As an indication of a celebratory day, the Litany of the Dead is not to be said on Saturday in the Morning Service. Hence, the prayer for the sick is to be said instead.

c. Creation and Light

The *Psalmody Book* and *The Agpeya* both share the same texts where creation is tied to the "light." In both books, for this morning time, the theme of creation emerges with light: "The night has passed; we thank You, O Lord, and we ask You to keep us this day away from sin and deliver us."[486] The liturgy continues with:

> O the true Light Who gives light to every man coming into the world, You came into the world through Your love for mankind, and all

---

[484] Ishaq, "Saturday," 2099.
[485] Ishaq, "Saturday," 2100.
[486] *Book of Seven Canonical Hours*, 5.

creation rejoiced in Your coming. You saved our father, Adam, from the seduction, and delivered our mother, Eve, from the pangs of death, and gave us the spirit of sonship. Let us, therefore, praise You and bless You saying...

As the daylight shines upon us, O Christ Our God, the true Light, let the luminous senses and the bright thoughts shine within us, and do not let the darkness of passions hover over us, that mindfully we may praise You with David saying, "My eyes have awakened before the morning watch, that I might meditate on Your sayings.

Even the "Light" is added to the invocation to Mary the Theotokos:

You are the honored Mother of the Light; from the risings of the sun to its settings praises are offered to you, O *Theotokos,* the second heaven, as you are the bright and unchanging flower...

Once the troparion is sung, the "Let us praise with the angels" is recited.[487] We will discuss this company of angels in more detail later in this chapter.

D. Angelology and the Luminaries

This section will focus on angelology and its connection to the Coptic Morning Service. The inclusion of angels in the Alexandrian liturgy appears to have been

---

[487] This Angelic Praise is recited two times: in Prime (*Book of Seven Canonical Hours*) and the Morning Service.

passed down from the early Jews who became Christians to the newly formed Alexandrian community. There are many instances that illustrate the similarities in types and roles.

1. *The Angel of the Blessed Day*

At the closing of the the Eucharist liturgy, the celebrant raises his voice and recites the priestly blessing:

> May God have pity upon us and have mercy upon us. Lord, save thy people and bless Thine inheritance, pasture them, raise them up unto the age. Exalt the horn of the Christians through the power of the Life-giving cross. Through the prayers and the intercessions of the *Theotokos*... (and of many saints), and he adds, "of the angel of this blessed day" (if it be the time of the Divine Liturgy) or "of the angel of this blessed sacrifice," closing his priestly blessing with, "May their blessing and their grace and their might and their favor and their love and their help be with us all unto the age. Amen."[488]

In the *Divine Liturgy*,[489] the priestly blessing shows two different angels ⲡⲁⲅⲅⲉⲗⲟⲥ ⲛ̄ⲧⲉ ⲡⲁⲓⲉϩⲟⲟⲩ ⲉⲧ ⲥ̄ⲙⲁⲣⲱⲟⲩⲧ (the Angel of this Blessed Day) and ⲡⲁⲅⲅⲉⲗⲟⲥ ⲛ̄ⲧⲉ ⲧⲁⲓⲑⲩⲥⲓⲁ ⲉⲧⲥ̄ⲙⲁⲣⲱⲟⲧ (the Angel of this Blessed Sacrifice).

---

[488] Burmester, *The Egyptian or Coptic Church*, 340.
[489] *Divine Liturgy*, 250.

2. *The Angel of Sacrifice*

This angelic praise that took place in the heavenly sanctuary was suitable for the Jews of the late Second Temple era: "This sanctuary was conceived as a place of worship without the blood of sacrifices."[490] The angels were offering a sacrifice of praise that seemingly could have been either praise or a qorban. The presence of this "angel of sacrifice" is believed to be present during the whole Eucharistic Service. The liturgy itself does not mention when the angel arrives during the service, but the celebrant, after washing the vessels, asks him to go back to heaven, to the throne of God, and intercede for the congregation. Archbishop Basilios calls him the "guardian angel." Burmester rightly calls him the "angel of the sacrifice," which is the Arabic appellation in all the Euchologions.[491] The article of Basilios states:

> The Coptic Church believes in the guardianship of a certain angel to the oblations offered in the liturgy. Accordingly, the last words said after washing the vessels and while sprinkling a little water on the altar are, "O angel of this oblation ascending unto the Highest with our praise: remember us in the presence of the Lord, that He may forgive us our sins."[492]

---

[490] Penner, *Patterns of Daily Prayer*, 102.

[491] Burmester, *The Egyptian or Coptic Church*, 79, 341.

[492] Basilios, "Guardian Angel," 1186; Cf. Basilios, "Liturgical Instruments," 1448. For the Coptic version of this invocation, see DL, 246.

Various tales and anecdotes have been created around these two angels. Some hagiographical writings claim that these two angels could have been visible to some saintly priests or bishops.

3. Archangels and Luminaries

In the Coptic *Book of Psalmody*, archangels and angels represent a significant part. In "Doxologies," the angels and archangels are a subject of praise during the Morning and Evening Service. The "Doxologies," as mentioned, are highly poetic compositions, characterized by their many stanzas and formulaic structure. They usually are addressed to the Virgin, to the angels, to individual saints, or to a particular category of saints. Such "Doxologies" are for everyday liturgy in the Coptic Church.[493]

The Archangels, in the "Heavenly Doxology,"[494] demonstrate many elements tied to the late Second Temple writings. Archangels are luminaries. Some excerpts from this doxology clarify this:

> Stanza 1   Seven Archangels,
>
> always praising as they stand,
>
> before the Pantocrator,
>
> serving the hidden mystery.
>
> Stanza 2   Michael is the first,

---

[493] Cody, "Doxology," 923–24.
[494] HPE, 305–306.

Gabriel is the second,
Rafael is the third,
a symbol of Trinity.

Stanza 3   Souriel (and) Sedakiel,
Sarathiel and Ananiel,
the luminous and holy,
asking him for the creation

These four luminaries—for Coptic tradition considers that Michael, Gabriel, Rafael, and Surial are the only four archangels—might reflect the creatures as seen in Ezekiel 1:4–21. However, this verse does not mention the names of the four archangels. The Gnostic literature describes the archangels as sources of light. In the *Apocrypha of John*, Birger Pearson talks about several emanations that originate from the supreme God. These creatures are the "Thought" of God (*Enonia*) being the chief among them, *Autogenes* ("Self-begotten"), and also the four "Luminaries" whose names are different from those that are included in the Bible: Armozel, Oriel, Daveidthai, and Eleth.[495]

4. Praise with the Angels

In the Coptic Morning Service, there is an interesting hymn called the "Hymn of the Angels" or "Praise of the Angels" (mentioned above). The prelude to this hymn consists of the following words:

---

[495] Pearson, "Jewish Sources in Gnostic Literature," 462.

Let us praise with the angels, saying, glory to God in the highest, and on earth peace, good will toward men. We praise you; we worship you, we confess you, we glorify you, we give thanks to you for your great glory, O Lord heavenly king, God the father, the Pantocrator. O Lord, the only begotten Son, Jesus Christ, and the Holy Spirit...[496]

This Angelic praise with its prelude is reminiscent of the liturgical feature in 4Q503, *Daily Prayers*. This imperative of "Let us praise with the angels" shows the counterparts and the unison between the angels and the human beings, a resonance of the Second Temple concept that allows the assembly of the worshippers to live in coordination with, and to be correspondent to, the praises of their angelic counterparts in heaven above.

The witnessing angel in 4Q503 is also present in the text of the Coptic Midnight Praise (before the start of the Morning Service). The celebrants cry out to the angel of the day (in singing): "O Angel of the day, flying up with this praise. Remember us before the Lord, that he may forgive us our sins."[497]

3.Conclusion: Luminaries in Second Temple Writings and Future Coptic Interrelations

The theme of luminaries that I have presented in this chapter is clearly multifaceted. The primary resources, which are the liturgical books, and the secondary resources,

---

[496] DL, 32.
[497] HPE, 241.

which are the rabbinic sayings and the sayings of early Alexandrian Fathers, hold abundant evidence that this topic is cherished in both Jewish and Coptic traditions. Further exploration of rabbinic literature and the scarcity of sayings of the Fathers would certainly further confirm their similarities and would also, I believe, help to decipher many enigmatic topics in the Coptic liturgy that may have a connection to the Jewish liturgy.

In the elements that I have been able to explore in this chapter, I have shown significant correspondence between the Qumran writings, the *Seder Amram Gaon* Book, and the liturgy of the Alexandrian Church. This section decodes some of the origins of the massive liturgical corpus in *The Book of Psalmody* where prayers ("Doxologies," "Psalis," and "Theotokions") are arranged in a particular sequential structure and large passages are sung just before and during the Coptic Morning Service, all pointing to Jewish influence, patterns, and precedents.

The arrangement of the Coptic *Psalmody Book* alongside everyday laudatory texts is analogous to that of 4Q408, 1QS, 4QS and 1QH. The angelology of the Alexandrian Church tradition has liturgical features that tie closely to 4Q503, 4Q504 and 4Q506 and the Morning Service in *Seder Amram Gaon*.

Chapter 5
Overall Conclusion and Possibilities for Future Research

This present, and I believe, unprecedented study, which further illustrates "the Jewish anchorage of the early Church of Alexandria"[498] through its liturgy, strengthens the scholarly consensus[499] that has attempted to find the linkage between the traditions despite the scarcity of the historical primary resources. Their findings opened one's eyes to consider the potentiality, but these scholars did not effectively demonstrate concrete conclusions. My findings as illustrated in the previous chapters (specifically in the Introduction, and in chapters 3 and 4) provide further insights and observations in relation to the theoretical body of knowledge concerning the history of the Jewish liturgy—starting from the late Second Temple era (200 BCE–70 CE) to the Period of the Tannaim (10–220 CE)[500] —and its survival in the shaping of the Alexandrian Church liturgy during the first centuries. Subsequently, historians and liturgists who are engaged in reconstructing the origins of the Coptic Church and its liturgy should take into greater consideration the massive Jewish liturgy and the writings of the Second Temple era that undoubtedly influenced it.

---

[498] The title of an important article by a French scholar, "l'Ancrage Juif de la Première Eglise d'Alexandrie." See footnotes 148–149.

[499] See Chapter 1, Research History.

[500] The Tannaim Period is important for further researches on reconstructing the early Coptic liturgy. It is during that time that the rabbis organized and elucidated the Jewish oral law. Their dictums are contained in the *Mishnah*, *Baraita*, *Tosefta*, and various Midrash compilations.

Throughout the restricted scrutiny of this study, at least I could confirm that the reverberations of many Jewish sources were not found just in marginal areas in the Coptic tradition but are deeply embedded in the most fundamental Coptic rituals: the Morning Service (as well as the Evening Service), and the Holy Psalmody, the Coptic Synaxarium. Undoubtedly, there are others. Further constraints prevented me from examining many of the early church documents, such as *the Apostolic Constitutions*,[501] *Didascalia Apostolorum*, and the *Apostolic Church Order*,[502] and how the early Jewish liturgy and rabbinic works impact them. Such investigational projects are important to pursue in the future because the Coptic Church, from its early era, considers these early texts as authoritative sources for the legislation of many canons and regulations. Here, I will outline the paucity of Alexandrian Patristics in explaining the Church liturgy and its effects and will argue that the Halakah is critical for Copts.

1. Early Alexandrian Church Fathers on the Liturgy

One possible, even likely, reason for the paucity of writings by Alexandrian Fathers about the worship of their

---

[501] Fiensy, *Prayers Alleged to be Jewish*.

[502] Bradshaw, *Search for the Origins*, describes these three pseudo-apostolic texts: "they are potentially valuable sources of evidence for the thoughts and practices of the periods in which they are composed." See pp. 80–84. It is important to note that the *Apostolic Church Order* comprises an important document called *The Egyptian Church Order*, which deserves dedicated meticulous study.

time is that the Jewish liturgy survived with its entire legacy during the early days of the Alexandrian Church. It regally imposed itself on the church leaders of Alexandria. Its authority was so strong that before the settlement of the Coptic Church, Jews of Alexandria who believed in the Messiah (some of whom may have been promoted to lead the church) continued to carry on worshipping with the same familiar laudatory texts. These Jewish prayers were always considered in their tradition as authoritative while holding a strong legacy in Scripture and have been strengthened and nurtured by a sturdy corpus of rabbinic dictums.[503]

The oral Jewish tradition of using the same core prayers for morning and evening, as well as for feasts, and of avoiding new forms of worship, stems from the Jews' decision to base their liturgy on a biblical pattern. I believe this serves as a starting point for the Alexandrian Church Fathers, who did not investigate, argue or explain its features in any detail. This is not due to a lack of interest, but rather because they tend to preserve the tradition as

---

[503] On this point, Heinemann, in *Prayer in the Talmud*, attests that the strong Jewish attachment to the Scripture-like created prayers and hymns followed the model of the book of Psalms, which served as stylistic, formal, and linguistic sources for the new forms of prayers. He even sees that the members of the Dead Sea sect "who began the formulation of the fixed prayers take it upon themselves to compose completely new and original hymns and prayers in the classical style of psalms. They limited themselves instead to much more modest and simple prayers, which however, made use of biblical prayer motifs and employed biblical phraseology and formulae" (Heinemann, pp. 17). Heinemann illustrates his concept with patterns of the Berakah (supplications) that are prayed during the Morning Service (Heinemann, pp. 90–103).

they received it, whether orally or in writing. They believe that this liturgical heritage originated with the apostles, who were all Jewish. Paul himself is no exception: he tells the Corinthians, "I commend you because you remember me in everything and maintain the traditions even as I have delivered them to you" (1 Cor. 11:2), and he commands the Thessalonians, "So then, brethren, stand firm and hold to the traditions which you were taught, either by word of mouth or by letter" (2 Thess. 2:15). He even instructs them to "keep away from any brother who is living in idleness and not in accordance with the tradition that you received from us" (2 Thess. 3:6). Paul instructed Timothy to ensure the apostolic tradition would be passed down after the apostles' deaths. "What you have heard from me in the presence of many witnesses, entrust to faithful men who will be able to teach others as well" (2 Timothy 2:2). In this passage, I interpret 'faithful men' as referring to the first four generations of apostolic succession: Paul's generation; Timothy's generation; the generation Timothy will teach; and the generation they will teach in turn. The early Church Fathers, who were part of the apostolic succession, recognized the importance of the traditions handed down from the apostles. The undermentioned quotations demonstrate the great care they took to protect these traditions.[504]

---

[504] See the sayings of Papias in Eusebius's *Church History*, 3:39 (fragment); 4:21. Also see Irenaeus, *Against Heresies*, 1:10:2; 3:4:1; 3:3:1–2 and Clement of Alexandria, *Miscellanies*, 1:1. Origen, *The Fundamental Doctrines*, 1:2. Cyprian of Carthage, *Letters* 75:3. Athanasius, *Festal Letters,* 2:7, 2:29. Basil the Great, *The Holy Spirit*, 27:66. Epiphanius of Salamis, *Medicine Chest Against all Heresies*, 61:6. Augustine, *Against the Donatists,*

Through the massive writings of the Alexandrian Church Fathers, we find that they made just a few allusions to the liturgy, as noted by Srawley.[505] Assuming each author's awareness, a brief illustration of their sayings about worship is beneficial for understanding the necessity of locating a better resource for interpreting the origin of the Coptic liturgy and its structure.

Srawley finds that Clement of Alexandria (c.150–215 CE), instead of describing the liturgy, "was more concerned with prayer as an inner converse of the heart with God than its public expression in worship."[506] Apparently, his excessive use of allegorical language in explaining liturgical segments does not shed any light on its setting and its legacy. Origen (c. 184–254 CE) only briefly speaks of liturgical formulas such as gifts to Christ, the kiss of peace, and the offering of the gifts of bread and wine.[507] On the other hand, Dionysius (died 264 CE), bishop of Alexandria, has a few passing allusions to liturgical customs such as the saying of "Amen" and of the communicant standing at the altar, putting forth his hands

---

5:23[31]; 5:26[37]). John Chrysostom, *Homilies on Second Thessalonians*.

[505] Srawley states in *The Early History of the Liturgy*, 41: "The vague and scanty references contained in the Christian writings of Alexandrian origin, and the comparatively late date of our earliest manuscripts of the liturgies connected with the Church of Egypt, rendered the task of reconstructing the course of liturgical development in this part of Christendom extremely precarious."

[506] Srawley, *The Early History of the Liturgy*, 41. As an example, the author mentions a passage from *Stromates*, 6, 14.

[507] Srawley describes Origen talking about prayers to God "that may be worthy to offer Him gifts, which he may restore us in Christ Jesus heavenly things in exchange for earthly" (*Luc Homily*, XXXIX).

to receive the holy food.⁵⁰⁸ Athanasius (296–373 CE) describes a vigil service that preceded the communion, and mentions the reading of lessons (*Hist. Arian,* 81; *De Fuga* 24). From a monastic setting, Macarius (c. 300–391 CE) similarly refers to the lessons and psalmody, which precedes the celebration of the mass (*De Caritate*, 29). At the same time, Synesius (c. 411 CE) refers to the 'Holy table' τράπεζα and the 'sacramental/mystic curtain' μυστικόν παραπέτασμα (the altar veil) (*Ep.* 67) by name, but provides no specific details.

By the time of Cyril of Alexandria (378–444 CE), it is noticeable that many Jewish elements are revealed in the Alexandrian Church, but the uttering of their legacy remains unspoken. Cyril, for example, refers to the deacon's various proclamations concerning binding to stand for prayer at the beginning of any congregational service,⁵⁰⁹ and makes some allusions to prayers to the emperor (*de Ador., in Spir. et Verit*, XII).⁵¹⁰ He further refers to the salutations, "Peace with you all." On the other hand, in *The Sacramentary of Sarapion*,⁵¹¹ which Srawley considers "the most important discovery of recent times for the knowledge of the early liturgy in Egypt,"⁵¹² the author traces many elements that are revealed in 1 SAG (some of which I noted in Chapter 3): the deacon's proclamation "to

---

⁵⁰⁸ Srawley mentions *Ep. ad Fab.* (Ed. Feltoe, 58).

⁵⁰⁹ See chapter 3, 1 SAG, 73, 75, 79.

⁵¹⁰ A possible reverberation of *Birkat Mishpat* ("Justice"), where the worshipper asks God to restore righteous judges as in the days of old. See 1 SAG, 92.

⁵¹¹ Sarapion becomes bishop between 337–339 CE.

⁵¹² Srawley, *The Early History of the Liturgy*, 50.

arise and pray,"⁵¹³ many petitions related to the Tefillah: a prayer for the people, a "benediction" (Berakah) of the people, a prayer and a benediction for the sick,⁵¹⁴ a prayer for fruitfulness,⁵¹⁵ for the Church, and for the Bishop and the church; and, finally, a "prayer for bending of the knee."

The result of such limited comments from the Alexandrian Fathers is that their writings have not adequately revealed the unacknowledged legacy of Jewish liturgy in the Egyptian Christian rituals, nor have they helped scholars⁵¹⁶ or faithful churchgoers to understand the unobserved wisdom and historical legacy that stands behind the Coptic liturgical worship texts and rubrics. This paucity of patristic information directly affects the most important aspect of the Copts' spirituality: their communal worship. It is also the cause of a widespread mythology and mistaken ideas,⁵¹⁷ which constitutes theories and fantasies that circulate in Coptic religious circles without appreciating the genuine grandeur of the textual spirituality, or the liturgical reasoning that is related to its core prayers.

---

[513] 1 SAG, 73, 75, 79, a replicate from Cyril's writings.

[514] 1 SAG, 89.

[515] 1 SAG, 89–90.

[516] Usually, for Egyptian scholars such as Athanathius Al Makary in *Salawat Raf Al'Bekhor*, when their specific research into some aspect of Alexandrian patristics is unsuccessful, they focus on the Middle Age Arabic writers, such as Ibn Al Muquaffa, Ibn Sebaa, and Ibn Kabar.

[517] The mythology includes the notion that these liturgical elements and worship music are directly inherited from the Old Egyptian Civilization.

If the core of the Coptic liturgy, such as I have shown exists in the Morning Service, has this kind of connection with the Jewish prayers texts, their similarities and textual and thematic correspondences (as demonstrated in Chapters 3 and 4), it is reasonable to consider the rabbinic Jewish literature of the late Second Temple period, which explains, exegetes, and clarifies their own liturgy, as a primary resource for genuinely understanding and deciphering many of the incomprehensible elements of the Coptic liturgy. I believe that in the twenty-first century, the Coptic catechist should leave parochialism behind and look more broadly for answers to some of the enigmas of the Coptic liturgy. Dix discusses the pitfalls of liturgical segregation and invites academics to link the Christian liturgies together to create the "first formation of the semi-Jewish church of the apostolic age."[518] The common similarities in the Morning Service in both Jewish and Coptic traditions provide compelling motivation for further Halakhic study of the Coptic prayers and services that will validate a strong correlation with the early Jewish liturgy, but will attempt to avoid unscientific conclusions or skeptical emotional inferences.

2. Could the Jewish Halakah Dissipate the Cloud over the Coptic Liturgy?

A. Definition of Halakah

The Hebrew word "Halakah" means "a way of acting," "habit," "usage," "custom," and especially "guidance" and the norm of practice. "Halakah" stands also

---

[518] Dix, *The Shape of the Liturgy*, 11 (Introduction).

for the whole legal part of Jewish tradition, in contrast with the Haggadah,[519] comprising thus the whole civil law and ritual law of rabbinical literature.[520] Regarding these canons, I will be concerned to uncover how the Halakah is critical to understanding the Coptic liturgy, especially the Halakah related to the Morning Service. The following Halakhic excerpts resonate clearly with the Coptic mindset concerning the setting of the liturgy.

B. The Talmudic Liturgical Halakah

In *To Worship God Properly*, R. Langer devotes part of her first chapter, "The Principles of Talmudic Liturgical Halakah," to many segments that echo with the Coptic liturgical reasoning. For instance, the author mentions that the obligation for Jews is not just to pray but also "to pray properly." [521] This is very important to the Coptic worshipper. Praying properly is to distinguish between "acceptable" and "unacceptable" prayers. Consciousness of the best way of worshipping is known, according to Langer, by accessing the "hundreds of laws"

---

[519] The Hebrew noun "Haggadah" usually means a tale, a narrative, and a homily. It contains stories and legends bearing upon the lives of biblical and post-Biblical Jewish saints. Such topics as astronomy and astrology, medicine and magic, mysticism, and similar topics, falling mostly under the heading of folklore, pass also under the name of "Haggadah." Thus, the text of the Haggadah is considered as the non-legal part of the old rabbinical literature. When applied to the Scriptures in order to indicate interpretation, the word used is "Midrash." See, Jahvist, "Haggadah," 141.

[520] Jahvist, "Halakah," 163.

[521] Langer, *To Worship God Properly*, 19.

generated by the Tannaim (10–220 CE)[522] and Amoraim (230–500 CE).[523] The fundamental source of these Halakhic liturgical principals is derived from the Babylonian Talmud.

C. Halakah for the Communal Nature of Prayer: Some Talmudic Principles

As seen in the petitions of the Tefillah,[524] the prayers must always be composed in the first-person plural.[525] A "*Davar shebikedushah*"[526] or "holy matter" requires a quorum of ten, as discussed in Mishnah Megillah 4:3. This is a strong principle for any Coptic Church service, even today. This Mishnaic passage[527] decrees that certain rituals, such as reciting the Kaddish in the "Pseuque de Zimra,"[528] the repetition of the Amidah (the Eighteen Berachot), the Priestly Blessing, and many other rituals may not be recited

---

[522] The time of Jesus on earth and the establishment of the newborn church.

[523] The period between 230 and 500 CE was a transformative era for the Coptic Church. It was marked by intense Roman persecution, the birth of monasticism, and a major theological split that shaped Coptic identity. Theological leadership and councils were marked by the influential Catechetical School, which played a central role in Christian theology. Athanasius, the Pope of Alexandria who died in 373 CE, was a key figure at the First Council of Nicaea in 325 CE, where he staunchly defended the divinity of Christ against Arianism. St. Cyril of Alexandria (Pope of Alexandria, d. 444 CE) led the Council of Ephesus in 431 CE, which condemned Nestorianism.

[524] Chapter 3, note 277.

[525] This principle is discussed in B. Berakhot 29b–30a; see Langer, *To Worship God Properly*, 20.

[526] See J. Levin, *With All Your Heart*, 199–213.

[527] Mishnah doesn't address this – this would be an anachronism.

[528] See its reverberation in the Coptic liturgy in Chapters 3 and 4.

without the presence of such a quorum. The spirituality and Jewish perception of these principles have great bearing on the deeper understanding of the Coptic liturgy.[529]

An important notion for modern Copts, which is well-explained and discussed in the Halakah, is that "prayer requires intentionality."[530] Obviously, both traditions are dependent on fixed prayers that are accompanied by permanent rubrics. The interesting point is that the rabbis of the late Second Temple period established a scheme to remediate undesirable attitude during attendance at any synagogue service. It is also called "Kavvannah."[531] Resources on this are found in B. Berakhot 13a, B. Eruvin 95b, and Pesahim 114b.[532]

D. The Blessings in Rabbinic Prayer

Langer's work also draws attention to the genuine legacy of many specific Jewish prayer structures that survive in the Coptic framework; in recognizing this, the rabbinic concept of "acceptable" and "unacceptable" prayers clarifies a Coptic perspective. There are many

---

[529] Langer, *To Worship God Properly*, 188–24.

[530] Intentionality is a philosophical concept defined as "the power of minds to be about, to represent, or to stand for, things, properties and states of affairs." Langer in *To Worship God Properly*, mentions this term, 23.

[531] Jacobson in *Meditations of the Siddur*, 46–48, also refers to many rabbinic dictums. Jacobson states: "The essential meaning of Kavvannah is that man should realize before Whom he is standing and pouring out the meditations of his heart; he should realize that in his Tefillah, insignificant man stands in the presence of the Infinite, Omnipotent God," 47.

[532] Langer, *To Worship God Properly*, 23, note 93.

specific Jewish structures for the composition of early prayers and hymns. For instance, the rabbinic literature explains why and how the blessings should be arranged (replicating Langer's framework): a liturgical blessing must begin with the word *"barukh,"*[533] must mention God's name,[534] must mention God's sovereignty,[535] and must not include multiple topics in one blessing.[536] This clarifies the features of many Coptic texts, where Copts need to find the Scriptural reasoning that stands behind the rule of their own prayers and blessings.[537]

E. Specific Liturgical Principles

Both Jewish and Coptic traditions hold a regulated system of prayers, blessings, and hymns "that would

---

[533] Sources for this principle: Tosefta Berakhot 1:9, B. Berakhot 46a; B. Pesahim 104b. This a common feature in the numerous Coptic blessings. See DL, Evening Service, 31. Three successive Coptic Berakhot start with "Blessed are you O Lord." The Third Ode counts many others with the same beginning; see *The Holy Psalmody*, 31–32, also 283. It is interesting to note that these characteristics of blessings in Rabbinic prayer emerged after the destruction of the Temple in the 6th–7th centuries. Thus, it is difficult to determine when the Coptic Church adopted this concept.

[534] B. B. Berakhot 40b.

[535] B. Berakhot 40b; P. Berakhot 9:1, 12d; Langer, *To Worship God Properly*, 25. She mentions several studies that could further support investigation of similar features in the Coptic texts.

[536] This is characteristic of Ode 3. Langer includes a long list of scholars who tackle this topic. See, Langer, *To Worship God Properly*, 27–28, note 13.

[537] These are all emerging after the destruction of the Temple, through the 6–7th centuries.

preclude response for the needs of the moment..."[538] Usually, these Talmudic principles, according to Langer, "are developed to allow the liturgical texts [as for the Coptic tradition hymns, deacon responses, etc....] to incorporate appropriate timely themes into the regular cycle of holidays."[539] For example, how should the requirements of two overlapping systems, such as when a holiday falls on Shabbat, be settled? In such a liturgical question, many rules, rabbinic dictums, and regulations are plenteous in the Talmudic principles.[540] The same questions and requirements exist regularly at the beginning of each Coptic Euchologion and *Khedmat Al Shamas* book that contains instructions for prayers, which strongly resonates with this type of liturgical overlapping. The vast regulated system in *Khedmet Al Shamas* provides many parallels.[541]

Thus, considering the Talmud as a source for more fully understanding the unusual features of the Coptic liturgical regulations could constitute a useful Halakah or guidance for the Copts, for Copts still wonder why they have this ritual setting and why there is such a strictness in following these rules. One logical reason is provided in Langer's following passage:

---

[538] Langer, *To Worship God Properly*, 23, note 93.
[539] Langer, *To Worship God Properly*, 31.
[540] See Langer's list of primary sources and related studies, in *To Worship God Properly*, 31–36.
[541] *Khedmet Al Shamas* 9–11; see also the three volumes of *Tartib Al Bayaa*, compiled by Bishop Samuel; also Liturgical Seasons in DL, preface 8–9.

Because Jews [and, I insert, Copts] understand worship to be one of the key pillars supporting their covenantal relationship with God, they want to be certain that their prayer is acceptable, that it reaches God and has beneficial effects, and that it does not transgress divine commandments and cause offense or worse in Heaven. To these ends, rabbis have struggled to define the details of proper worship, encoding these details in Halakhah.[542]

F. Model of a non Halakic Dictum Related to the Morning Coptic Service

It is impossible here to deal even superficially with what the Halakah has to say about the different parts of the Jewish Morning Service that could be valuable to study of the Coptic liturgy. Perhaps it is enough to cite one profound Jewish aphorism that personally, as a Copt who has practiced for many years the prayers of the Morning Service, has helped me to understand more about the specific program of preparation that is required before attending the Morning Service, as well as to visualize the connection between all parts of the Service:

> When one rises from his bed, he should not occupy himself with any mundane activity whatever. He should not even talk of anything else. He should attend his bodily needs, wash his hands and think

---

[542] Langer, *To Worship God Properly*, 245. Here, interested scholars will get further not by pointing to parallels as suggesting common historical origins, but by investigating Jewish liturgy from the perspective of comparative theology.

of the Creator of the world, focusing his thoughts on the fact that He is the One, the only unique Unity, that he is the supreme King of Kings, the Holy One, blessed be He. He is the Sovereign, the Ruler, the Source and Root of all worlds. One should contemplate the heaven and the earth, and meditate on this verse (Isa. 46:26): "Lift up your eyes on high and see: Who has created all these?" ...Then he should contemplate the greatness of God's work in creating earth and all it contains... And the wonders of the ocean and all it contains... And all of these are but as tiny seeds as compared with the world of spheres... And all of them are nothing in comparison with the angels... And altogether are as non-existent in comparison with the exalted and elevated throne, is nought as compared with His Divine Glory which, is the ultimate cause and ground of all existence. There is none beside Him. Then the person will be filled with the awe and love of God... And the desire to cleave to Him will enter his Heart. With these thoughts, the worshipper begins his Berakah: "Blessed are You O God..."[543]

---

[543] Jacobson, *Meditations on the Siddur*, 51–52 (excerpt from Habarith Shelah, *Sha'ar Haothioth, Oth Aleph*). This is not a halakhic text, but one meant more to be edifying and inspiring.

3. Possibilities for Further Research

A. The Embryonic Stage of a New "Judeo-Coptic" Scholarship

The Jewish literature in general, to my knowledge, has not yet been fully used, exploited, or even linked with the Coptic tradition on a significant scale. My thesis is about a new orientation towards studying the Coptic Church's liturgical origins through a new perspective on Jewish primary sources from the late Second Temple period. More concrete evidence could completely change many theories and assumptions related to the early age of the Alexandrian Church and the domain of Coptology in general (including Jewish influence on Coptic art, patristics, hagiography, and, of course, its liturgy).

I consider the present research as simply a brief preview for future Judeo-Coptic studies. I have showed many examples where numerous Jewish elements, rituals, rubrics, and writings reverberate in the Coptic liturgical tradition, as they were undoubtedly active in Jewish liturgies and prayers during the time of the Alexandrian Church's advent. The potential of locating many ties between the two traditions should fuel the excitement of liturgical scholars for ongoing productive research in this new academic field.

Also, as mentioned previously, identifying the liturgical roots of the Christian Church of Egypt is not only beneficial for Coptic history, but also an important element for the history of Early Christianity. Researchers in this new field of Judeo-Coptic studies should not think that the findings of such scholarship would be inadequate. From the results of my initial investigation, I believe that "the harvest is plentiful," and I pray that the workers shall not be few.[544] For example, areas that would require deeper knowledge of the Jewish traditions and more advanced knowledge of Hebrew and Greek languages, would provide a great opportunity to engage in semantic comparisons of Septuagint texts in both Koine Greek and Coptic, as well as comparisons of Hebrew and Arabic Old Testament texts.

B. Network of Scholars for the New Scholarship

My future vision towards a collective Judeo-Coptic study would involve a network of professors and scholars of Jewish studies (specifically the ones mentioned in my Research History, Chapter 1),[545] as well as some Coptologists. A connection between them could provide research interests, and shared commitments and purposes. The goal of such a network would be to nurture this embryonic scholarship for developed research and shared intellectual practices and expertise. Documentation of this shared learning would be available to others through publishing the conference presentations, and blog posts, and would provide a basis for future scholars to build their studies.

C. Academic Projects

Throughout many parts of this thesis, I mentioned that several topics need further study. Some would be

---

[544] Matt 9:37–38.

[545] Scholars who consider a potential Jewish seed in the Alexandrian Church, such as Griggs, Pearson, Cannuyer, Broadhead, and Paget.

major projects, and some minor, although not necessarily less important. Major projects would refer to studies that call for specific requirements: such as working on manuscripts that are dispersed in different worldwide libraries, collaborating with other scholars in examining the semantics of different texts (Greek/Hebrew/Coptic/Arabic); translating and publishing the massive literature of Christian Arabic and/or Jewish Arabic texts into English. Minor projects would not be on such a large and international scale.

1. Major Projects

The following is a summary of what I believe could be a very productive study.

a. The Midnight Praise [546]

Several years ago, I began to compile many notes on this core worshipping piece in the Coptic liturgy. Many pieces of evidence adhere to my contention that this Coptic text is a survival from the Jewish liturgy. One major part, such as the third Ode (*Hos*), is directly derived from Greek Jewish texts, while both the Coptic and Greek forms have

---

[546] This nocturne service consists of four odes, two of which are from the psalter. As described earlier, the four praises are also known in Coptic *Hos*. First and third *Hos* are biblical canticles (Exod 15: 1–21 and Greek Dan 3:1–67); the second and fourth *Hos* are Ps 136 and Pss 148, 149, 150. PhD dissertation, 2026. Research and translation of M574, a Greek-Coptic Sahidic manuscript held at the Morgan Library in New York. Under the supervision of Prof. André Lossky, Institut de Théologie Orthodoxe Saint-Serge, Paris.

similar features.[547] Nickelsburg observes that the two texts, "Prayer of Azariah" and the "Hymn of the Three Young Men," are in accordance with the synagogal Hellenistic prayers of the late Second Temple era.[548] Common features include that they appear to be antiphonal, they have a repetitive refrain, and they imitate the repetitive refrain of Psalm 136, which is the Second Ode or *Hos*, preceding this Danielic Hymn in the Coptic *Holy Psalmody*.[549]

This project would deal also with the lengthy Midnight Praise recited at The Bright Saturday (which occurs at the beginning of Saturday of Easter Eve), which also includes many Jewish apocryphal prayers,[550] including the apocryphal Psalm 151. To reach adequate conclusions, this assignment would necessitate the study of the earliest Greek and Coptic manuscripts that contain the Midnight Praise.

b. Early Coptic Church Sources and the Jewish Cachet

In this thesis, I have compared Amram's text (1 SAG) with the Coptic-Arabic Euchologion (Massoudy)

---

[547] For the Greek text, see Horst and Newman, *Early Jewish Prayers in Greek*, 181–215; Oegema, "Reception of the Book of Daniel in the Early Church," 243–52.

[548] Nickelsburg, "The Bible Rewritten and Expanded," 149–52.

[549] HPE, 554.

[550] Many prayers that are alleged to different prophets, such as Prayers of Manasseh, of Azariah, of Jacob, and many others. For that, see Azmy, *The Book of Holy Pascha*; van der Horst and Newman, *Early Jewish Prayers in Greek;* and Stone (ed.), *Jewish Writings of the Second Temple Period*.

and its English version (the *Divine Liturgy*). It is my intention to work further on the early Jewish and Coptic prayers that date from the first four centuries.

These texts are believed to originate in Egypt. In 1967, Deiss published the following sources:[551] the *Sacramentary of Serapion* (c. 350 CE), the *Strasbourg Papyrus* (fourth to fifth century), and *The Euchologion of Deir Belyzeh* (a Greek papyrus that dates from the sixth century but, according to Deiss, preserves very ancient elements).[552] Another important colossal Euchologion, titled by E. Lanne, *Le Grand Euchologue du Monastère Blanc*,[553] also needs close attention and sturdy erudition in order to analyze it and compare it to the Jewish repertoire. Finally, the Liturgy of Saint Mark (Greek text) as well as the Anaphora of Saint Cyril (also called Saint Mark) should not be omitted, as the petitions of this liturgy are clearly tied with the Tefillah of the Jewish Morning Service. Both liturgies have been translated and were first published in English by Brightman in 1965 in Oxford.

c. The Coptic-Arabic Synaxarium and the Pseudepigrapha

I started to work on the Arabic Christian literature in 1996, under the supervision of Father Samir Khalil, a well-known Orientalist and a specialist in the domain of the literature written by Christians after the conquest of Islam

---

[551] Deiss, *Springtime of the Liturgy*.

[552] Deiss, *Springtime of the Liturgy*, 243.

[553] "The Colossal Euchologion of the White Monastery," text edited and translated by E. Lanne, "Le Grand Euchologue du Monastère Blanc," 270–406.

in Egypt in 639 CE. Much of this massive production is still unknown to western academia due to slowness in translating these texts. A simple reading through these works shows that there is a potential to trace many Jewish Pseudepigrapha throughout it, where many Coptic hagiographies represent Old Testament figures that can be paralleled in the Jewish Apocrypha. Also, many stories that recount the conversion of some Jews to Christianity could be tied to and compared with some Arabic and Judeo-Arabic manuscripts in the Cairo Genizah collections.[554] Also, the writings of converted Jews, such as al-Wadih ibn Raga, and the Jew Abd al-Masih al-Isra ili, who wrote three works intended to convert Jews to Christianity, are still unknown to the non-Arabic speaking world.[555]

2. Minor Projects

a. Conclusion of the Morning Service (1 SAG)

Many minor projects must be completed in order to assemble all the pieces, including further puzzles in the Morning Service in both traditions. These puzzling liturgical elements are mentioned here as per their liturgical order in 1 SAG, Morning Service, starting with the leadership of the Chazzan in reciting the prayers,[556] and the Seliach Zibbur in the Synagogue as a primitive form of prayer leaders in the Coptic Church. The *Beraka*, "My

---

[554] Shivtiel and Niessen, *Arabic and Judeo-Arabic Manuscripts*. See manuscripts nos. 4205, 4598, 5782, 7385, 7901, 8741, 7901, 7902, and 8741.

[555] Hamilton and Ebrary, *The Copts and the West*, 28.

[556] 1 SAG, 6.

God: luminaries, soul, and resurrection,"[557] needs more enquiries and gathering of information. The "Pseuqe de Zimra," reciting Pss 146–150 or Pss 145–150, and other passages from the Book of Psalms, also needs to be compared and tied to the Palestinian Psalter, which originated in Jerusalem.[558] The same goes for the reciting of the Shema,[559] and the prevalent use of key words and phrases: luminaries, Lord of hosts, King of the Universe, and the Quedusha: "Holy, Holy, Holy is JHWH of hosts: the whole earth is full of his glory." Details in Chapter 4 above were necessarily restrained due to thesis restrictions. The Quedusha needs to be studied separately and in detail, for it is a major hymn in both Jewish and Coptic traditions. Studies of the rubrics in both liturgies related to the Shema and the Tefillah could benefit from further investigation of resources from the Christian Arabic literature of the Middle Ages, such as those that deal with the act of covering or uncovering the head,[560] whispering to God,[561] and many others. Each of these has potential to shed light on the origins of the Coptic liturgy.

b. Judaism and Further Coptic Observances

As shown in the Introduction, the survival of some Jewish concepts in the Coptic Church tradition strengthens the evidence of a Jewish cachet that may lead to further

---

[557] 1 SAG, 8–9.

[558] In that, see Zanetti, "La Distribution des Psaumes dans l'Horlogion Copte," 323–69.

[559] 1 SAG, 46–50.

[560] 1 SAG, 64.

[561] 1 SAG, 120.

investigation. These customs include circumcision, menstruation, dietary patterns, keeping the Sabbath, and many others that strictly comply with the Mosaic Law, are also required and legislated by the Copts.

c. Letter of Aristeas

The *Letter of Aristeas*, a letter believed to be a composition of an Alexandrian Jew from between 170–100 BCE and concerning the translation of the Torah from Hebrew to Greek, is found in the Coptic Synaxarium in different forms, and deserves serious study from a Judeo-Coptic perceptive.

d. Hellenistic Jewish Writings and Early Alexandrian Patristics

As discussed above, Hellenistic Jewish writings and Early Alexandrian Patristics were quoted by some early Church Fathers such as Clement of Alexandria, Origen, and Dydimus the Blind. Paget reckons and asserts Clement's knowledge of Jewish sources in Greek.[562] Clement's familiarity with the Jewish sources may open doors to further investigation into early Christian Alexandrian thought and extent to which Jewish sources may have influenced the Alexandrian liturgy and Church tradition.

---

[562] All the Jewish writings that Clement cites in his writings are in 93, note 9. Paget refers to Demetrius (*Strom* 1.141.1–2; 1.150.2); Aristobulus (*Strom* 1.72.4; 1:150:1; 5.97.7; 6.32.5); Aristeas (*Strom* 1.148.1–149.3); Artapanus (*Strom* 1.154.2); Pseudo-Hecataeus (*Strom* 5.113); Ezekiel the Tragedian (*Strom* 1.155.1–1.156.2); and *The Assumption of Moses* (*Strom* 6.132).

e. Thse Incense

In an earlier paper on liturgy, I discussed how the concept of incense in the Jewish tradition in many ways is paralleled in the Coptic practice, especially in the Morning and Evening Service, as well as in the Eucharist. However, much more detail needs to be added to my primary research.

4. Conclusion

My last word for this thesis is that we must not overlook the Torah as the foundation of the entire Jewish liturgy. Many of the Jewish Morning Service liturgical practices were in use before, during, and after the time of Christ. This feature should constantly influence the understanding of the transfer of Jewish liturgical customs to the newborn Church of Alexandria during the first century CE, via the early Christian missionaries. The Halakhic details provide an essential source in explaining the strictness of the Coptic Church in following its liturgical rules. This also benefits the contemporary Coptic Church, for it would help the Copt to pray with more understanding (1 Cor 14:15), to better evaluate their spiritual heritage, and to reasonably credit the origin of their laudatory corpus to a genuine source.

I completely agree with Bradshaw: "There is in fact much more than is often assumed,"[563] commenting on James Charlesworth's catalogue of what he "describes as an abundance of unexamined data" relating to forms of

---

[563] Bradshaw, *Search for the Origins*, 15.

Jewish hymns and prayers that predate 70 CE. [564] In order to assure a connection between Alexandrian Judaism and Egyptian Christianity, it is necessary to synthesize this data, and to explore the relationships of shared themes, perceptions, symbols, and metaphors held in common in Jewish and Coptic traditions.

---

[564] Charlesworth, *Old Testament Pseudepigrapha*. The Scriptural references listed in these two volumes strengthened Steve Delamarter's resolve to publish a book just to index the 7897 references. Cf. Delamarter and Charlesworth, *Scripture Index*.

Related Essay I

Art Scholars: The Matter the Jewish and Coptic Art in Egypt

The release of associating Jewish art with early Christian art in Egypt makes disappearing from any study the identity of Jewish art as an important heritage which, when studied in its genuine context, will reveal valuable information for the understanding of the Jewish community in Egypt at the birth of Christianity. The aim of surveying the books where the Christian Art in Egypt is treated is to highlight how the scholars (which are many) observe the origin of the church through the early Christian art in Egypt, known as the Coptic Art.[565] In this part, I will focus on the most famous scholars in the field. J. D. Cooney (1943)[566] observes that this Christian art witnesses a slow development to become an art where Christian themes are distinctively exhibited. He states that, "With rare exceptions, Christian subjects are not found in objects produced in Egypt before the fifth century. The earliest Christian objects from Egypt, mainly reliefs, usually depict a cross or saint in a Hellenistic or pagan setting." [567] Cooney traces the cause of this slow development to the

---

[565] G. Maspero, *Guide de Visiteurs au Musée du Boulaq*, 128. Gayet, *l'Art Copte*. Beckwith, *Coptic Sculpture, 300–1300 CE,* starts his Study with the fourth century. Some scholars investigate the Coptic art through archeological Studies, such as U. de Villard, Les *Couvents près de Sohag*; *Les Premières Eglises d'Égypte Copt*; Maspero, *(see* Fairman, H. W.) *"Fouilles Exécutées à Baouit."*

[566] Cooney, *Late Egyptian and Coptic Art,* 9–11.

[567] Cooney, *Late Egyptian and Coptic Art,* 9.

pervasiveness of Greek culture, which at the time of the beginning of the Christianity in Egypt replaced the Egyptian ethnicity. Even the Coptic language —the latest form of the ancient Egyptian language—was written in Greek characters. He illustrates his book with many photos demonstrating how Greek or Hellenistic subjects, particularly scenes from Greek mythology, are common.

In 1965, the German scholar K. Wessel, in his book, *Coptic Art*, observes how bewildering it is to define the common characteristics of early Coptic artistic forms. He states: "Anyone who looks at works of so-called Coptic art for the first time will speedily give up hope of finding a common factor in their intrinsic contradictions, the irreconcilable differences in their forms of expression, and the great contrasts of their subject matter." [568] He expresses his doubt about the origins of that art and questions: "Is that art a new national art (as per Ebers)"?[569] An offshoot of Byzantine art (as per Maspero and Gayet)?[570] Or "a reservoir of often very diverse streams?[571]" In his chapter entitled "Egypt Under the Roman Empire," he wonders how Egypt became Christian? He mentions the familiar New Testament passages and Eusebius' traditions about Mark's founding of the church, and he continues by summarizing the early centuries' history without any

---

[568] Wessel, *Coptic Art*, 46.

[569] Wessel refers to Ebers without mentioning the page number, *Sinnbildiches. Die Koptishe Kunst*, see Wessel, *Coptic Art*, 240.

[570] Wessel refers to Ebers without mentioning the page number, Maspero, *Fouilles Exécutées à Baouit*, (Drioton's edition); See Wessel, *Coptic Art*, 241, 243.

[571] For more details about the different opinions, see Wessel, *Coptic Art*, 46–47.

prompt answer to his questions.⁵⁷² Later in his book, Wessel depicts a Jewish funerary chapel known as the Necropolis of El Bagawat,⁵⁷³ in Khargah Oasis and usually associated with fifth-century Coptic art. Asserting from Fakhry,⁵⁷⁴ a famous Egyptologist, that among the chapels [of El Bagawat] "one is particularly striking" the Chapel referred to by the Egyptologist as the Chapel of Exodus, because the most distinctive theme represented is that of the flight of the children of Israel from Egypt. In this chapel, other scenes are also found, which, according to Wessel, hold "a rich Jewish tradition"⁵⁷⁵ of Adam and Eve, Daniel in the lions' den, the three young men in the fiery furnace, the sawing asunder of Isaiah,⁵⁷⁶ the history of

---

⁵⁷² Wessel, *Coptic Art*, 65. And in order to complete this historical picture, he mentions the pilgrims who usually their ships arrive at the port of Alexandria, on their way to the Holy Land in order to visit places associated with Joseph and Moses and States "that the shrines of the archangels, originally no doubt founded by the Jews."

⁵⁷³ The Khargah Oasis is the southernmost of Egypt's five western oases. It is located in the about 200 km to the west of the Nile valley. "Khargah" or "El-Khargah" is also the name of a major town located in the oasis, the capital of New Valley Governorate.

⁵⁷⁴ An Egyptian archeologist, see A. Fakhry, *The Necropolis of El-Bagawat in Khargah Oasis*. See, Wessel, *Coptic Art*, 241.

⁵⁷⁵ Wessel, *Coptic Art*, 162.

⁵⁷⁶ The Bible doesn't refer to Isaiah being sawn in half while hiding in a tree .That's contained in *The Martyrdom of Isaiah* 1:7–10; 3:1 (according to R.H. Charles version, *The Apocrypha and Pseudepigrapha of the Old Testament)*, 162–163. Coptic Synaxarium, under Tout 6, commemorates Isaiah 's torture: "On this day, the great Prophet Isaiah, the son of Amos, was killed by the hand of Manasseh the King who sawed him with a wooden saw." Seemingly the Synaxarium quoted it from this pseudepigraphic Jewish writing that was well circulated during the close of the First century of our era.

Jonas, and so on.[577] Wessel ends his description of the chapel by considering the great Jewish colonies in the Nile Valley for the existence of this art with these themes, and the allegorical interpretation of Philo's text for keys to understanding the Jewish symbolism in a Christian context.

Du Bourguet, in his book *l'Art Copte* (1968), shares Wessel's insights into the unclear picture of early Christian art in Egypt prior to the fifth century.[578] Similarly, to Wessel, he studies the paintings of El Bagawat, uncertainly dates them to the fourth century, and asserts that they are Coptic art.[579] He thinks that the inscriptions designating the painted figures or places are written in Greek. Thus, make [us] think that this work is executed by Greek Christians, probably from Alexandria, settled in this oasis, which we know that it was a place of exile for suspect persons for the authorities.[580] Later Du Bourget associates El Bagawat paintings with the catacomb of Karmouz in Alexandria,[581] Stating that they do not demonstrate any Coptic Style. Without pursuing this phenomenon, he adds two studies to

---

[577] For the plates illustrating the Old Testament's episodes in El Bagawat, see Wessel, *Coptic Art*, 167.

[578] Du Bourguet divides the development of the Coptic art in different phases under different appellations: the earliest period, he calls it the "pre-Copt" art ["l'Art précopte"] 54–72; followed by the proto-copt ["l'Art protocopte"] 72–99, and the last one, the Coptic art ["l'Art copte"] 99–129.

[579] Du Bourguet, *l'Art Copte,* 100.

[580] Du Bourguet, *l'Art Copte*, 104.

[581] Karmouz Catacomb was found in 1857, southwest of the Serapeum hill. For more information, see McKenzie, *The Architecture of Alexandria and Egypt, C. 300 B.C. to AD 700,* 237–238.

his endnotes and at least one of them demonstrates Jewish appearances in El Bagawat and Karmouz sites.[582]

A. Badawy, in his *Coptic Art and Archeology* (1978), quotes from Bardy that the beginnings of Christianity in Egypt are shrouded in darkness.[583] Badawy seems to be convinced that there is a Jewish presence in the history of the Coptic Church.[584] He agrees with Du Bourguet of on Coptic art development. He assesses the monastic murals of Bawit[585] dated from the fourth century, where many Old Testament scenes are depicted with additions from the Apocalypse. To the subject represented in the murals, usually a theophany, are added crosses as apotropaic elements (Chapel XLV). And because of certain similarities between the treatment of the theophany at Bawit with those of Palestinian ampulae (at Bobbio, Monza), Badawy mentions the suggestion of Gabar that it originated from the repertoire of the Hellenized Jewish

---

[582] Du Bourguet, *l'Art Copte*, 130. He also refers to H. Stern, "Quelques Problèmes d'Iconographie Paléochrétienne et juive"; and J. Shwartz, "Nouvelles Études sur des Fresques d'El Bagawat," in cahiers Archéologiques, 13, 1–11.

[583] Badawy, *Coptic Art and Archeology,* 2, quoting from Bardy, *Les Premiers Temps du Christianisme*, Paris 1940, 203.

[584] Badawy refers to the Egyptian Jews pilgrimages to Jerusalem before and during Jesus' time, the large community of the Jews in Alexandria, the 54 C.E. Jewish revolt and its impact on the Alexandrian Jews, Philo and his writings Eusebius tradition concerning Mark's introducing Christianity in Egypt. See Badawy, *Coptic Art and Archeology,* 2–6.

[585] The town of Bawit is located between Dayrut and Asyut in Upper Egypt.

art.[586] But Badawy sees that "this hypothesis applies, however, with better chances of credibility to the iconography of Bagawat."[587]

M. Martin the author of a very interesting article, highlights some implications for the history of Judaism and early Christianity within his historical investigation on the Necropolis of El Bagawat. He finds that "such interpretation of the art of the Exodus Chapel at El Bagawat has important implications. A Strong case can be made for considering these paintings as examples of a Jewish Christian art."[588] Furthermore, after describing in detail all the necropolis iconography and scrutinizing their possible Jewish Christian background, he even posits that with this funerary chapel, "we are dealing with an evangelized Jewish population."[589]

Many Christian art scholars (in general) and especially in Egypt omit to study Jewish art in the Roman Greco-Roman period prior to making assumptions. Many early believed Christian motifs, iconography's scenes and symbols existed in the Jewish repertoire of that era before being transmitted to Christian art in general.

---

[586] Badawy quotes Gabar, *Martyrium*, 2, 230–40. See Badawy, *Coptic Art and Archeology*, 260.

[587] Badawy, *Coptic Art and Archeology*, 260.

[588] Martin, "The Necropolis of El Bagawat in Khargah Oasis," 2, 1422. This suggestion is evidenced by the piece of information provided by the *Coptic Synaxarium*, 1, 1–2 states: "To this Apostle fell the lot to go [preach] to the oasis Al–Khargah."

[589] Martin, "The Necropolis of El Bagawat in Khargah Oasis," 2, 1421.

In Related Essay II, I will raise the re-consideration some of the correlations between the Egyptian Jewish heritage and early Coptic architecture and art.

Related Essay II[590]

The Jewish-Egyptian Heritage and its Impact on Coptic Church Architecture

The impact of the Pre-70 CE Jewish-Christians on the Alexandrian church was often overlooked from scholars' world widely. For the last twenty-five years, curiosity about a possible Jewish core at the heart of Egyptian Christianity has been on the rise. However, many structural components from ancient Egyptian synagogues correlate with many old Coptic churches. Torah and Rabbinic sources reflect the uniqueness legacy of the earliest Egyptian synagogues which might provide a better understanding, not only on the layout of churches in Egypt but moreover on the rituals and the Jewish worshipping customs connected to it. While this paper tackled many shared architecture components, with a brief methodological consideration, I emphasized on many architectural components shared by the Jewish and Coptic traditions such as: the partitions, the 'bema', (table and platforms), the torah shrine, the Eternal light, 'Cathedra of Moses', women seating, fonts and building orientation towards East. The writings of Philo are of inestimable importance for the Alexandrian synagogue as a *viva voce* of his time.

---

[590] Paper submitted at The First International Conference Coptic Archeology in Cairo 24–26 September 2022. Conference organized by the Faculty of Archeology – Ain Shams University, Institut Français d'Archéologie Orientale and Société d'Archéologie Copte. Article "The Jewish-Egyptian Heritage and its Impact on Coptic Church Architecture" is under publication.

This study aims to assess the layout of the two religious' institutions with their potential common liturgical components to have a better understanding of some of the potential roots of the early Coptic layout assembly. The correlation between church-synagogue architecture in general, is not a new discipline in the field of Jewish Christians studies.[591] Many scholars have tackled such important topic aiming to locate the historical flow of synagogues (in Palestine and Diaspora) and its tie with early churches. In the case of Egypt, hence synagogue and the Egyptian Church hold many shared rituals; and obviously the layout of the sacred place increases the worship performance: these two factors might help to realize rationally a promising impact of Jewish-Egyptian heritage on Coptic Church architecture.

Jewish-Coptic Common Rituals and layouts

Before the destruction of the Jerusalem Temple (70 C.E.), many synagogues existed in the Land of Israel as well as in the Diaspora. Levine reasonably concludes the following regarding the importance of such institution, stating: "The synagogue, one of the unique and innovative institutions of antiquity, was central to Judaism and left indelible marks on Christianity and Islam as well."[592] The Synagogue reveals a step towards the existence of the

---

[591] Will, Ernest. "Lee I. Levine (éd.), The Synagogue in Late Antiquity,"487–8. Porter, Stanley E., and Andrew Pitts. *Christian Origins and Hellenistic Judaism*. Hachlili, Rachel. "The Origin of the Synagogue: A Re-Assessment."

592 Levine, *The Ancient Synagogue*, 1.

Church.[593] This edifice was revolutionary in preparing a common ground to Jewish settlements and later a seed from which the church will grow. After the destruction of the Temple in 70 C.E., the Jew would find the synagogue to be the only place for worship, to study and to have fellowship with his community. The priests were no longer required for the sacrifice. The participation of the congregation was not limited to certain functionaries. Worshippers could share in Scripture readings and in the prayers. At the Temple, the presence of non-Jews was not tolerated, but the doors of the synagogues were open to everyone. Levine adds, "In many places, particularly in the Diaspora, non-Jews attended the synagogue regularly and in significant numbers."[594] This explains why Christ and later the Apostles went to preach in the synagogues, since "The synagogue became universal in nature."[595]

The following schema illustrates the common architecture components in church and synagogue. Some of Jewish designated names were kept the same in church

---

[593] Dugmore, *The Influence of the Synagogue Upon the Divine Office.* Kaufmann and Enelow, *The Origins of the Synagogue and the Church.*; Dix, Gregory. *The Shape of the Liturgy*; Oesterley, The *Religion and Worship of the Synagogue*; Runesson, *The Ancient Synagogue from Its Origins to 200 C.E.*

[594] Levine, *The Ancient Synagogue*, 2.

[595] Levine, *The Ancient Synagogue*, 2.

and others took a new one according to the new ritual functionality.

Figure 1 Coptic and Jewish Layouts

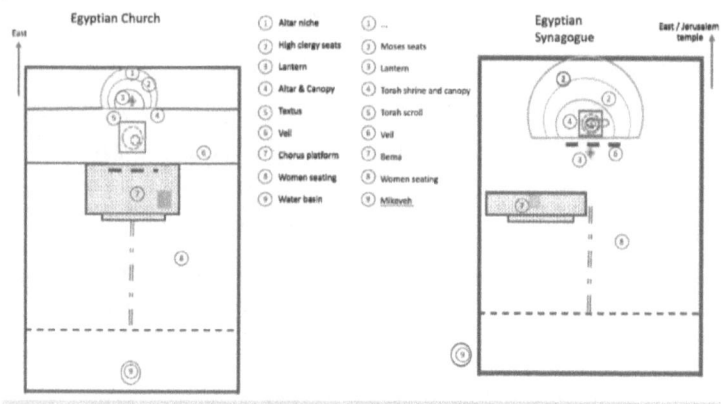

- The torah shrine, related components:
- Shape, the partitions (concept of praying towards East)
- Torah scrolls
- the Eternal light "Tamid"
- 'Cathedra of Moses'
- the 'Bema', (table and platforms)
- Purity Requirements: fonts and building.
- Women seating/partitions

In this section, emphasizing of the common rituals of the Jewish early worship and the Egyptian Christianity. I will focus only on the most Jewish architectural components that survived in the Coptic Church.

A. The Altar الهَيْكَل (alhaykal) and the Torah Shrine in the Synagogue

The apse was an integral part of the ancient synagogue where the Torah shrine is to be kept.[596] Levine notes that in the Amoraic literature, the apse is called "aron," which is associated with the biblical ark containing the tablets with the Ten Commandments that was placed in the holiest precinct of the Tabernacle and later in the Temple.[597] The apse, called also "aedicula,"[598] is where the Torah Shrine had previously stood in the first phase of the synagogue. This may have been used to emphasize the sanctity of the Torah shrine area as compared to the rest of the synagogue or the congregation. In old Coptic churches and monasteries, the apse has the same shape as that of the synagogue. Generally, the apse is only slightly narrower than the nave and usually is in the east of the Altar هيكل. Churches in Egypt, more than in other Roman provinces, made great efforts to decorate the apse richly where

---

[596] As the only synagogues dating from the beginning of the late antiquity were found during different excavations, Levine believes that the phenomenon of keeping the Torah scrolls in the apse dates from this era. This idea could be wrong, as many synagogues were destroyed or are still unexcavated. Also, the New Testament did not attest the existence of an apse. Many questions remain unanswered.

[597] Levine, *Ancient Synagogue*, 202–203 quoting from Meyers, "Torah Shrine" 303–308 in the Ancient Synagogue: Another look of the evidence" *JSQ* 4, 1997.

[598] Levine, *Ancient Synagogue,* 275, the apse has different form as a "aedicula" (in synagogues in Dura, Sardis and Ostia; as a niche (in Priene, Geraza, Apamea); as an apse (Elche, Aegina), and as a bema (in Bova Marina, Stobi).

traditionally the triumphal Christ is painted enthroned with majesty as king.[599]

It remains to mention that it seems the apse for the Torah shrine entailed the whole synagogue building against the Jerusalem-oriented wall.[600] This orientation of the synagogue is also a vast area for future investigation to explore further correlations between the synagogue and the Coptic Church.[601]

Rabbinic tradition feels the sanctity of the shrine almost entirely in terms of the sacred scroll within it.

Potentially, the altar niche or Torah Shrine resembles the Coptic altar and its location at the far East point, known also as *Sherkiah* شرقية. In the synagogue, the focal point of the centrale hall was the Torah shrine, a repository for the Ark of scrolls located at the East side or towards Jerusalem.

Ancient synagogues had 3 different forms of Structure:

a. An aediculae usually survived as a raised stone platform (Galilee, Golan)
b. Two flanking aediculae added to the Jerusalem oriented wall (Chozarim, Capernaum)

---

[599] Grossman, "Architectural Elements of Churches," 194–226.

[600] Levine, *Ancient Synagogue*, 237.

[601] The topic is stimulating in sighting this common liturgical architecture concept between the synagogue and the Coptic Church. See: Basilios (Archbishop). "Orientation towards the East."; Ryken, Leland, et al. "East." (In this *Dictionary* editors do not mention the author of each article); Levine, *The Ancient Synagogue*, 326–330.

c. A niche built into the wall (Eshtemoa, Khirbet Susya)

Without going into details, we uncover Goodenough's amazing discernment:

> No one has noticed, however, that the shrine also survived in Christian usage upon Coptic tombstones." .... that acroteria are important symbols, whether they are horns, birds, acanthus, or a combination of these, is strengthened by the fact that for acroteria the Copts used a variety of devices as birds; fishes; hares or AΩ. A close similarity with Jewish shrine during Greco-Roman period: wine, presence of Shekinah (bust of Christ). Shrine in these Coptic representations is usually a frame for a sacred object, but sometimes to be also a doorway to the next world."[602] It is sufficient to indicate that Goodenough made this correlation between Coptic altar and the Torah shrine based on Gayet's[603] and Crum's[604] collections of some Coptic monuments.

---

[602] Goodenough, *Jewish Symbols in the Greco-Roman Period*, vol. 4, 197–198.

[603] Gayet, Albert. *Les Monuments coptes du Musée de Boulaq.*

[604] Crum, W. E. (Walter Ewing). *Coptic Monuments : Catalogue Général Des Antiquités Égyptiennes Du Musée Du Caire.*

Correlation Torah Shrine and Coptic Altar

Figure 2 Coptic Altar Shapes

- Goodenough (1954): Correlation between Coptic Altar and Jewish Torah Shrine

B. The Sherkiah الشَرقِية (alshārqīā)

Another interesting survival form of the torah shrine in the Coptic Church, is in the concept of *Mizrach*[605]

---

[605] מִזְרָח (*mizrach, miz-rawkh'*): Sunrise, i.e. The East (side, -ward). "Mizrach" is found in Exodus 27:13, 38:13; Numbers 2:3, 3:38, 21:1, 32:19, 34:15; Deuteronomy 3:17.

(means 'East'), kind of drawing or diagram put upon the east wall of a room. The Jew will look at it while worshiping outside of the synagogue. It seems that this type of tapestry or gravure usually holds decorative tablets displaying "the name of God," scriptural verses, and representation of the Temple of Jerusalem. The theological concept, prayers said by a worshiper facing such tablet would be oriented toward the Shekinah,[606] and this idea is vividly presented by all symbols in a way which, emphasises on the presence of God.

The Copts call the eastward side of the altar the *Sherkiah* الشرقية which collates with the meaning of *Mizrach*. When a Coptic priest officiates outside of a church, the same tradition is held. The focal point becomes this Coptic *Mizrach* by facing the Pantocrator icon, which is hung towards East.[607] Jews and Copts, seems for centuries, hold the same theological and ritual concepts.

I will mention just one example of an old unique Mizrach as illustrated in *Figure 10* where the decorative symbols explicitly convey theological notions which stimulate reverence and piousness.

---

[606] Heb. שְׁכִינָה word meaning The majestic presence or manifestation of God which has descended to "dwell" among men.

[607] This priestly perception is still in use, when the priest is officiating in areas where there is no a church building.

C. The Veil or الحِجاب (ạlḥijāb)

The veil or the *ạlḥijāb* is the curtain that separates the Holy of Holies from the Holy in the Tabernacle.[608] It is traceable also in the ancient synagogue. It is known under the name of *Parokhet* and it is a covering of liturgical vessels or a veil for a sacred place.[609] In the synagogue, the *Parokhet* gains its sanctity because it was covering the Torah shrine[610] or was hung as a curtain to protect the Torah shrine and to be opened when the scrolls are to be taken out for the reading of the Scriptures and closed after returning the scroll to the shrine. Eventually, the function of this veil or curtain is well supported by the etymological significance of the word *Parokhet*. Emil Hirsch explains it:

> It [Parokhet] is more properly a *portière*, at the gate of the court; and, in fact, it occurs in conjunction with another Hebrew word, 'Parokhet' which is derived from a root, still extant in Assyrian, meaning 'to shut off,' and is found in Exodus 26:31, and elsewhere, as the designation of the curtain that divides the Holy of Holies from other parts of the Tabernacle. In

---

[608] The Greek liturgical appellation of the veil is καταπετασμα, see Clugnet, *Dictionnaire Grec-Français*, 78.

[609] Levine, *Ancient Synagogue*, 643. Levine states that the *Parokhet* was found in Bet Shean (Levine, 216), and in the synagogue of Smyrna as a curtain for the Ark which was covering a portal, (Levine, 216). It was found also in an old synagogue in Smyrna, see Jacobs and Hirsch, "Curtain," 390–394.

[610] Levine, *Ancient Synagogue*, 351. The author notes that by the second century C.E., the Torah Shrine was considered the most sacred of liturgical objects in the synagogue.

Assyrian 'parraku,' by metonymy, signifies the apartment and shrine which are 'shut off'; while the Hebrew has retained the active sense, and denotes the means used for 'shutting off.'[611]

The apse, where the Torah shrine is kept, correlates with the Coptic altar (the Holy of Holies). The *Parokhet* is theoretically associated with the altar veil[612] that the Coptic priest opens at the beginning of any liturgical services and closes it immediately after the service is accomplished.

Furthermore, in both Jewish and Coptic traditions, this curtain is made of expensive materials: velvet, brocade, and silk of various colors. For liturgical symbols, the color of the curtain is changed according to certain feasts. In the Synagogue, on the 'awful days' (Rosh ha-Shanah and Yom ha-Kippur), hangings made of white fabric are used. In the Coptic tradition, the velvet curtain remains for the whole liturgical year and the dark blue or black is for the Holy Week, white is for joyful days as Easter (Jesus' resurrection and the following 50 days).

Wealthy Jews and Copts hold almost the same artistic concepts when offering a veil to their Synagogue or church. It is usually complete with wealthy fringe with gold borders, fringes, and tassels, and were often embroidered in gold with inscriptions commemorating the pious donors and the event that occasioned the gift. They also

---

[611] Hirsch, "Curtain," 393.
[612] Synesius (c. 373–c. 414 CE), Bishop of Ptolemais in ancient Libya (which was and still is an eparchy under Coptic patriarchate) speaks about the altar veil as καταπέτασμα μυστικόν, which means 'mystic curtain' in the "Sacramental Curtain" or Ep. 67.

embellished the veils with verses and quotations from the Bible. As seen by me, in Eliyahu Hanavi Synagogue in Alexandria: there is no doubt the altar-curtains are richly embroidered with Torah verses and figures in needlework of gold. Figures 1 and 2 are self-explanatory. Though, A. Butler[613] noticed at Abu Sargah Church in Old Cairo an old interesting tradition about the altar veil. Here, he is emphasizing on the fact that the discussed veil is not hung at the altar door but on columns surrounding the eucharistic table *Al Mesbah* [614]. He observed two of the columns stand at a distance of 2 ft. 9 in., two at 3 ft. 31/2 in from the nearest corner of the altar; so that there remained enough room for the celebrant to move round the altar inside the curtains. At Abu Sifain's the shortest distance is 2 ft., which leaves rather a narrow space for movement. This curtain, which was surrounding the *Mesbah*, was an old tradition: to be closed while the Coptic priest sanctifying the eucharistic elements.

---

[613] Butler, The Ancient Coptic Churches in Egypt, vol. 1, 114–115.
[614] Coptic: ⲘⲀⲚⲈⲢϢⲰⲞⲨϢⲒ means 'place of making sacrifice'.

Figure 3 Left: Photo taken in Eliyahu Hanavi Synagogue in Alexandria - Torah Shrine with its veil.

Figure 4 Right drawing by A. Butler Al Mu'allakah church - Altar Veil, (vol. 1, 31).

At the present day such curtains are not used in the Greek Church any more than in the Coptic ritual. The purpose of closing the veils provide "an air of mystic sanctity to the precincts of the altar, was to veil the celebrant at the moment of consecration." [615] This practice was abandoned probably due to the fact that the iconostasis formed an effectual screen in itself.

---

[615] Butler, *The Ancient Coptic Churches in Egypt*, vol. 1, 31.

D. Tamid תָּמִיד قَنديل الشَرقية (qandyl alsẖārqīāïa)

In both Jewish and Coptic traditions, the presence of God is symbolized by an uninterrupted light in the sacred place. In Jewish tradition, a lamp is usually situated in front of the Torah shrine; and in Copts' mindset, it should be hung at altar entrance and in from the Sherkiah in the Altar.

The Jews call it *Tamid* [616] 'eternal light', and Copts *qandyl alsẖārqīāïa* قنديل الشرقية.

The concept is purely related to ritual theology: Yahweh is present and inhabitant in this holy place eternally: would impress upon a devotee the implication that he is standing before the Shekinah a feeling of reverence. Rabbinic literature stresses on the obligation of the prayer to well reflect on the presence of the Divine: "When you Pray, know before Whom you are Standing.[617]"

Just proving with one example, in Dair Tadrus, Butler well-regarded a bell-shaped cups and rimmed bowls of plain white glass suspended by chains are common in all the Coptic churches, and are before the altar-screen, or in the niche of the eastern wall [Al Sherkiah]. But the most important one is the niche of the eastern. Figures 13 (*JSGRP*, vol 4, 116) and 14 are self-explanatory.

---

[616] Ps. 16:8, 1 King 8:29, 44, 48; 9:3.
[617] Berakoth 28B.

Related Essay III
'Cosmic Music' (or 'Praise') from Greek Philosophy to Church Fathers:

A Potential source towards Singing with a Melismatic Style?

Throughout history, from antiquity until today, numerous pieces have been published on the subject of "cosmic music" or the "music of the spheres based on ancient writings and archeological substantiations."[618] Though it is not stress-free to write about this topic, it is nevertheless interesting to see how this exposé offers the understandings of some of the most famous intellectuals from Ancient Greek to early days of church in Egypt.

The definition of 'Cosmic Music' is still ambiguous within scholarship, and it is rarely found in any well-known music dictionaries or reference books. It is a classical musical concept rather than a style of music. In ancient Western culture, there was a connection between the cosmos and music, as boldly presented in texts of praise from Egypt, Greece and Asia Minor. References to this perception can be found in various verses of the Bible. Classical Greek did not use "musikè" to mean what we currently refer to as "music." The language had no word for that. Etymologically, the word means 'the business of the Muses.' The music of classical Greece was extended to cover all imaginative uses of language and dance. The term 'cosmic music' (or 'paise') is what we are dealing with here. The word 'cosmos'(κόσμος) means 'ordered world', which

---

[618] James, *The Music of the Sphere*.

is the opposite of 'chaos'. Broadly speaking, a cosmos is an orderly or harmonious system.

The interpretation of mysticism that surrounds the practice of Coptic liturgical songs requires a study of the parallelism between various fields of science relating to liturgy and ancient musicology. Sacred music is an art that refers to several historical, biblical, and local traditions factors that make up its characteristic. Aristoxenus had already advised his disciples to better know this art: "It is necessary to acquire much more knowledge to know music, and the study of harmonics is only one part of what constitutes the musician, in the same way as rhythmic, metric and organic."[619] In this section, (adhering to the recommendation of Aristoxenus), I will undertake a difficult task tracking the development of the concept so called 'Cosmic music' starting from Egyptian and Greek philosophical ideas, the biblical tradition in the Book of Psalms, Philo of Alexandria and subsequently the Fathers of the Egyptian Church. It will be perceived in what way this topic is packed with multiflued mystical and ritual implications in regard to the custom of Coptic singing, precisely in melismatic[620] style and or by performing long vocalisation based on a single Greek/Coptic vowel,[621] associated with an imperceptible genre of 'cosmic' praise or music.

Potentially, singing with vowel alphabets appears to be —in ancient world culture—as an element of cosmic

---

[619] Ruelle, *Aristoxène, Éléments Harmoniques*, 49, Livre II, chap.1, para. 5.

[620] A group of notes sung to one syllable of text.

[621] Coptic language shares the same Greek seven vowels.

music, by way of a harmonious mighty noise produced from the planets upon their rotations. However, have said previously, the theme of "Cosmic music" is still undefined by most specialized works dealing with the science of music. To put it in a comprehensible approach: Early Egyptians and Greek civilizations, biblical tradition, and theologians, each treated the concept of 'cosmic' music according to local beliefs and traditions. Each one who contributed to the 'field,' their threshold is the universe created (by the divine or God) where planets or stars are composing a universal blare, shout, harmony (as we will see later. Universe is the purely inspiration which upon it they elaborated ideas and aspirations. It might be a foundational layer of the singing practice of early Christian era. A quick survey on some old texts,[622] it appears that the music of human beings goes back to the same source: universal music. The elements of this music constitute a celestial lexicon: 'stars' that praise, the sound of vowel alphabets heard from the 'seven stars.' The ancients went even further associating the rotation of the 'stars' (planets) which causing the seasons, suggesting that the melody of the song should be changed correspondingly to the three seasons of the year. Later, they took it to another level, they established a doctrine based on the concordance between the notes of the musical scale and its musical-astral vowels (as we will see later). It was an imaginary imitation of the universe for a musical production in the service of their worship. The musicological study in this respect is very interesting.

---

[622] Démétrius, *De Elocutione*; Diodore de Sicile, *Histoire Universelle*; Aristote, *Du Ciel*.

Part I – Observations and Dictums from Greek Philosophers

1. The Concept of Cosmic Music in the Ancient Greek Philosophy

A. Pythagoras[623] (c. 570 BC--c. 495 BC)

None of Pythagoras' works have survived, Pythagoras achievement sinks in murkiness. Everything we know about his life and his philosophy comes down to us recycled by his later devotees: through their writings and their commentaries. Pythagoras –conceiving philosophy in abstract– was the first to take note of the relevance of certain small-number ratios to the intervals recognized as consonant and invariant in the music of the day. His observation was based on mathematical calculations. He compares the length of string or the weight of bells (musical intervals) with the distance of the planets. For Pythagoras, music embodies numerical principles and somehow answers to the laws of nature. His ideas seem already to have been accepted everywhere in the ancient world. According to the Pythagoreans, ratios found in musical intervals were sought in the distance of the planets,

---

[623] The bibliographical outlines of the historical outlines of historical Pythagoras are few and quickly sketched: according to most accounts of his life, Pythagoras was the son of a gem engraver names Mnesarchus, born on the island of Samos, in the Aegean Sea near the cost of Asia Minor.... He studied geometry in Egypt, where he was the first to initiated into the mysteries of Egyptian religion; in Phoenicia p. 26 he learned about "numbers and proportions;" he received his instructions in astronomy from Chaldeans. See James, J. (1993). *The music of the Spheres*, 25.

in the souls of good men, and in everything that contributed to cosmic order. The Pythagoreans attributed to Pythagoras the concept of the 'harmony of the spheres', thus explaining that planets and stars moved according to mathematical equations, which corresponded to musical notes, producing a symphony.

The cosmos as originated by Pythagoras is the concept of a divine order, or divinely ordered creation. At the time, the Sun, Moon, and planets were thought to revolve around Earth in their proper spheres. The spheres were thought to be related by the whole-number ratios of pure musical intervals, creating harmony. This is known as 'musica universalis,' during the pagan period, when humans were unable to complete its purpose: Creatures were producing 'music' to an unknown Creator.

B. The Pythagoreans and His Followers

The Pythagorean conception of the universe as a musical-numerical system rapidly became the standard through the Mediterranean world. While there were refinements and variations (as we will see later), some more successful than others, the basic keywords remained those established by the Pythagoras. Aristotle (384 BCE-322 BCE),[624] not pleased with a cosmos that made sophisticated mathematical awareness, attempted to create a mechanical model of the universe that would work. He

---

[624] Ancient Greek philosopher and scientist, one of the greatest intellectual figures of Western history. He was the author of a philosophical and scientific system that became the background and vehicle for both Christian Scholasticism (i.e. Anslem of Laon, St. Anselm of Canterbury and medieval Islamic philosophy (i.e., Al Kindi and al-Rāzī).

failed to explain the seemingly casual and disconnected movement of the stars. His exploration ended by concluding that fewer than fifty-five spheres, each driven by its own spirit—;'Its Intelligence'—to explicate for the motions of the seven planets.

In the Mediterranean realm, the Pythagoreans extended the concept of the Cosmic Music into distinct platforms. Some fails in comprehending the Pythagorean concept. In Alexandria Egypt, Ptolemy (c. 100 CE- c. 170 CE),[625] astronomer, His great work, the *Almagest* was nothing more than a collection of astronomical observations – immensely useful to navigators only far from any celestial music produced pitched tones.

Cicero (106–43 BCE) [626] as academic sceptic, he examined Pythagoras' –amateur of nature principles – cherished his concept and integrated it into a drama (theatre). In the works of Cicero *Somnium Scipionis* (Scipio's Dream) written in Latin (as its title indicate), Cicero's description of the universe is presented as an abstract literature, disconnected from the phenomenal world. He adapted the Pythagorean view in an innovative method as narrative of a dream—putting his perception in

---

[625] Claudius Ptolemaeus, an Egyptian astronomer, mathematician, and geographer of Greek descent who flourished in Alexandria during the 2nd century CE. In several fields his writings represent the culminating achievement of Greco-Roman science, particularly his geocentric (Earth-centred) model of the universe now known as the Ptolemaic system.

[626] Roman statesman, lawyer, scholar, and writer who vainly tried to uphold republican principles in the final civil wars that destroyed the Roman Republic. His writings include books of rhetoric, orations philosophical and political treatise.

the mouth of a mortal dreamer named Scipio. This visionary —while he was traveling the Universe—asked a simple question: "What is that great and pleasing sound that fills my ears?" Scipio Africanus reply is an admirably clear and concise account of the great theme:

> By the onward rush and motion of the spheres themselves; the intervals between them, though unequal, being exactly arranged in a fixed proportion, by an agreeable blending of high and low tones various harmonies are produced; for such mighty motions cannot be carried on so swiftly in silence; and Nature has provided that one extreme shall produce low tones while the other gives forth high. Therefore, this uppermost sphere of heaven, which bears the stars, as it revolves more rapidly, produces a high, shrill tone, whereas the lowest revolving sphere, that of the Moon, gives forth the lowest tone; for the earthly sphere, the ninth, remains ever motionless and stationary in its position in the centre of the universe. But the other eight spheres, two of which move with the same velocity, produce seven different sounds, —a number which is the key of almost everything. Learned men, by imitating this harmony on stringed instruments and in song, have gained for themselves a return to this region, as others have obtained the same reward by devoting their brilliant intellects to divine pursuits during their earthly lives.[627]

---

[627] Cicero, *On the Republic*, Book 6. Translated by C.W. Keyes (1928). *The sixth book ends with the Somnium Scipionis* para 18, 19.

Did Cicero perceive this majestical spheric music (tones) by any manner? If it is heard in reality: it should an amazing human experience. But why Humans are not witnessing this 'orchestral' production. Cicero puts straightaway the answer to this metaphysical phenomenon immediately in the end of the above quotation:

> Men's ears, ever filled with this sound, have become deaf to it, for you have no duller sense than that of hearing. We find a similar phenomenon where the Nile rushes down from those lofty mountains at the place called Catadupa, the people who live nearby have lost their sense of hearing on account of the loudness of the sound. But this mighty music, produced by the revolution of the whole universe at the highest speed, cannot be perceived by human ears, any more than you can look straight at the Sun, your sense of sight being overpowered by its radiance.[628]

The Pythagoreans extended the concept of the Cosmic Music into two distinct stages. The first was the association of the seven planets with their sounds to the seven Greek vowels; the second was the making of a ligature of vowels and consonants in their laudatory textsThe Pythagoras' followers view had triumphed utterly by the first century BCE and seemingly was preserved in the mind of the thinkers before the naissance of the church.

---

[628] Cicero, *On the Republic*, para 9.

C. Seven Planets Sound and The Seven Greek Vowels

Nichomachus of Geraza, known also as the Pythagorean, (c.60–c.120 CE),[629] was the first who associated the seven planets with their sounds to the seven Greek vowels α (alpha), ε (epsilon), η (eta), ι (iota), ο (omicron), υ (upsilon), and ω (omega);[630] in his *Manual of Harmony* he uttered this connotation:

> The sounds of each of seven spheres produce a certain noise, the first making the first sound, and these sounds were given the names of the vowels. These are things inexpressible in themselves among scholars, as well as all that is formed since the sound, here, has the same value as the unit in arithmetic, the point in geometry, the alphabetic letter in grammar. If these things are combined with material substances, such as consonants, just as the soul is united to the body and harmony to the strings, they realize things animated this one of tones and songs, that of tones and songs, that of the active and productive faculties of divine things. This is why the theurges, when they honor the divinity, symbolically invoke it with *Popisms* (clapping of the lips) and whistles, with inarticulate sounds and without consonants.[631]

The above analysis by Nichomachus also reflects the testimony of Demetrius of Phalerum (c.350–c.280

---

[629] Roman philosopher and mathematician.
[630] In Coptic, the vowels are: ⲁ, ⲉ, ⲏ, ⲓ, ⲟ, ⲩ, ⲱ.
[631] Translation as per H. Leclercq, "Alphabets vocaliques des Gnostiques", 1268–1288.

BCE)[632] regarding the Egyptian tradition of praising gods. Phalerum's statement is important for our study, since it will help us understand the purposes of the Christian writers, which will follow in this paper; an attempt to decipher some of the mysticism of the long vocalism in chanting the many of the old Coptic liturgical songs. He wrote in *On Style*:

> In Egypt the priests, when singing hymns in praise of the Gods, employ the seven vowels, which they utter in due succession; and the sound of these letters is so euphonious that men listen to it in preference to flute and lyre. To do away with this concurrence, therefore, is simply to do away entirely with the music and harmony of speech. But perhaps this is not the right time to enlarge on these matters.[633]

Digging in the archeological monuments, we find some justifications about Phalerum's statement. The beliefs and traditions of the Egyptian and Greek civilizations demanded, while evolving, a rapprochement between the planets, the vowel alphabets, and the three, five, and, later, seven tones of the musical scale. According to Lise Manniche: "This link between the alphabet and musical notes is a fairly natural one: all letters represent a sound, although some lend themselves to musical sound more easily than others."[634] As noticed by Manniche The

---

[632] Athenian orator Demetrius of Phalerum (late fourth century BC), who took refuge in Egypt with Prince Ptolemy Soter (306–385) helped to found, under his direction, the Library of Alexandria.

[633] Démétrius, *De Elocutione*, chap. XXI (French translation version).

[634] Manniche, *Music and Musicians in Ancient Egypt*, 13.

ancient musicological theories were the fruit of a certain 'Wisdom.' This term is used also to 'Intelligence' by Aristotle when he attributed to the reason of the stars' movement. His exploration ended by concluding that fewer than fifty-five spheres, each driven by its own spirit an Intelligence' – to clarify the motions of the seven planets. The philosophy of music at this early stage had from the 'Universe' a conceptual model preventing from acknowledging earthly music, giving higher values to the celestial or the heavenly music or praise. These early philosophers as lovers of 'wisdom,' practiced through a discipline of self-transcendence, philosophy promised unworldly joys that exceed the common, sexual and immediate pleasures enjoyed by musicians and their audience. Priority was given in antiquity to the vocal and seemingly the vowels as per their natural phonetics is the best to avoid instruments.[635]

Apparently, Ancient Egyptians find that the use of vowel alphabets is as a substitute for musical instruments. This does not deny that the Egyptians did not celebrate their gods without accompanied songs but demonstrates the Egyptian preference for vocal songs. The sung vowel was the ideal and exemplary instrument for praise. True glorification of the "divine" does not require a sound emitted from a man-made musical object or tool, but a clear voice gushing from the heart to the world of the hereafter. A scene unique to Beni Hassan[636] shows us another aspect, not only of the use of vowel alphabets, but also of the fact

---

[635] Bowman, Wayne D., and Ana Lucía. Frega. *The Oxford Handbook of Philosophy in Music Education,* 90.
[636] Governorate of Minyeh, South of Cairo.

of the extension of a syllable. Here is Lise Manniche's description and commentary. A scene depicting singers in a Middle Kingdom tomb at Beni Hassan may contain some clues as to which letters might have conveyed musical sounds. Each of two hieroglyphs (I, h) is repeated in a row beside each singer, they have been interpreted as representing the sounds produced by the singers. The row of repeated c signs may either refer to a singing exercise at the end of each phrase, prolonging a particular word (as in Coptic liturgical practice) or it may signify the lens of the entire phrase.[637] Which reminded us of Diodorus of Sicily (c.100 BCE–c.1 BCE),[638] Thoth[639] was the first to observe the order of the arrangement of the planets and, consequently, the harmony and nature of the musical sounds arising from the stars. Egyptian belief also wanted that this god made a three-stringed lyre, to adopt three tones; imitating in this the number of seasons of the year: the high for the summer, the low for the winter and the medium for the spring.[640] This legend led musicologists to believe that each string symbolized a specified season of the year and that each season had its musical tone. This seasonal music, three-stringed lyre is only an abstract

---

[637] Lise Manniche, *Music and Musicians in Ancient Egypt.*

[638] Greek historian, the author of a universal history *Library* known in Latin as *Bibliotheca Historica*, that ranged from the age of mythology to 60 BCE. He traveled to Egypt 60–57 BCE.

[639] Thoth often depicted as a man with the head of an ibis. His wife was Ma'at (symbolises concepts of truth, balance, order, harmony, law morality and justice. He was the god of the moon, wisdom, writing, hieroglyphs, science, magic, art, and judgment. His Greek equivalent is Hermes.

[640] Diodore de Sicile, *Histoire Universelle* I, 16.1.

concept, like uttered by the Greek philosophers (as seen above), but its interest lies in the clandestine type of the transmission of this very ancient belief in the ritual of the church. The Christians of Egypt still change the tone of some songs according to the season[641] while keeping the same liturgical text. This system is entirely established according to fixed criteria and rules, which cannot be neglected by the ecclesiastical hierarchy and the faithful. The invariable liturgical texts with a musical tone relative to the season are the doxologies (*Zoksologiate*),[642] the responsa of the Gospel of the Mass and Psalm 150 sung during Holy Communion. This ritual phenomenon deserves a devoted study.

Furthermore, as praising the gods, it should be related to the unchanged system of the universe (day and night rotation, rotation of seasons), Egyptians considered certain genres of music susceptible to break morals and that they could never be adopted. They had defended any kind of innovation and any practice tending to move away from prescribed modes. It is therefore not a question of the proscription of music in general. This defense of all change also extended to sculpture, painting, as well as laws and mores. It even forms one of the main features of the physiognomy of this people.[643]

---

[641] This term season is not used here in its strict sense, but rather refers to a religious event limited in time during a specific season.

[642] *Psalmody Book.*

[643] Pierre Larousse, *Grand Dictionnaire Universel du XIX siècle*, « Musique » 2200.

Part II – Psalms Recognition of Cosmic Praise

1. Biblical Tradition and Cosmic Praise

Genesis 1–2 discloses the act of Creation where God orders the cosmic elements to come into existence. As the Creator, He "made,"[644] "separated,"[645] and "placed" [646] all features in order to transform the chaos into an orderly world. He is the unique God who, through the days of creation, "said,"[647] "saw,"[648] and, "called"[649] for an extensive variety of creatures. Once the chaos was demolished and the heavens and earth were accomplished, he created human beings in his own image[650]. Irrevocably, God proclaims his delight to his creation by stating that "it's good"[651] which means that his making is 'perfect.'

This delight is not only streaming from God, as seen in Job 38–41,[652] but appears also in the Book of Psalms, demonstrating the gladness that the creation takes in its creator. [653] Thus, all creation is summoned to praise the Lord in Psalm 148 in a natural response by worshiping

---

[644] Gen 1:7, 16, 25, 31.

[645] Gen 1:6, 7, 14, 18.

[646] Gen 1:9.

[647] Gen 1:3, 6, 9, 11, 14, 20, 24, 26, 28–29; 2:18.

[648] Gen 1:4, 9, 11, 18, 20, 24, 31.

[649] Gen 1:3,6,9.

[650] Gen 1: 26–27.

[651] Gen 1:3, 9, 12, 14, 20, 24, 31.

[652] When God responds to Job's complaint, he reminds him the greatness of his creation and how he takes delight in the variety of his creatures. *Cf.* Ps 104:3.

[653] Pss 19:1; 98:4; 100:1.

the Lord the Creator. A mutual delight creates a harmony in the cosmic praise that overflows from huge creatures such as the Sun, the moon, and the Earth, snow, and everything that breathes.

In the book of Genesis, the cosmic elements are created, blessed, and placed in the cycle of life within an eternal system; but in the book of Psalms the cosmic proportion is multifaceted and holds a profound theology uttered through metaphors and images. This section will outline the cosmic system in the Book of Psalms by first defining the term of 'cosmic praise'. Secondly it will tackle how the Hebrew poets described this concept. Thirdly it will study the Hebrew poets' motivation to emphasize on the whole universe and its connection with the history of Israel, the other nations and their mythological beliefs. Finally, it will highlight the eschatological hope in the coming reign of God over all nations as judge. The conclusion of the research will concisely explain the Church of Egypt's appreciation of specific scripture unfolding the cosmic system and placement of that scripture at the core of the daily psalmody since the early centuries.

In biblical literature, the term 'cosmic praise' holds two elements: 'cosmic' and 'praise'. According to the Septuagint the Greek verb 'κοσμεω' (*kosmeo*) means: to put in proper order, to decorate (literally or figuratively), to adorn, garnish, or trim.[654] This word's definition is evident

---

[654] 2 Chr 3:6; Esth 1:6; Jdt 12:15; 2Mac. 9:16; 3Macc. 3:5; 3Macc 5:45; 3Mac. 6:1; Eccl 7:13; Sir 16:27; Sir 29:26; Sir 38:28; Sir 42:21; Sir 45:12; Sir 47:10; Sir 50:9; Sir 50:14; Mic 6:9; Jer 4:30; Bar 6:10; Ezek 16:11; Ezek 16:13; Ezek 23:40.

throughout the New Testament writings. The New Testament Greek Lexicon states that 'κοσμος[655] (*Kosmos*) is an apt and harmonious arrangement or constitution, order, decoration, adornment, e.g., the arrangement of the stars, 'the heavenly hosts', as the ornament of the heavens. In 1 Pet. 3, the meaning is extended to 'the world', 'the universe', 'the circle of the earth', 'the earth' and 'the inhabitants of the earth'. The word "Cosmos" fundamentally refers to the arrangement and order. However, the term 'Praise' originally meant to 'set a price on' or to 'appraise'. This led to another meaning for 'praise', which is to commend the worth of someone or something. The psalms of praise celebrate and revere the worthiness of God through his creation not only for his making but also for establishing the 'Cosmos' as an orderly created universe in place of the chaos, which is figuratively seen in the image of the formless earth and its emptiness as well as the darkness that was covering the deep water.[656] 'Praise' also means psalm,[657] 'Praise Hymns' is the second largest category of psalms following the lament that specifically praise God.[658]

2. *Order in Universe and Human life in Hymns*

The hymns often "praise God for the orderliness of his creation."[659] Psalm 148 summons the whole heavenly

---

[655] The word κοσμος is mentioned 151 times in the NT.

[656] Gen 1:2.

[657] Ryken, et al., *Dictionary of Biblical Imagery*, 658–659.

[658] Just to mention some of these psalms: Pss 8; 19; 33; 103; 104; 145–150.

[659] Futato, *Interpreting the Psalms,* 146.

creatures (vv. 1–6) and the earthly creatures (vv. 7–14) to offer a hymn of praise. The psalmist starts with the spiritual beings (angels, his heavenly host), followed by the lights (sun, moon, shining stars) and finally the clouds (water above the skies). Amazingly, other elements are called to join this universal choir: the lightning, clouds, winds, hail, snow and clouds, stormy winds, wild animals, even cattle, small creatures, and flying birds.

The themes of the cosmos as a well-ordered universe by the divine ruler and the status of orientation and disorientation of the human life are amazingly tied in the text. 'Hymns' are known to be composed when no trials exist, nor perils menace the human peacetime. In Psalm 105, in the days when the Israelites suffered famine (v.6), worship is given to God as the redeemer of Israel's ancestors (vv. 12–15), Joseph, (vv. 16–22), Moses and the Egyptians (vv. 23–26), the exodus and wilderness (vv. 37–41) which are all events that took place when Israel was in the stage of the disorientation. As Futato states that: "When our lives are well ordered, they are a microcosm of the well-ordered universe. By celebrating God's good creation, we celebrate the goodness of God that we are currently experiencing.[660]" This notion matches the meaning of the word 'κοσμος', the 'ordered world', which opposes the concept of 'chaos'.

The Hymn Psalms celebrate the Creator and his ordering of all the element of creation (e.g. Psalm 104), the mighty Lord in the history of Israel and his powerful use of cosmological elements from the cosmos for imposing his plagues (as in Psalm 105). When the Jews sing this hymn,

---

[660] Futato, *Interpreting the Psalms*, 146.

they are exalting God's name within a festival congregational context and also expressing their personal faith in him who restored their lives from the chaotic state. Likewise, when Christians meditate on the orderly created world, they sing the faithfulness of God and his steadfast love and mercy. At creation, God ordained the universe to remain in harmony, peace, and joy for mankind. He had set natural laws such as the order of day and night and the sequence of seasons that provide stability, prosperity, and peace for the creatures. As the world fell into sin, causing chaos and destruction, God the Father sent his only begotten Son to restore the initial peace and order. Christ's incarnation, salvation and resurrection demonstrate the eternal restoration plan to save the chaotic sinful world. Such amazing grace that the Lord bestowed on mankind is worth to be sung.

3. The Victory of God over Destructive forces in Kingship Psalms

Unsurprisingly, the cosmic element is found within the psalms of this category. The king is the creator; the ruler of the universe and mighty warrior who opens the Red Sea to let His people flee Egypt. In this section, the cosmic proportion is viewed through the context of the Babylonian civilizations. Ancients were always terrified of the destructive natural forces: flood, earthquakes, thunders, the sea roars,[661] etc., but Israel saw her king's supremacy over the gods of nations through the works of his creation. In face of the deep. Throughout the bible, waves that run irregularly in all directions and liberally interspersed with

---

[661] Keel, *The Symbolism of the Biblical World*, 61–77.

whirlpools were seen as a source of grievous disasters.[662] The waves with their roar indicate the uncertainty that prevails upon the waters. "All sorts of unexpected, fabulous creatures emerge between the fish, turtles, and prawns: a man with a body of a fish, a bull-man with wings and a winged bull." [663] However, in Ps 93:1, the Divine king is seen as mightier than the chaotic water because "the Lord reigns, he is robed in majesty".

In Psalm 29, the lordship claims victory over the chaotic forces of nature "the earth is the Lord's, and all it contains, the world and those who dwell in it. For he founded it upon the seas and established it upon the rivers."[664] The mighty creator manifests himself as the warrior who "defeats," "vanquishes" the chaos and re-establish the cosmic order. In this psalm, as also in Genesis 1, his voice is uttering creation, dominion and royalty over the whole universe. "The voice of the Lord is over the waters; the God of glory thunders, the Lord thunders over the mighty waters. The voice of the Lord is powerful; the voice of the Lord is majestic. The voice of the Lord breaks the cedars; The Lord breaks in pieces the cedars of Lebanon."[665]

Ps 104:2–4 is another cosmic imagery used by the Hebrew poets pointing at the domination of God over the destructive forces (wind and fire). It is obvious that the poet is familiar with the Babylonian myth of creation where it is

---

[662] Pss 48:7; 107:23–29, Jonah 1:3–16; Acts 27.
[663] Keel, *The Symbolism of the Biblical World*, 74–75.
[664] Ps 98:1–2.
[665] Ps 29:3–5.

told that Marduk,[666] the god of Babylon, vanquished Timiat, the dragon and the powerful, destructive enemy of the ordered world. In opposition to that myth, in this psalm, God of the Hebrew has a privilege over all other gods,[667] he is not only defeating them, but he is furnishing his chariot by the clouds (v.3) and marches royally on the wings of the wind. Neither flames of fire nor winds are believed to be as scary and destructive as it is for the other nations; at the contrary, he makes them 'his messengers' and 'ministers' (v.4). In Psalm 68:4, the psalmist summons the congregation to exult in God who rides the steppes between Sinai and Canaan, 'Who came from Sinai[668]' to save his people and to bring them the fructuous rain:[669] A divine transformation of the water from being a destructive force to become a source of blessings.

Psalm 29 is "unique in the Psalter"[670] and is also called the 'song of the thunderstorm.' In the time of Moses, God's theophany was through thunders, lightening, clouds on Mount Sinai[671] and the divine voice of God is heard cosmologically. A thunder's physical property lies in its' terrifying power and that is has the loudest noise produced over the universe impacting heavens and earth; however, in (Ps 29:3) "The voice of the Lord echoes above the sea. The God of glory thunders. "The Lord thunders over the mighty sea." The whole psalm describes the power of the

---

[666] Leslie, L. *Psalms,* 141–142.

[667] Ps 136: 3, "Lord of lords."

[668] Deut 33:2.

[669] Futato, *Interpreting the Psalms,* 67; Leslie, *Psalms,* 68.

[670] Oesterley, *The Psalms,* 1: 199.

[671] Exod 19:16–19; 1 Kgs 19:11–12.

voice of the Lord: a reminder of the Lord's creative voice in Gen 1. Similarly, to Ps 104, the metaphor of thunderstorm is to state God's power over nature's forces, controlling the thunder and blessing his people with rains as a source of life for vegetation and crops. God rules the thunder, not for destruction but for his people's abundance.

4. *The Coming of the Judge: A Cosmic Joy for Divine Restoration*

There is another reference to the cosmic proportion in Psalm 96. It is the image of the Judge who will come to rule and to govern the earth, which is the reason for the cosmic praise.[672] In this psalm, the congregation admires their Lord who governs so that "the world is firmly established, it cannot be moved" (v.10). The congregation utters a universal joy and stands in awe facing the kingship of God, his creative deeds, and his involvement in judging the nations. This joy will not be expressed individually or by the nations but by all creation: the heavens, the earth, the sea, the fields and the forest.[673] In a summons style (v.11) and because the "kingship of Yahweh is too stupendous,"[674] the voice of the cosmic structures is heard for the "earth to rejoice," "the sea to roar," "the field to exult" and 'the trees of the forest to shout for joy."

Ps 96 displays how the ancient Israelites welcomed God's judgment over the nations, through a call to all creation to celebrate this event. Summoning the creatures

---

[672] Ps 96:10–13.

[673] Broyles, *Psalms,* 377; Futato, *Interpreting the Psalms,* 88, *Cf.* Ps 47:2; Is. 55:12, Ps 29:5; Isa 42:10–11; Ps 104.

[674] Oesterley, *The Psalms,* 2, 424.

is to simply invite them to collectively distinguish the kingship of Yahweh from the other Gods (vv. 4–5). The cosmos (heaven, earth, field) greets God's intervention in the world and are singing (v.13) his 'justice' and 'truth' as they are glad that the will of God is put in effect.[675] The creation is jubilant for the hope of the coming of the divine of king as the rains come to regenerate the earth after five months of drought. Futato, quoting from Clifford states "The exultant rejoicing of the nature is a metaphor for its blooming and fruitfulness in the wake of the onset of the rainy season." [676] In Psalm 98, the universe is singing the salvation of the Lord. All the earth is singing with instruments: harp and trumpets (vv. 5–6), for his wonders (v.1), for his salvation (v.2) for his revelation. Nature joins the applause of the Nations in this great divine event to praise the greatness of the creator. It also brings mankind closer to the understanding of the forthcoming Divine Mission that will be assigned by the father on the Son so that Jesus as "Son" and the "heir" achieves judgment.[677]

The purpose of the Cosmic Praise to the Lord as the coming judge over the earth, perfectly matches the concept of the Cosmos, i.e. the orderly world. Futato clarifies the meaning, drawing our attention that the word "judge" in Hebrew means not only "to pass judgment" but also "to rule/govern."[678] 'To judge' means to govern in such a way as to put all things in the right order, as an author says,

---

[675] Dunlop, *Patterns of Prayers in the Psalms*, 78.

[676] Futato, *Interpreting the Psalms,* 122. (Quoted from Clifford, *Psalms 73–150*, 122).

[677] Jacquet, *Les Psaumes et le Coeur de l'Homme*: 2, 826. Ps 98:9 "judge the world with justice, and the nations with fairness."

[678] Futato, *Interpreting the Psalms*,90. (Quoted from Halot,4).

"judge, designates an action that restores the disturbed order of a community."[679]

5. Global focus on God's deeds in Creation and History

Ps 66 displays the unity of all creatures in one cosmic choir; "all the earth" (v.4) shouting with joy to God. It is an invitation to come and see what God has done. God's people have heard their fathers when they told them what God did in the times of Old.[680] A focus on the cosmic wonders that God did as mention in the psalm shows: The story of Noah recounts the destructive flood that God ordered and executed as a punishment; the plagues where God used different creatures to demonstrate his supremacy over the king of Egypt; and finally, the wonder of crossing the Red Sea (v.6). A variety of elements are arranged together by the poet to proclaim that all in under God's control. Spurgeon declares that: "the poetry [of this psalm] is such as would suggest itself to one familiar with mountain scenery; power everywhere meets you... massive grandeur, and stupendous force all around you and God is there, the author and source of all."[681]

6. Blessings for the Nations and the "Cosmic Scale"

In Ps 108, David expressed his intention to praise the Lord among the nations and to sing about the Lord among the peoples (v.3). His aim is to sing of the expansive nature of God's mercy and faithfulness (v.4). As in Psalms

---

[679] Futato, *Interpreting the Psalms,* 91. (Quoted from G. Liedke).

[680] Ps 44:1,4.

[681] Spurgeon, *The Treasury of David*: 3, 163.

96 and 98, here too, David's prayer is that the nations, along with the whole cosmic order, be covered with the glory of God.

Ps 114 says "In the Exodus of Israel from Egypt, of the house of Jacob from a savage people, Judah became his sanctuary, Israel his domination" (vv. 1–2). The Lord's great power over the Red Sea called for a congregational adoration in a liturgical praise. St John Chrysostom interprets this divine authority when "the sea saw and fled", Jordan turned back" (v3): "... the creation gave ground and yield and turned backwards on seeing its commander and giving way to the leader of the people"[682] as well as the "sea fled" marks the speed of yielding. The creator of nature (v.8), who "turns the rock into pools of water and the flint into springs of water" is the same God of Genesis 1 "who made everything out of nothing."[683]

In Ps 108, a hymn of praise, these cosmic creatures are commanded to praise following a certain sequence. First, the highest order of heavenly things: heavens, angels, heavenly hosts (vv. 1–2) then the sun, moon and stars (v.3) and the lesser heavens (v.4) and lastly the waters beneath the heavens (v.7). Then in (v.8): hail, snow, frost, stormy wind; (vv. 9–10) the exhortation targets mountains, hills, beasts, and all the cattle, even the flying birds are not forgotten. In (vv. 11–12) comes the invitation to the kings, young men and women. It is noted that the cosmic proportion covers the known and the unknown world. Verses 13–14 explain the reasons for this cosmic praise to

---

[682] Chrysostom, John. *Commentary on the Psalms*, 77.
[683] Chrysostom, John. *Commentary on the Psalms*, 88.

Yahweh: "He is supreme over all creation and is the protector of his people Israel."[684] The name of God is greater than any creature: His glory is above all the created cosmos, above earth and heaven.

> Praise him, sun and moon; praise him all the stars and the light. Praise him, heavens of heavens, and let the water above the heavens praise the name of the Lord. *Because* he spoke and they are created, he commanded, and they were brought forth. He established them forever and ever. Praise the Lord, angels, powers, heavens, moon star, water above the heaven (vv. 1–5).

St John Chrysostom[685] wonders how do these things praise while not having voice or tongue, spirit, reasoning or brain, phonetic instrument, or mind? The psalmist means that each of the created things is worthy of the wisdom of the Maker, and is full of awesome wonder, as Moses said at the beginning as a way of summary, "God saw all he had made and, lo, it was very good" – so good as to glorify the Maker and lead the viewer to praise of the Craftsman.

Certainly Psalm 148 articulates praise for God on a cosmic scale. This cosmic doxology (Pss. 146–150) summons the universe to praise the Lord, first by extending the call to worship to the "heavens" (vv. 1–6) and then extending it to the earth (vv. 7–14). It is the same idea manifested in the canticle of the three Hebrew children in

---

[684] Bratcher Robert and Reyburn William, *A translator's Handbook on the Book of Psalms,* 1184.
[685] Chrysostom, John, *Commentary on the Psalms,* 66.

the Greek additional book of Daniel.[686] Among those on earth who are called to praise the Lord are the "kings of the earth", "all nations", "the princes (of the earth)" and "all rulers on the earth" (v.13) and "his blessing of Israel" (v.14). Furthermore, In Psalm 150, we encounter for the last time the praise of God in Cosmic proportions. Apart from all the elements, there is a characteristic verse (v.6): "Let everything that has breath praise the Lord."

Though, in this section, it is impossible to cover the whole Old Testament writings, I wish to conclude with a relevant biblical glance that is found in the Book of Job: "while the morning stars sang together and all the angels shouted for joy?"[687] In Hebrew Bible 'shouted for Joy' is a one verb רָנַן (ranan, raw-nan'); holding 'to shout' 'for joy' together in one verb. The verb has different meaning: to creak (or emit a stridulous sound), i.e. to shout (usually for joy): —aloud for joy, cry out, be joyful (greatly, make to) rejoice, (cause to) shout (for joy), (cause to) sing (aloud, for joy, out), triumph. The Septuagint offers an interesting lexicon: ὅτε ἐγενήθησαν ἄστρα, ᾔνεσάν με φωνῇ μεγάλῃ πάντες ἄγγελοί μου.

The verb "οἐγενήθησαν" doesn't exist in the Hebrew text, ἐγενόει (3rd sg.), means to come into existence; to be created, exist by creation, as in Jn. 1:3, 10; Heb.11:3; to arise, come on, occur, as the phenomena of nature Mt. 8:24, 26; 9:16, et al.; to come, approach, as

---

[686] Apocrypha Dan 3:51–90, called also known as the Prayer of Azariah.
[687] Job 38:7.

morning or evening, Mt. 8:16; 14:15, 23; to be kept, celebrated, solemnized, as festivals, Mt. 26:2, et al.

As for the word 'ἄστρα,' ἄστρον (*astron*) means a constellation; a star; ἤνεσάν: 'αἰνέω aineō expresses to praise, celebrate. φωνῇ : has a vast champ lexique: φωνή (*phōnē*) : a sound, Mt. 24:31; Jn. 3:8; Rev. 4:5; 8:5; a cry, Mt. 2:18; an articulate sound, voice, Mt. 3:3, 17; 17:5; 27:46, 50; voice, speech, discourse, Jn. 10:16, 27; Acts 7:31; 12:22; 13:27; Heb. 3:7, 15; tone of address, Gal. 4:20; language, tongue, dialect, 1 Cor. 14:10 → language; sound; speech; voice. μεγάλῃ: μέγας (*megas*) great, large in size, Mt. 27:60; Mk. 4:32; great, much, numerous, Mk. 5:11; Heb. 11:26; great, grown up, adult, Heb. 11:24; great, vehement, intense, Mt. 2:10; 28:8; great, sumptuous, Lk. 5:29; great, important, weighty, of high importance, 1 Cor. 9:11; 13:13; great, splendid, magnificent, Rev. 15:3; extraordinary, wonderful, 2 Cor. 11:15; great, solemn, Jn. 7:37; 19:31; great in rank, noble, Rev. 11:18; 13:16; great in dignity, distinguished, eminent, illustrious, powerful, Mt. 5:19; 18:1, 4; great, arrogant, boastful, Rev. 13:5 lastly, πάντες ἄγγελοί : all ἄγγελος (*angelos*) one sent, a messenger, an angel.

A philological analysis is needed here. The Greek translation of the Hebrew verse shows a wealthier meaning for each word in line with the spirit of the Greek culture and philosophy in what concerns cosmic praise as seen with the Pythagorean school. In KJV "When the morning stars sang together, and all the sons of God shouted for joy?" doesn't show what we argue. Because "when" is replaced by "οὲγενήθησαν" which something is to be created (by the Creator), a loud sound φωνή μεγάλη: that could be as per the meaning of φωνή, an articulate sound, voice, speech, discourse. Having a melody? Certainly, as it is an intoned (αἰνέω *aineō* expresses to praise). Here we come to 'stars' and 'angels' or 'son of men' (in some translations), it is a shared joyful glorification to God from two celestial elements. A parallelism with Pythagoras and the concept of the 'harmony of the spheres', planets and stars moved according to mathematical equations, which corresponded to musical notes, producing a harmony. This joyful harmony between two choirs of stars and angels (or son of man) – on a cosmic scale – is fitting (as indicated above) to magnify God as Creator and displays the reverential attitude of 'all' creation to the 'One.' The motives are specific and well described: God is worthy to be praised as he is the one who maintains the order in the Universe, stabilizing life conditions of mankind and protecting it against catastrophes. He vanquishes the destructive forces and consequently the Nations perceive his Kingship over all the earthly kings. He holds the supremacy in judging all the earth and the restoration of his kingdom; and finally, he blesses the Nations so abundantly that his people praise him and summon the cosmos to acknowledge his faithfulness. The concept of the universe and its components, with their daily and seasonal mechanisms, illustrates a theology of praise from nature to God. The biblical text emphasises a jubilee: a majestic praise from nature and believers, as well as from natural elements, without adding a mathematical notion or pitched tone, as shown.

The 'cosmic psalms' concept is fundamental to understanding whether this idea was embraced within the laudatory repertoire of the early Church, given that the Psalter is the oldest Jewish book of praise in the form of poetic songs, predating Christianity. None of the psalms can be proven to date from a period later than the time of Ezra and Nehemiah, meaning the entire collection spans approximately 1,000 years. The Psalter is referenced directly 116 times in the New Testament.

Part III – Philo of Alexandria

Philo (c. 15–10 BCE, Alexandria—died 45–50 CE)[688] did not work directly on the ratios found in the musical intervals and on the music of the spheres. As a Pythagorean, he developed the Pythagorean concept of 'Cosmic Music' according to his Jewish/biblical beliefs. The reason for inserting such philosophical concepts into religion is simple: Jewish believers, who discover the majesty and the complexity of the gift of God in the Universe, strive to give thanks to the Creator "as it should be." This means 'creatures offer' a praise to the 'Creator' using their best existing tools in offering these praises to God: lyrically and musically.

Philo was the first Jewish writer to use the idea of the music of the spheres, by uniting Greek and biblical elements of Greek musical thinking. Laporte, in his book *La doctrine Eucharistique chez Philon*[689] linked the term 'Euchristia' (thanksgiving as sacrifice) to the cosmic

---

[688] Greek-speaking Jewish philosopher, the most important representative of Hellenistic Judaism. His writings provide the clearest view of this development of Judaism in the Diaspora. As the first to attempt to combine to revealed faith and philosophic reason, unique of his biblical philosophy. He is also considered by Christians as a forerunner of Christian theology.

[689] La Porte, *La doctrine Eucharistique chez Philon*, 89.

concept. He argues how based on Scriptures, Philo built a logical argument, following the Pythagorean concept.

Leonhardt summarizes well Philo's theory of singing and music.[690] Philo claimed that the wordless music (instrumental) originated in nature and imitates it.[691] However, he said that the word 'music' is superior: it can express an articulate meaning. He argues, music which is sung in words, is greater since it can precise articulate meaning.[692] The reason for this superiority is that human singing occurs in two styles: in singing of the voice and in singing of the mind.[693] Philo's reasoning will now take different paths in order to achieve harmony between the human song of the mind and the perfect music of the heavens. A closer look at his laudatory philosophy is needed here. Firstly, the mind sings the 'pure song' to God Himself, making it better than any other music. Logically, the singing of the mind (psyche) can only happen through voicing praise to the Creator.[694] Therefore, in order to form 'the pure song', speech and rhythm are required. Together, they constitute the entirety of human expression. Speech (words) addresses the mind and influences it through ideas. Tune (the rhythm of singing) influences the senses by controlling the passions.[695] Classifying a song as 'pure' implies a chaste life, as it influences the human

---

[690] Leonhardt, *Jewish Worship in Philo of Alexandria*, 159–163
[691] Philo, *Post.*, 103–111.
[692] Philo, *Post.*, 106.
[693] Philo., *Plant.,*126, 135, *Ebr.*, 94.
[694] Philo, *Agr.* 80f
[695] Philo, *Agr.*, 78–82; *Plant.*, 126); *Ebr.*, 105–121; *Sobr* 13, 58; Som II 268.

mind and senses, improving the soul. Human singing reflects virtues and vices. 'Pure song' is powerful and necessary for achieving harmony of the soul; as such, it is offered to the Creator of all creatures.

Once again, this concept is taking on a new dimension. The development of praising God is characteristic of Philo, as it progresses from a microcosmic element to a macrocosmic extension. The mind and body create a different kind of 'harmony' (more important than that between speech and tune) where male and female voices sing together in a chorus. According to Philo, the perfect model is the Song of Moses as recounted in Exodus 15, which he regards as a prototype of 'the pure song.'[696] This harmony extends further to become macrocosmic. Having dealt with this notion, he further emphasizes the importance of 'harmony' by concluding that human choral praise is accompanied by the perfect music of the heavens. In Som. I, 35–37, he reveals his Pythagorean background, explaining how the connection occurred between 'the mind' and 'cosmic' music. This occurs when the mind is in a state of conscious contemplation and the spheres are in perfect order. Their perfect order is when they (the spheres) praise the glory of God, who created this variety and continues to rule and maintain it. Humans (believers) should give thanks ('eucharistia') to God for his great wisdom in governing all components and features of the universe.

The essence of the Father (macrocosm) vis-à-vis of the believers (microcosm) is elucidated as follows: God (the Creator) shows kindness to His creation. He owns everything: the creature does not have anything to give

---

[696] Philo, *V. Moses*. II, 256.

Him, except praise and thanks, the proper expression of which is the hymn. Therefore, the main purpose of 'pure song' is a 'thanksgiving' as modeled in Exodus 15 (the Song of Moses). Since the mere performance of sacrifices and offerings does not suffice to acquire God's favor, it is the creature's (humans and spheres) duty to sing hymns of praise. This singing assembly represents the harmony of the mind and body (controlling passions and sin). This spiritual harmony of mind and body is represented by the two choirs presided over by Moses and Miriam (his sister), who thank him with the 'pure song'. This harmony of mind and body[697] is transformed into a polyphonic song, connecting human praise to the music of the spheres — the perfect music, as articulated by Philo.[698]

Returning to the Song at the Red Sea, Philo refers to this biblical passage as 'the great song' or 'the greater song'. The Song of Moses is also explicitly depicted as a model for a thanksgiving hymn. Moses is depicted as 'singing a hymn', which constituted his 'final thanksgiving.'[699] Moses calls upon the entire creation of elements and beings, both mortal and immortal, to join him in his hymnody, which incorporates every kind of music and harmony so that both men and the administering angels may listen. Mankind listens to it and learns about thanksgiving, while the angels listen to see if there is any discord in the singing. Finding none, they express their surprise that a mortal man can be so in tune with the heavenly harmonies of the spheres and the universe. This

---

[697] i.e. Beleivers (male and female).
[698] *Som.* I 35, 37,
[699] *Virt.* 72–75.

passage conveys Philo's belief that Moses had a profound understanding of the concepts and connections within the universe and its Creator. Celebrating the Israelites' crossing of the Red Sea, Moses presided over all the men and Miriam the prophetess led the women. Philo considered it to be the perfect hymn to God, the mighty warrior of the Israelites, in which the two highest creatures sing in harmonious concord.

At the time of Philo, the Kedushah was already an important hymn in the Jewish liturgy. This Jewish doxology was accepted and cherished by Alexandrian Church leaders. It proclaims God's creatures participating in worshipping "His Holy Glory." The Kedushah states: "Holy, Holy, Holy, the Lord of Hosts, the Whole Earth is Full of His Glory!" To this day, it is still a cherished praise that is chanted during the Coptic Church's Divine Liturgy. A scene where is depicted Heaven (heavenly hosts) and earth with all what exist enjoy His glory by singing to Him.

Late in the Second Century AD, the large Jewish community in Alexandria impacted the development of Christian liturgy as seen in Chapters 3 and 4 of this book. Alexandria was not only a great capital city, well known at that time as the Hellenistic world's leading learning center, but it also had a well-established Jewish community, with their own noteworthy faith and folkloric heritage. This society would generate new converts to the Egyptian Church, creating a new Alexandrian Hellenistic Jewish heritage. With his cosmic view, Philo, with his theological exegesis combined with Greek philosophy paved the way for the early Alexandrian Church leaders to construct their aesthetics regarding sacred music and worship. It was neither about aesthetics in lyrics nor musical performance:

as we will see later, the cosmic concept in praising God seemingly had been probably the perfect dogma to implant the best adulatory principles into the ritual scheme of the Alexandrian Church. As Discussed in above chapters, such transmission may occur with the converted Jews in the second half of first century CE, or simply impacted by both Greek and Jewish views.

Part IV - Vowel alphabets: Gnostic legacy

Leclerc and Ruelle have a substantial study helping to pursue our topic investigation.[700] The Gnostic texts of Egypt provide us with songs written only using vowel alphabets. These documents therefore have no Christian faith itself, but their importance exists because of this aspect so curious as its composition. Papyri I and II of Parthey and W of the Leiden Library, as per Leclerc, contain significant formulas related. Papyrus I: col 1 lig.26: There is an invocation to Saint George. The vowel alphabets are repeated successively as if to show a text to be sung following the compositive order of these vowels. Col.2, line.220: α α α α α α; Col.2, lign.139: αεηιωχωοιηεα; Col. 3, lign.227: ααααααα ιι ωωωω ιεω ιεω ιεω ιεω ιεω ιεω ιεω.

Papyrus II: Col. 1, line. 12-16: The text is more inquisitive. It presents a hymn formula "that must be recited or sung before going to bed."[701] This passage

---

[700] H. Leclercq « Alphabet Vocaliques des Gnostiques », 1270.

[701] Ruelle « Le Chant des sept voyelles grecques », 38–44.

reminds us of the famous popular lullaby[702] that mothers in Egypt vocalize all the vowels Arabic alphabets in this concise melody, until today, sing to put babies to sleep. The common point between this text and that of the Egyptian mothers is the presence of the vowels, singing with a certain extension. The W papyrus of Leiden bears notions dating back to Nichomachus' time; correlation between the seven vowels and the seven stars: «τῶνέπτά ἀστέρων α ε η ι ο ν ω ». Further folio of the papyrus, (14, line 31), it is the direct link between the use of singing vowels and the glorification of God's Almightiness: "I invoke you Lord, by a hymn sung, I celebrate your holy power ΑΕΗΟΥΩΩΩ.". A similar passage: "Your name [God] composed of seven letters following the agreement of the seven sounds that have intonations (φωνάς) corresponding to the twenty-eight lights of the moon." [703] To emphasize this divine attribute, the narrator writes in the context a "mise en place," an arrangement of words, which according to him perfectly suits the fundamental idea of the song.

Part V – Utterances of the Church Fathers on 'cosmic music'

This high moralistic view of music, praise and sound from the planets and stars seems extreme to us in the

---

[702] Ragheb Muftah, "Coptic Music from Mothers Chanting to Mlm. Mikhail El-Batanony Hymns", in http://www.redway.com/newbies/copt.xmas95.htm): «*Ho ho Nam Nam Wadbahlak Goz Hamam Waffarrak hulak al giran. Oskot, Oskot wadbahlak goz kot kot.* »

[703] Twenty-eight days of the lunar month.

modern era, but the early Christian fathers found it congenial. They believed that the profound philosophical perceptions, which they may have inherited from past generations, corresponded to biblical truth about the universe as created by God. They also considered it useful and necessary for the structure of church praise. Most likely, Greek and Egyptian views, as well as Alexandrian Judaism as presented by Philo and the Book of Psalms, laid the foundation for ritual theology in the Coptic Church. This is reflected in two areas: the way of singing and the selected biblical laudatory texts used for worship. Given the vital role played by Hellenistic culture in the theology of the early Church Fathers, I would argue that this high ethical view of music and praise seems to be a fruitful ground.

In 1966, Bouyer wrote an important statement:

> In the first place the knowledge we have today of Hellenistic Judaism is enough to convince us that the Christians used the materials and even the instruments of Greek thought as a medium of expression, or of reflection, has nothing specifically Christian about it, and especially nothing that would permit to oppose Christianity to Judaism. Nothing is clearer than that the Jews did this long before the Christians, and if there ever was any effective hellenization of early, if not primitive, Christianity, it was first all a

product of the school of Jews and not a reaction against them.[704]

1. Athenagoras

Athenagoras (c. 133–c.190)[705] lived in the 2nd century, was a Christian philosopher and an apologist. Athenagoras's chief treatise, titled *Presbeia peri Christian* (177 AD), is one of the earliest works to use Neo-Platonist concepts—which are based on the ideas of Greek philosopher Plato, to interpret Christianity. Athenagoras may have been a native of Athens, Greece. He is known as one of the founders of the catechetical school in Alexandria and as its renowned teacher. He observed:

> Now if the cosmos is a harmonious instrument set in rhythmic motion, I worship Him who tuned it, who strikes its notes and sings its concordant melody, not the instrument. Nor do the judges at the contests pass over the cithara players and crown their citharas.[706]

As one of the first Christian philosophers, the harmony of the cosmos was already accepted as a hypothesis. Pagans used to attribute different musical instruments to gods and goddesses. Consequently, Christians had to worship the Creator, not the musical instruments of the harmonious Universe set in rhythmic motion. Just as citharas were connected to the pagan

---

[704] Stapert, *A New Song for An Old World*, 4.

[705] Unknown biography (Ancient Greece or Alexandria, Egypt?)

[706] All patristic dictums in this section were grouped by McKinnon, *Music in Early Christian Literature*. Athenagoras, *Supplications for the Christians*, 16, *PG* vi, 921.

musical tradition. Athenagoras tried to push aside instrumental music from the praise of God.

2. Clement of Alexandria

Clement (c. 150–c. 215) was a theologian in the early stages of the Egyptian Church and the head of its Catechetical School in Alexandria. He is best remembered as Origen's teacher. He combined Greek philosophical traditions with Christian doctrine and believed that gnosis was essential for understanding theological concepts. The Greek word for 'ratio' is 'logos', which also means 'word, thought, and reason'. To early Christian philosophers, it had special significance in light of the opening words of the Gospel of John. While the evangelist is referring to Jesus, what he meant by the word 'Logos' was very similar to the Pythagorean ideal. This equation was crucial in rationalizing the acceptance of pagan philosophical teachings within Christianity. Clement of Alexandria's writings could be interpreted as arguing that the Pythagoreans' identification of ratio, or logos, with the divine principle of universal order harmonized with the Gospel's identification of logos with God, of which Jesus was the manifestation.

Eager to adapt it to their own ends, the early Christians readily embraced the Pythagorean concept of cosmic harmony. In his late second-century treatise *Exhortation to the Greeks*, Clement of Alexandria used music as a principal metaphor to reveal the errors of paganism and the perfect truth of Christianity.

In order to encourage pagan conversion to Christianity, Clement provided a wealth of information on ancient pagan cults, particularly concerning the mysteries of their rituals and related myths. He claimed that pagan songs were delusions inflicted on their singers by demons and sorcerers through evil arts. He then launched into a rhapsody on the saving power of Jesus, who is known as the 'New Song'. In Protrepticus, Clement states that the New Song is the Logos, who presides over Cosmic Music. The Logos' triumph is over the Greek myths and poets in a cosmic contest. The elements of discord in the universe (under Christ's sovereignty) shall be arranged in harmony:

> It ordered the universe concordantly and turned the discord of the elements in a harmonious arrangement, so that the entire cosmos might become through its agency a consonance. It let loose the rolling sea yet checked it from advancing upon the earth. It stabilized the receding earth and established it as boundary to the sea. And indeed, it even softened the raging fire with air as if tempering the Dorian harmony with the Lydian.[707]

Clement aimed to attribute the marvelous properties of Orphic song to Jesus while transmitting Pythagorean philosophy. Furthermore, it is this 'new song' that organised the entire creation into a melodious order, tuning the discord of the elements into correct harmony, thereby bringing the whole universe into harmony with it. It was a clever approach to involve Jesus, the 'New Song', through whom the whole universe could be in harmony.

---

[707] Clement of Alexandria, *Protrepticus* I,5; *PG* VIII,57.

Remarkably, as music impacted the minds and hearts of Hellenistic people, Clement explicitly associated the human body with musical instruments. The bodies of Christians are like David's harps and trumpets, and Jesus is the musician playing a hymn of joyful thanksgiving to God the Father with them. Clement thereby succeeded in conveying the Christian doctrine of the harmony between the Father and the Son, Jesus, to the pagans, albeit indirectly:

> He who from David, yet before him, the Word of God, scorning the lyre and cithara as 'lifeless instruments,' and having rendered harmonious by the Holy Spirit both this cosmos and even man the microcosm, made up of body and soul — he sings to God on his many voiced instruments and he sings to man, himself an instrument: 'You are my cithara, my aulos and my temple, a cithara because of harmony, and aulos because of spirit and a temple because of the word, so that the first might strum, the second might breathe and the third might encompass the Lord. Now this David whom we mentioned above, a king and citharist, urged people to the truth and dissuaded them from the idolatry; indeed, he was so far from hymning demons that they were actually put to flight by his music, when simply singing he healed Saul who was plagued by them. The Lord made man a beautiful breathing instrument after his own image,' certainly he is himself an all-harmonious instrument of God, well-tuned

and holy, the transcendental wisdom, the heavenly Word. This is the New Song, the shining manifestation among us now the Word, who was in the beginning and before the beginning.[708]

In *Paedagogus*, Clement proposes an allegorical musical instrument that combines the different instruments referred to in Psalm 150, and offers a new interpretation of them for Christian believers. His approach combines macrocosmic and microcosmic views:

> The Spirit, distinguishing the divine liturgy from this sort of revelry, sings: (quoting from Ps 150, which I will be outlined here for a better understanding, linking a divine attribute to each instrument showing the mighty power of Jesus Christ – the New Song)
>
> [verse 3] 'Praise him with the sound of trumpet,' and indeed he will raise the dead with the sound of the trumpet
>
> [verse 3] 'Praise him on the psaltery,' for the tong is the psaltery of the Lord.
>
> [verse 4] 'And praise him on the cithara,' let the cithara be taken to be the mouth, played by the Spirit as if by a plectrum.
>
> [verse 5] 'Praise him with tympanum and chorus' refers to the Church mediating on the

---

[708] Clement, *Protrepticus* I,5; *PG* VIII, 60–1.

resurrection of the flesh in the resounding membrane.

[verse 4] 'Praise him on strings and instrument' refers to our body as an instrument and its sinews as stings from which derives it harmonious tension, and when strummed by the Spirit it gives off human notes.

[verse 5] 'Praise him on the clangorous cymbals' speaks of the tongue as the cymbals pf the mouth which sounds as the lips are moved.

[verse 6] Therefore he called out to all mankind, 'Let every breath praise the Lord,' because he watches over every breathing thing he has made.[709]

In the same book, we can see Platonic ideas about 'harmony' clearly influencing Clementine's interpretation of Psalm 149. These are terms that are typically associated with cosmic harmony and encourage new believers to achieve it through hymns to God:

… But let erotic song (ancient Greeks) be far removed from here (church); let hymns to God to be our songs.

[verse 3] 'Let them praise his name in dancing,' it is said;

---

[709] Clement, *Paedagogus* II, 6; *PG* VIII, 441.

> [verse 3] 'Let them play to him on tympanum and Psaltery. And who is this singing chorus? The Spirit will explain it to you.
>
> [verse 1-2] 'His praise is in the assembly of the faithful; let them rejoice in their king,
>
> And again, he adds, 'that the Lord takes pleasure in his people' [4]. Now temperate harmonies are to be admitted, but the pliant harmonies are to be driven as far as possible from our robust minds. These through their (Greeks) sinuous strains instruct one in weakness and lead to ribaldry, but the grave and temperate melodies bid farewell to the arrogance of drunkenness. Chromatic harmonies, then, are to be left to 'colorless' carousals and to the florid and meretricious music.[710]

From the following quotation, it appears that Clement has a unique opinion on Egyptian music, rejecting it as it contradicts Christian values such as idolatry and superstition. He exhorts Christians to distance themselves from 'our native choir':

> Let carousing be absent from our rational enjoyment, and also foolish vigils which revel in drunkenness... Let lust, intoxication and irrational passions be far removed from our native choir... The irregular movements of auloi, psalteries, choruses, dances, Egyptian clappers and other such playthings become altogether indecent and uncouth, especially when joined by beating cymbals and tympana

---

[710] Clement, *Paedagogus* II, 6; *PG* VIII, 445.

and accompanied by the noisy instruments of deception. Such a symposium, it seems to me, becomes nothing but A theater of drunkenness. As the Apostle would have it: "Let us then cast off the works of darkness and put on the armor of light; let us conduct ourselves becomingly as in the day, not in reveling and drunkenness, not in debauchery and licentiousness" (Rom 23:12–13).[711]

McKinnon also emphasised that, in Clement's 'new song', Christ is the Word prefigured in David. He added that this view contains one of the earliest examples of instrumental allegory in patristic literature. He also observed that instrumental music is redundant, since God created humans as beautiful breathing instruments in his own image. Indeed, the human being is an all-harmonious instrument of God.[712]

Stapert offered a fresh perspective on the concept of Cosmic Music in the early Christian community, based on Exhortation IX of Clement. Unity was important for Christians' identity. It was a longing that stemmed from Christ:[713]

> The Church sings her song 'with one voice'. That 'one voice', however, includes more than just her members on earth. Both the Old and New Testaments present the picture of all

---

[711] Clement, *Paedagogus* II, 4; *PG* VIII, 440–1.//
[712] McKinnon, *Music in Early Christian Literature*, 30.//
[713] John 17: 11b–20, 23.

God's creatures joining in praise. The concept of the 'unity of one voice' in praising Abba Father is a result of a divine grace in order to live in harmony with each other, in accord with Christ Jesus, so that together with one mouth you may glorify God and father of our Lord Jesus Christ....The union of many in one, issuing in the production of divine harmony out of a medley of sounds, becomes one symphony following one choir-leader, the Word, reaching and resting in the same truth, and crying Abba, Father. "[714]

Thus, the 'harmony of the cosmos', which glorifies the Creator through a 'pure song', impacts the harmony of the soul. The harmony of an ordered cosmos was also a source of inspiration for some of the Fathers of the Church and monastic leaders in Alexandria, as we will see in the rest of this essay. This inspiration would subsequently influence the rhythm of sung praise and, by extension, the harmony of the soul.

3. *Athanasius of Alexandria*

Athanasius (296–373 CE) was Bishop of Alexandria and a confessor and doctor of the Church. He wrote the Nicene Creed. He explored a new area related to Cosmic Music, and he is the first in the Alexandrian Church to discuss the harmony among the four elements of the Universe, a topic that links musical tunes and their effects on the moods and the soul. The elements of nature—fire, cold, dry, and wet—are essential substances

---

[714] Stapert, *A New Song for an Old World* 25–27; see Rom 15:5–6.

in music, such as the Octoechos system, which is influenced by Greek musical philosophy. Athanasius, in Against the Heathe, claims:

Athanasius (c. 296–373 CE) was the Bishop of Alexandria, as well as a confessor and doctor of the Church. [715] He wrote the Nicene Creed. He explored the concept of Cosmic Music and was the first in the Alexandrian Church to discuss the harmony of the four elements of the universe, a topic relating musical tunes to mood and the soul. The four elements of nature — fire, cold, dryness and moisture — are key components of music, as exemplified by the Octoechos system,[716] which draws upon Greek musical philosophy. In *Against the Heathen*,[717] Athanasius claims:

> Who that sees things of opposite nature combined, and in concordant harmony, as for example fire mingled with cold, and dry with wet, and that not in mutual conflict, but making up a single body, as it were homogeneous, can resist the inference that there is One external to these things that has united them?

---

[715] He was the chief defender of Christian orthodoxy in the 4th-century battle against Arianism heresy.

[716] The Octoechos it is one of the most utterances of Cosmic music. It deserves a devoted article. For further studies, see Villecourt, "Les observances Liturgiques et la discipline du Jeûne dans l'Église Copte", 249–66; Werner, *Sacred Bridge,* Part 1 and 2, 370–409; Strauven and Reeth, "De Harmonie der Sferen en het Ontstaan van de Muzikale Modi" 95–118; Kuhn, *Koptische Liturgische Melodien*, 34–41.

[717] The passage is from Section 41.

Athanasius, who was undoubtedly influenced by Philo, emphasizes the theme of 'harmonia'. He defines it as unity, since the Greek word 'harmonia' means 'fitting together'. To him, the harmony of words was a sign of the harmony of the soul.

For who that sees the circle of heaven and the course of the sun and the moon, and the positions and movements of the other stars, as they take place in opposite and different directions, while yet in their difference all with one accord observe a consistent order, can resist the conclusion that these are not ordered by themselves, but have a maker distinct from themselves who orders them? Or who that sees the sun rising by day and the moon shining by night, and waning and waxing without variation exactly according to the same number of days, and some of the stars running their courses and with orbits various and manifold, while others move without wandering, can fail to perceive that they certainly have a creator to guide them? [718]

Building on Philo's ideas, Athanasius considers 'singing with mind' to be of the utmost importance. The melody of the words stems from the rhythm of the soul and its harmony with the spirit. Different notes have different effects on the souls of the singers and those who hear them. Spiritual harmony significantly impacts the character of

---

[718] *On the Incarnation*, often cited as Section 35 in English translations. McKinnon, *Music in Early Christian Literature*, 55.

believers. It is not a harmony based on individualism; rather, it is a harmony exemplified by the members of a monastic society, as Athanasius explains: "Harmony between desert monks produces in the mountains monasteries like tabernacles filled with saintly choirs."[719] The Alexandrian bishop also said that, just as a musician blends the sound of each string into a harmonious symphony, the Creator rules an entire harmonious order over the world as a whole.[720]

4. *Serapion of Thmuis*

Serapion Bishop of Thmuis (ca. 330 to 360 CE)[721] in the Nile Delta was a prominent supporter of Athanasius in the struggle against Arianism. In his ancient Egyptian Anaphora,[722] he depicts such a unity as is found in 1 Cor. 10: 17. In the liturgy the priest prayed:

> For just as this bread
>
> Once scattered upon the hills,
>
> Has been brought together and become one,
>
> So too, deign to gather your Church
>
> From every people, from every land,

---

[719] *Vita Antonii,* Section 44. McKinnon, *Music in Early Christian Literature,* 155.

[720] *Against Heathen* 3, 42-44. McKinnon, *Music in Early Christian Literature,* 55.

[721] Egyptian monk, theologian, and bishop of Thmuis (Delta, Egypt).

[722] Also known as the *Sacramentary of Serapion* of Thumis, Section 29 (on Eucharist). Stapert, *A New Song for an Old World,* 27.

From every town, village and house,

And make of her a single Church, living and catholic.

Part VI – Cosmic Music Concepts: Lyrics and Performance

The ancient concept of linking the terms 'cosmos' and 'musikè' creates a logical distinction: 'Cosmic music' is a synchronization originating from an orderly world. Musical sounds are produced from all of nature's elements and microcosms, and share the same arrangement and musical pitch as the macrocosm. Understanding this imagined hypothesis involves grasping several different elements. The cosmos generates cycles, seasons, days and nights, all of which are based on mathematical principles. Numbers determine musical scales and link tunes to language, i.e. vocalism and syllables. The harmony among these elements creates 'Cosmic Music'. (or 'praise'). More specifically, all constituents of the cosmos produce harmonious music, which pagans used to praise their deities. The early Church adopted this philosophical framework and adapted it to praise the One true God, who created and still administers the entire universe. Commentaries on the 'Way of Singing' related to this philosophical perspective and its development over the centuries are presented below.

In light of the points I made earlier, the focus will now shift to two main themes. Firstly, we will explore passages focusing on universal elements in praise of the Lord, most of which are rooted in biblical teachings.

Secondly, we will examine the direct and indirect impact of hymns on performance. The melismatic style is the most important characteristic of the Coptic chant.

1. *Liturgical Extracts*

The theme of cosmic praise is clearly evident in the liturgical books of the Alexandrian Church.

A. Euchologion

A striking example of the concept of the microcosm and the macrocosm is found in the book *Apostolic Constitutions*, VIII, 12:27. In it, the people join the angels in singing the Sanctus:

> The Cherubim and six-winged Seraphim, their feet covered with two, their head with two, and flying with two', saying together with thousand times thousands of archangels and ten-thousand times ten-thousands of angels, without ceasing and in loud voice; and let all the people ay with them, Holy, Holy, Holy, Lord of Sabaoth, heaven and earth are full of his glory; blessed be he forever, Amen.

B. Psalmody Book

The selection of the biblical hymns and psalms for a laudatory purpose is remarkable. The recitation of the passage of the Red Sea seems to be a cherished part in the tradition of the Jews when celebrating the Passover. It was to be read and contemplated at night. This pure thanksgiving song was transmitted for the Midnight Praise. No document supports a direct inheritance from the Alexandrian Jewish liturgy by the time of birth of the Church. Exodus 15 is also called First Ode. According to Baumstark,[723] this Ode is deriving from the ancient synagogue rites. Also, a fragment of papyrus, brought from Fayyum by W. A. F. Petrie, published by W.E. Crum, and identified as a leaf from an ancient Egyptian office book, contains parts of the First Ode. The Second Ode Psalm 135 (136) has the same trend towards the Cosmic Music concept. The Third Ode is the song of the three Holy youth found in the book of Daniel (in the Septuagint). They sang this song when King Nebuchadnezzar threw them in the furnace, calling upon the whole of creation to bless (praise) the Lord. The Fourth Ode comprises of Psalms 148, 149, 150. When chanting this Ode, the believers share with all of creation by offering praises to their Creator. These psalms express the state of joy, victory, and rejoicing from the whole heart and soul.

2. Grapheme[724] and Comments of the Way of Singing

The exceptional aspect of universal music, as described by the Neo-Pythagorean Nichomachus, who connected sound to the Greek vowels (which are the same in Coptic): α, ε, η, ι, ο, υ, ω, can be traced within the lyrics of the song. These long vocalizations in 'Tempo giusto'[725]

---

[723] Baumstark, *A. Comparative Liturgy*.
[724] Term to refer to the specific base of a given writing system.
[725] Tempo giusto (Italian term) is a musical expression that literally means 'in exact time', often directing a return to strict time following a

constitute the general character of Coptic songs. Ilona Borsai demonstrates the Coptic manner by singing these prolonged vocalizations. They are not 'melismas' of pure ornamentation, but rather long vocalizations sung with the same intensity and at the same time as the syllabic parts, forming an integral part of the melody. This melodic type is unparalleled in other Eastern liturgies.[726] The inventory of songs that apply this concept of vocalization is impressive. It includes at least those sung to the 'long melody'. This is what Borsai concluded after analyzing, for example, the hymn ϣερε νε Μαρια (Responsa du Praxis). This hymn consists of a single seven-minute poetic stanza: three minutes on the first syllable and two on the second. To facilitate singing these long vocalizations, Coptic cantors insert additional syllables: a, i, e-ye, o-wo. This singing practice has its roots in ancient cultures and moves away from conjecture. Examples of this melodic style can be found in Beni Hassan and in the interpretation of Maniche, and it is still practised by the Copts today.

Many of the Alexandrian Fathers, particularly in the early period of the Church's history, came from a Hellenistic culture where their parents encouraged them to pursue an education in various sciences, including astronomy, arithmetic, philology and rhetoric. When composing their laudatory texts, these early Church leaders may have had in mind a certain ideal grapheme, as shown in Gnostic papyri. This could be based on ancient rhetorical

---

period of rubato. It most commonly indicates a return to the main tempo after a temporary change.
[726] Borsai, I. "À la Recherche de l'Ancienne Musique Pharaonique," 25–42.

concepts. The composition of these texts aids the perception of Cosmic Music, where cappella and the concordance of phonetic elements such as rimes, alliteration, vowels, consonants and syllables are prioritized.

During the last century, Ragheb Muftah, Ilona Borsai and Ernest Newlandsmith[727] initiated the study of Coptic music. They all noticed that this music's main characteristic was the melismatic style. In their initial studies, Borsai and Muftah referenced the interpretations of Demetrius and Nicomachus (previously mentioned). Muftah stated: 'Until today, most Coptic hymns are sung on these vowels... Some are sung on "a", some on "e", as in the "Great Alleluia" and the "Offering Alleluia". Newlandsmith indicated the average tempo of some melismatic songs. "Several large hymns take as long as twenty minutes to sing, with pages of music for a single syllable."[728] In the Coptic Encyclopedia, Muftah, Robertson and Roy acknowledge that this musical style is:

> One of the most obvious characteristics of Coptic music, and one probably derives from the ancient times, (it) is the prolongation of a single vowel over many phrases of music that vary in length and complication. This phenomenon may take two forms identified by scholars as vocalize, when the vowel is prolonged with a definite rhythmic pulse, and melisma (pl. melismata), when the vowel is prolonged in a free, undefined rhythm. A melisma generally lasts from ten to

---

[727] Muftah, R., الموسيقي القبطية (*Al Musika al Kepteya*), 42–53.
[728] Newlandsmith, E. *The Ancient Music of the Coptic Church,* 7.

twenty seconds, but some vocalizes may continue for a full minute.⁷²⁹

Singing vowels or syllables with extended vowels is called melisma. According to the New Grove Dictionary of Music and Musicians, some scholars have recognized melisma because of its antiquity. The long vocalism found in many liturgical songs has necessitated a robust oral tradition for transmitting 'lengthy melismas." Robertson conducted several studies, recording songs between 1955 and 1968, and comparing them with the original transcriptions by Kamil Ghobrial (Cairo, 1916) and Newlandsmith (1926). She concluded that melodies had been faithfully transmitted from soloist to soloist for almost a century without any musical notation."⁷³⁰

In the Egyptian Church, chironomy, or flapping, is still used to teach liturgical songs. This practice dates back to the Fourth Dynasty of ancient Egypt (2723–2563 BC), as noted by Muftah. Due to their strong oral tradition, Egyptians preferred this method of entrusting their traditional songs to new singers. Cantors were always taught by counting the vocalises of a single musical phrase while clapping. Mathematical values also play an integral role in transmitting songs, particularly those with lengthy melismas.⁷³¹

The way in which early Christians viewed music and its connection to the cosmos is described by Stapert,

---

⁷²⁹Muftah, R. "Coptic Music," 1715–1747.

⁷³⁰ Robertson, M. "The Reliability of the Oral Tradition in Preserving Coptic Music", III, 93–105.

⁷³¹ Muftah, R. الموسيقى القبطية (Al Musika Al kepteya), 42–53.

who also explains how they incorporated this into their daily lives. While it is true that this idea was not expressed by an early Church Father, the essence of what he was trying to convey does support my argument:

> Music was not something early Christians thought about in isolation. It was involved in their thinking, from the cosmos to the details of daily living. In their speculative thought they looked at the Cosmos musically, and at music cosmically. And when they discussed life's activities of work and play, eating and drinking, worship, civic ceremonies, social events and the like, they often referred to music.[732]

Conclusion: From an Aesthetic to the Worship Ritual

While this appendix does not examine the concept of cosmic music in ancient Egypt and Asia Minor in depth, it is clear that it originated from Greek aesthetic theories based on the notion of a regulated cosmos and musical harmony.

As previously demonstrated, this highly prized musical concept was naturally transmitted to the writings of the Alexandrian Jews in the 1st century CE (e.g. Philo). Shortly after Philo's death, the Egyptian Church emerged within the same Greek milieu. Therefore, it is reasonable to conclude that converts to Christianity from Judaism developed the concept of cosmic music, followed by local

---

[732] Stapert, *A New Song for an Old World,* 52.

neophytes. It was subsequently incorporated into liturgical songs based on biblical principles. In order to praise the Creator, the elements of the universe had to be unified, as the universe is designed with 'wisdom'.

The early fathers of the Alexandrian Church deemed it necessary for praising God to be accompanied by specific graphemes representing this cosmology and its scriptural phenomenology, as the theology of this concept was majestic in their minds and faith.

The Coptic repertoire is another manifestation of these musical ideals. Incorporating all the aforementioned elements, it offers an unparalleled style of extended vocalism based on chanted vowels (see the Gnostic model). This intricate vocal technique means that some songs must be sung to different tunes on different days of the week. Furthermore, many hymns and praises have the same lyrics but different melodies according to the season or ecclesiastical celebration — a phenomenon which merits further study.

The diagram below shows the links between the theory's components.

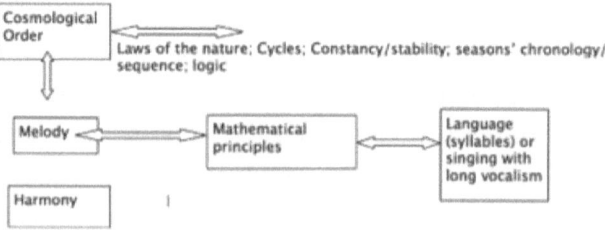

- Tunes: musical scales and structures
- Number of vocalism segments in the chanted piece

Emile Tadros 261

Related Essay IV

Documenting Oral Torah Tradition in Coptic Church and its Liturgy: Methodology and Anthology

What Is The 'Oral Torah'?

The rabbinic Jewish tradition has always maintained that God revealed a dual Torah ((תֹּרָה))[733] to Moses at Mount Sinai. The first was transmitted to the people of Israel in written form, while the second was passed down orally. This concept is reflected in Mishna, Tractate Avot 1:1:

> Moses received [from God] the Torah at Sinai and transmitted it to Joshua, Joshua to the elders,[734] the elders to the prophets, and the prophets to the Men of the Great Assembly.

The Oral Torah developed through a sequence of phases in Jewish tradition:

Phase 1: Source: Divine revelation (Orality)

---

[733] תֹּרָה Torah, (*to-raw'*): refers to a precept or statute, particularly the Decalogue or Pentateuch, and is often translated as "law." The fundamental principle of Mosaic law is its theocratic nature, meaning it is directly linked to God's commandments, forming the foundation of both religious duties and daily life. The root fundamentally means "to teach, instruct".

[734] Religious leaders first appeared during the construction of the Second Temple (around 500 BCE), as recounted in the Book of Nehemiah (8–10). The Hebrew term for 'elder' translates as 'old' and can refer to elderly individuals, ancient men, elders or senators.

Phase 2: Preservation through the memory of successive sages

Phase 3: Oral transmission across generations

Phase 4: The necessity to redact the Oral Torah after the destruction of the Jerusalem Temple in 70 CE

The rabbis[735] taught that the Oral Torah was transmitted orally for centuries persists into the late First millennium CE (after the destruction of the Temple of Jerusalem in 70 CE). In the Mishnah, this oral teaching is referred to as Mitzvot Zekenim.[736] This tradition ultimately led to the compilation of the Mishna[737] in 200 CE, followed by the completion of the Babylonian Talmud[738] in 500 CE. The Talmud expanded upon the Mishnah, incorporating additional rabbinic interpretations and employing various literary devices.[739] The destruction of the Temple played a pivotal role in the emergence of an extensive corpus of rabbinic literature, as illustrated below. This development is rooted in the structure of divine commandments as

---

[735] It is worthy to indicate that the Sadducees did not accept the principle of the Oral Torah at all. This was specific to rabbinic (or Pharisaic) tradition.

[736] B. Suk. 46a. The term Mitzvot Zekenim refers to the commandments, decrees, or instructions of the elders.

[737] The Mishnah (meaning "teaching") is the digest of the Oral Torah, compiled by Rabbi Judah the Prince at the end of the second century CE, and the beginning of the third century CE. Rather than being its author, Rabbi Judah acted as its editor, incorporating earlier collections and preserving some material in its original form.

[738] The Talmud, derived from the root limed ("to learn," "teaching," or "study"), contains the teachings of the Amoraim of Palestine and Babylon. probably the process was going on until closer to 700 CE. The Jerusalem Talmud was completed by 500 or a bit earlier – probably – and was known to the redactors of the Babylonian Talmud.

[739] Talmud is structured as a running commentary on the Mishnah.

conveyed in the Tanakh. Lauterbach suggests that the Jews found it necessary to formulate the Oral Torah because many Mosaic laws were presented in a concise manner, often unintelligible without certain presuppositions that were assumed to be commonly understood.[740]

It is important to highlight the impact of the destruction of the Temple and the emergence of new principles in liturgical Halakhah (later codified in the Mishnah and Talmud).

First, when the rabbis declared that all Jews were not only obligated to pray, but also to do so with precision, they assumed a formal teaching role. This led to the creation of a system of accessible rules — a liturgical *nomos* — designed to disseminate their framework throughout Palestine and the diaspora, ensuring its continuity and relevance. Second, by the time of the rise of Christianity, the Tannaim and Amoraim had established hundreds of regulations to distinguish between acceptable and unacceptable practices, shaping the landscape of Jewish worship. Many of these rules were highly specific, governing the wording and method of reciting prayers in particular circumstances. The theme of 'acceptable' and 'unacceptable' practices is extensively documented in the vast corpus of the Oral Torah, ensuring that only what was deemed acceptable remained as part of Jewish tradition, in accordance with divine will[741]. Thirdly, the period of the

---

[740] Lauterbach, *Rabbinic Essays*, 423–426.
[741] Langer, *To Worship God Properly,* 1–40. Langer describes the new principles of liturgical Halakha. Following the destruction of the Jerusalem Temple in 70 CE during the Jewish War against Rome,

Tannaim, which lasted approximately 210 years (10–220 CE), was crucial in the parallel development of codified worship rules within Judaism and the efforts of early Jewish Christians to structure the Christian way of life in relation to Halakhah. Notably, the six generations of these prominent Tannaim coincided with the birth of Christianity and its missionary movement. To my knowledge, their rulings have never been studied in connection with the liturgical fragments of early Christianity in general, and Egyptian Christianity in particular.

The Oral Torah and the Early Church Codes (see figure 1)

The timing between the compilation of the Mishnah and the emergence of early Christian canons is striking and warrants closer examination. At the beginning of the second century, foundational elements for shaping the Christian community continued to develop through letters written by early church leaders, such as *1Clement* (95 CE), *the Letter of Polycarp* (130 CE), *the letters of Ignatius of Antio*ch (117 CE), and the Letter of Barnabas (before 135

Jewish worship had to be adapted to take place outside of the sacrificial system. This resulted in the development of a valid non-sacrificial halachic framework that accommodated the new religious circumstances. However, most texts describing the emergence of fixed liturgical texts in the Tannaitic period are actually later Babylonian inventions and retrojections. While the basic structure of the core sections of the liturgy is Tannaitic, most of the words within them are not. There is also little evidence of this liturgical system spreading beyond rabbinic circles in the Land of Israel until around the Third century.

CE). However, the compositions that most significantly contributed to the development of Christian law in a formal sense were those classified as "Church Orders"—mostly anonymous compilations of traditions that regulated an increasingly broad spectrum of Christian life.

The earliest of these is *the Didache* (The Teaching of the Lord through the Twelve Apostles), likely composed in Syria around 90 CE. In addition to a catechetical section outlining the "Two Ways" of virtue, *the Didache* provides instructions for the celebration of the Eucharist and regulations concerning church leadership.

Other notable examples include *the Apostolic Church Order* (Egypt, ca. 300 CE), the *Didascalia Apostolorum* (Syria, third century), and the *Apostolic Tradition of Hippolytus* (Rome, third century). These works build upon earlier Church Orders, expanding their scope and detail.

The most comprehensive of these texts is *the Apostolic Constitutions*, a fourth-century compilation of ecclesiastical law from Syria. Its eight books provide detailed regulations for worship, the hierarchy of clergy, and general Christian practice. Christian emperors, along with regional and ecumenical councils, would later play a role in further developing these legal frameworks.

The historical sequence illustrated in figure 1 demonstrates that by the time the Mishnah was completed, three distinct forms of codification had emerged: the Didascalia Apostolorum and the Apostolic Church Order, along with the Canons of Hippolytus—two of which originated in Egypt. Later, after the completion of both

Talmud, the eight books of the Apostolic Constitutions were compiled.

I strongly believe that the codification movement on both sides was driven by a need to assert self-identity, as exemplified by the Birkat Ha-Minim (Prayer Against Heretics),[742] in Jewish worship of this period and its parallel, the (Litany of Assemblies) in Coptic liturgy.[743] The Berakah Ha-Minim was a petition recited during the Jewish morning service (which corresponds to the Coptic Morning Service as well), aimed at separating Christianity

---

[742] Rabban Gamaliel II, a second-generation Tanna, added the Birkat Ha-minim prayer. He was the first Nasi (president) of the Sanhedrin following the destruction of the Second Temple in 70 CE. He was the son of Shimon ben Gamaliel, a notable participant in the Jewish–Roman War, and the grandson of Gamaliel the Elder, who passed away in 114 CE. Rabban Gamaliel II lived during a crucial period in the early development of Christian liturgy, particularly among Jewish converts in Palestine and the diaspora. Given that Paul was a scholar in the School of Gamaliel, Hedegård's statement is particularly significant: 'At the time of Christ, the Eighteen Benedictions were recited in the synagogue service on weekdays and the Seven Benedictions on holy days. Ha-Minim is an exclusively weekday liturgical text. Both texts attempt to declare the other party as heretical, calling for divine eradication. This strongly suggests an issue of self-identity, whereby each group sought to define itself in opposition to the other. In Langer's monograph, *Cursing the Christians? A History of the Birkat Ha-minim* (Oxford, 2012), Langer indicates that this prayer may have contained early elements. However, in the same monograph, Langer (pp. 16–33) argues that theories claiming the prayer explicitly sought to create a break with Christianity cannot currently be substantiated (pending further research).

[743] The Birkat Ha-minim ('Prayer against Heretics') is presented as an untitled litany and forms the concluding section of the Coptic Litany of Assemblies.

from Judaism and suppressing false teachings.[744] Similarly, the Prayer Against Heretics appears as an unnamed litany concluding the Coptic Litany of Assemblies.

In the past (DL 80–81), this litany was originally unconnected to *the Litany of Assemblies* and focused on asking God to grant a secure environment for church gatherings. The prayer implores God to remove any 'obstacle' or 'hindrance' that might endanger the congregation, which was believed to stem from idol worship, the power of Satan, and especially from heretics (Christians), instigators, and dissenters. The priest prays for the Lord to scatter their plans, just as He did with the counsel of Ahithophel.[745]

However, the historical development and dating of the Berakah Ha-minim,[746] remain subjects of debate.[747] The term minim was used broadly in rabbinic literature[748] to refer to various types of heretics, including atheists, idol worshippers, and apostates to Christianity similar to the classifications found in the Coptic ritual. Both Jewish and Coptic liturgies call upon God for a swift and harsh

---

[744] Birkat Ha-minim in 1 SAG, 93.
[745] 2 Sam. 17: 1–23.
[746] This petition aimed at the separation of Jewish Christians from the synagogue. Over time, tensions grew between Jews and Jewish Christians, leading to the latter being identified simply as Christians.
[747] The dating of Birkat Ha-minim remains a subject of scholarly debate. Some Jewish scholars argue that it is not an early text from the formative centuries of the Coptic Church, but rather a result of early modern censorship. For further discussion, see Langer, *Worship God Properly* (in particular chapter 1).
[748] 1 SAG, 93.

response against these groups, often using strikingly similar language.

The Egyptian rabbinic literature preserved at least three texts relating to this Birkat. The textual variants do not represent remarkable variants:

A. The Prayer book of Rav Sa'adiah ben Joseph of Fayyum,[749] Gaon of Sura (third decade of the tenth century). The text of Birkat HaMinim in the prayer book of Rav Sa'adiah is as follows: "For the apostates let there be no hope and let the kingdom of arrogance be speedily uprooted and crushed in our days. Blessed are You, Lord, who crushes the wicked and humbles the arrogant."[750]

B. Maimonides' [the Rambam's][751] 'Order for Praying throughout the Year' is one of the earliest prayer books. This collection of prayers, is structured with a framework that includes, praising God, acknowledging needs, expressing gratitude, and seeking forgiveness, as well as incorporating scripture and reflection. This is the text of the twelfth blessing in Rambam's order of blessings: "For the apostates let there be no hope and may all the minim perish in an instant and the kingdom of arrogance be uprooted and crushed speedily in our days. Blessed are

---

[749] The Prayer Book was written in Babylonia about a hundred years after Rav Amram's time (SAG), apparently because of a request from the Jewish community in Egypt. for the text, see Teppler, 14.

[750] According to Teppler,14. "this text is the earliest sources for Birkat haMinim in the prayer books which have come down to us, if not the earliest."

[751] Moses ben Maimon, Talmudist, philosopher, astronomer, and physician; born at Cordova March 30, 1135; died at Cairo Dec. 13, 1204; known in Arabic literature as, Abu 'Imran Musa ben Maimun ibn 'Abd Allah. RaMBaM" is a Hebrew acronym for "Rabbi Moshe ben Maimon," which translates to "Rabbi Moses son of Maimon."

You, Lord, who crushes the wicked and humbles the arrogant."[752]

C. From Cairo Genizah (9–10th Century) we have another version which its particularity is the designation together with Minim (referring to heretics in general), and adding specifically the Nazarenes (Christian First Century term). The text reads: "For apostate (meshumaddim) let there be no hope, and no dominion of arrogance to Thou speedily root out in our days; and let Christians (*ve-ha-Notzrim*) and Minim perish in a moment, let them be blotted out of the book of living and let them not be written with the righteous."[753]

DL: "Satan, with all his evil powers, trample and humiliate under our feet speedily...the enemies of Your holy Church... strip their vanity, show them their weakness speedily ⲛⲭⲱⲗⲉⲙ 'Bring to naught their intrigues, their madness, their wickedness, and their slanders, which they commit against us."[754]

---

[752] Teppler, 2007,15. Critical edition: E.D. Goldschmidt, 'Maimonides' Rite of the Prayer According to an Oxford Manuscript, (Hunt. 80; Neubauer 577), Studies of the Research Institute for Hebrew Poetry, 7 (1958), 199.
[753] Translation taken from Katz (1984), 64. See also, Wilson, (1989), 65-66.
[754] DL, 80–81.

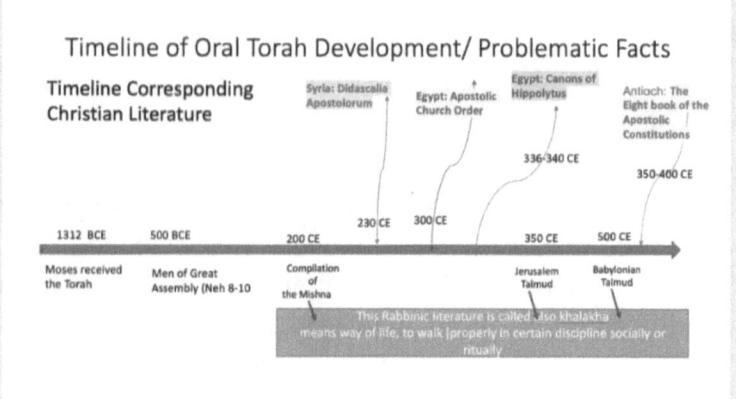

Methodology Dealing with Jewish Sources

Jaffee[755] investigates the concept of "Orality" in the Oral Torah, arguing that the earliest Jewish sources show little interest in explicitly demonstrating that rabbinic teachings were transmitted orally. In rabbinic literature, specific terms denote material passed down as tradition such as *qabalah*,[756] *masoret*,[757] and *halakha* [758] (as seen in Mishnah *Yadayim* 4:3; *Eduyot* 8:7, *Peah* 2:6), yet no term explicitly refers to "oral tradition" as a distinct category. He also expresses skepticism about the notion of verbatim oral transmission and raises doubts about the reliability of human memory in preserving tradition accurately.

---

[755] Jaffee, 1992: 53–72.

[756] *Kabalah* means "to receive" and literally translates to "the received or traditional lore." It refers to the esoteric or mystical doctrine concerning God and the universe, which is claimed to have been revealed to select saints in the distant past and preserved by a privileged few.

[757] *Masoret* is derived from a root meaning "to hand down" and has come to signify "tradition".

[758] *Halakhot* (pl.) of *halakha*.

Indeed, there is a significant span of time between God's revelation to Moses at Sinai and the finalization of the Babylonian Talmud—a period of 1,812 years, or approximately 18 centuries. The designation of an "Oral" Torah within rabbinic culture presents another challenge: How long was the process of memorization in effect? Did it extend from the time of Moses to 70 CE (the destruction of the Temple) and further into third–and fifth-century Judaism and early Christianity?

Jaffee questions whether the term Oral Torah in Jewish sources truly refers to a fully memorized oral tradition. If so, does this imply that all rabbinic traditions were transmitted solely through memory, or were only certain elements preserved and later canonized in the *Mishnah*?[759] or we would consider it a flexible process rather than an unchanging body of specific knowledge?

The term 'Apostolic Tradition', as understood by the early Church, may logically refer to new Christian forms
influenced by the writings of the Oral Torah—particularly those emerging during the eras of the Tannaim and Amoraim, who were the rabbinic authorities at the time of Christianity's birth.

The issue with the so-called Ancient Church Orders lies in their dubious claims to apostolic authorship, which casts uncertainty over their origins. Since at least the early twentieth century[760] scholars have universally rejected the notion that these texts were directly authored by the

---

[759] Jaffee, "How Much 'Orality' in Oral Torah?", 53–72.
[760] Bradshaw and Hoffman, *The Making of Jewish and Christian Worship*. 12.

apostles. Bradshaw, in Search for the Origins, describes these pseudo-apostolic writings as "potentially valuable sources of evidence for the thoughts and practices of the periods in which they were composed."[761] It is important to highlight that the Apostolic Church Order includes a significant document known as The Egyptian Church Order, which warrants meticulous and dedicated study. However, Bradshaw advises scholars to set aside claims of apostolic authorship when analyzing these texts. That being said, I acknowledge the continued use of the term apostles in these writings, which clearly reflects their Jewish roots and their commitment to the worship practices of their time, as described in the New Testament.[762] This is particularly evident in the frequent references to Jesus Himself being present in the Temple, where many key events took place.[763] However, contemporary understandings suggest that the rabbinic worship system emerged after the Temple's destruction (and gradually took over the pre-existent synagogue which was a place of study of scripture originally).

Many studies have been published highlighting the influence of Jewish heritage on these early Church Orders—a significant topic that warrants dedicated research and scholarly publication. Given the constraints of this article, I will provide only a concise bibliography.[764]

---

[761] Bradshaw *The Search for the Origins of Christian Worship,* 80.
[762] Luke 24:53. Acts 2: 46; 3: 1; 5: 20, 21, 25; 22: 17; 24: 12, 18; 21: 27; 26: 21.
[763] Matt 21:12; 14; 21; 23. Mark 11:11; 15;27; 12:35. Luke 19:45; 22:53. John 2:14; 5:14; 7:14 8:2; 10:23; 7:28; 8:20; 18:20.
[764] For a concise bibliography see Jones, C. et al. *The Study of Liturgy*; Berkovitz and Letteney, *Rethinking 'Authority' in Late Antiquity*; Fonrobert, "The Didascalia Apostolorum; Boyarin, "Introduction: Judaeo-Christianity Redivivus;" and many others.

The question remains: Is this Oral Torah what later came to be known as 'Church Tradition'?

The transmission of the Jewish Oral Torah to the early Church involved several factors, including psychological aspects such as self-identity and the human capacity for memory. Abel, in the title of his article, does not explore in detail the transmission of Jewish liturgical practices; rather, he focuses on how the story of Jesus was recorded in the New Testament. Nevertheless, his work offers valuable insights relevant to my study—particularly regarding how Jesus' sayings were transmitted by early believers (*Kerygma*) and how this process shaped practical concerns. Furthermore, he raises an important question: "Did Christianity have as rigid and supervised a program of oral transmission as existed in the Jewish schools of that time?"[765]

The exploration of Jewish liturgical traditions has been the focus of only a handful of scholars. Rouwhorst,[766] for instance, published an article demonstrating his interest in this topic, particularly in the context of the Syriac Church. He examined traces of the Jewish Sabbath and certain architectural elements in Syriac Christianity that may be linked to liturgical practices. His conclusion raised the question of a possible Jewish-Christian origin of Syriac Christianity.

However, Rouwhorst also discussed elements common to all early churches, such as the bread and wine

---

[765] Abel, "The Psychology of Memory and Rumor Transmission," 270–281.
[766] Rouwhorst, "Jewish Liturgical Traditions in Early Syriac Christianity," 72–93.

rites associated with baptism and immersion, without specifically addressing how liturgical minutiae embedded within oral traditions may have influenced the Syriac repertoire—a focus more aligned with the present article. Another important contribution comes from Verhelst,[767] who studied key topics based on Oral Torah literature (Mishnah and Talmud/Gemara), including the Trisagion and its origins in the Kedushah, prayers related to incense offerings, and Jewish supplications. His research is particularly valuable and warrants a comparative liturgical analysis between Jerusalem and Alexandria.

The perspective of Coptic intellectuals regarding the transmission of the *Oral Halakhic* tradition is shaped by a distinct hermeneutical approach. The most prominent researcher in this area is Bishop Mettaous, who, in his book *The Spirituality of the Rites of the Holy Liturgy*,[768] explains how the Coptic Church received its liturgical rules.

    a. Oral transmission from Jesus Himself: Acts 1:3 "He (Jesus after His resurrection) presented Himself alive to them after His suffering by many proofs, appearing to them during the forty days and speaking about the kingdom of God."[769]

---

[767] Rouwhorst, "Jewish Liturgical Traditions in Early Syriac Christianity," 72–93.

[768] https://accot.stcyrils.edu.au/wp-content/uploads/2020/07/The-Spirituality-Of-The-Rites-Of-The-Holy-Liturgy-In-The-Coptic-Orthodox-Church.pdf.

[769] ESV version. "speaking" holds a variety of connotations. Λέγω (*legō*): *to lay, to arrange, to gather; to say*, Mt. 1:20; *to speak, make an address* or *speech*, Acts 26:1; *to say* mentally, in thought, Mt. 3:9; Lk. 3:8; *to say* in written language, Mk. 15:28; Lk. 1:63; Jn. 19:37;

b. This oral transmission should entail an order (called *Taksis*, طقس) as per Mettaous: "God endorses the rites of the church, He has set an order for everything, especially in the worship offered to Him by man." Based on verse 1 Cor. 14:33: "For God is not a God of confusion but of peace. As in all the churches of the saints."[770]

---

to say, as distinguished from acting, Mt. 23:3; *to mention, speak of,* Mk. 14:71; Lk. 9:31; Jn. 8:27; *to tell, declare, narrate*, Mt. 21:27; Mk. 10:32; *to express*, Heb. 5:11; *to put forth, propound*, Lk. 5:36; 13:6; Jn. 16:29; *to mean, to intend to signify,* 1 Cor. 1:12; 10:29; *to say, declare, affirm, maintain*, Mt. 3:9; 5:18; Mk. 12:18; Acts 17:7; 26:22; 1 Cor. 1:10; *to enjoin*, Acts 15:24; 21:21; Rom. 2:22; *to term, designate, cull*, Mt. 19:17; Mk. 12:37; Lk. 20:37; 23:2; 1 Cor. 8:5; *to call* by a name.

[770] The ESV version presents this verse in a context unrelated to any liturgical idea. Verses 33–36 address an aspect of the role of wives in the church. Some commentators attempt to resolve the issue by suggesting that this section ia later addition and not authored by Paul. However, every manuscript includes this passage. Three key points should be considered in understanding this passage: "Wives prayed and prophesied in Christian gatherings" (1 Corinthians 5 :11. This was a common practice in all the apostolic churches (v. 33b). The context is crucial, particularly regarding the evaluation of prophecy (v. 35). The law requires acknowledgment of the distinctive roles of men and women (v. 34), likely referring to Genesis 2:20–24 or 3:16. Paul has already cited the former in 1 Corinthians 11:8–9. The wife is instructed to seek clarification at home, which could imply that her husband was the one who delivered the prophecy (v. 35). While absolute certainty is lacking, the present writer holds the view that in this public gathering, wives are not to engage in the public weighing of prophecy, which involved interrogating its content. The Greek word for "confusion" is ἀκαταστασία (*akatastasia*) means strictly: instability; hence, an unsettled state; disorder, commotion, tumult, sedition in a socially context.

c. Divine punishment by God will apply in case of breaking God's rituals' order. As per Mettaous based on Num. 3:4: "Now Nadab and Abihu, the sons of Aaron, each took his censer and put fire in it and laid incense on it and offered unauthorized fire before the LORD, which he had not commanded them."[771] Mettaous interpreted it as: "God explained to Moses and Aaron all such details relating to the rites of worship. His command was very strict and whoever disobeyed it would not escape the heavenly punishment, which was exactly what happened to the sons of Aaron - Nadab and Abihu - who disobeyed the rites, and instead offered profane fire in the censer. The Lord sent fire down from heaven to consume them and they died before the Lord." This punishment occurred as a consequence of outrageous transgression, against God's commandment in Ex. 30:9.

Item C connects to a widely recognized Graeco Roman concept, leading me to explore the notion of *Felix Culpa*–an expression that pertains to ritual failure in Early Christianity and the underlying theory of failed rituals. Smit examines common early New Testament rituals, such as circumcision, Christian meals, and baptism in Pauline writings, drawing parallels with

---

[771] ESV version. Mettaous, 9. אֵשׁ זָרָה ; both Hebrew and Aramaic hold the same meaning of burning, fiery, fire, flaming. However, זָר (*zer, zare*); (in the sense of scattering); a chaplet (as spread around the top), i.e. (specifically) a border or crown. A Hebrew word that is considered unique in this verse.

Bishop Mettaous' interpretation of Nadab's account. He argues that instances of ritual failure prompt evaluation and renegotiation within a community as it develops its identity. [772]

He identifies several reasons why a ritual may fail:
a) Not following the script of the prayer
b) Not adhering to the rubrics
c) The celebrant not being in a state of purity

Smit also raises the question of whether early Christian voices had the proper perspective when interpreting these ritual failures.

Questions

Did Jesus and the Apostles engage with the teachings of the rabbinic Oral Torah?
Mark 1:22 highlights that Jesus' teaching method was notably di3erent from that of the religious leaders,
who were deeply preoccupied with rules and regulations concerning social conduct and piety. When examining the backgrounds of most of the Apostles, it becomes evident that their social status and intellectual pre-requisites were rather modest, confined to their immediate circles. As C.K. Barrett observes, the Apostles were "often of the lowest intellectual class, [men] who could spare but little time from the labor needed to sustain life."[773] Conversely, many early Christian texts contain ritual regulations. As

---

[772] Smit, *Felix Culpa*, 7–22.

[773] Barrett, *Jesus and the Gospel Tradition*, 9.

Bradshaw describes in *Search for the Origins*,⁷⁷⁴ these pseudo-apostolic writings "are potentially valuable sources of evidence for the thoughts and practices of the periods in which they are composed." One particularly significant text within this category is *The Egyptian Church Order*, which merits a thorough and dedicated study.

Another question arises: Who were the transmitters of the halachic corpus into the Coptic Church—Philo, the frequent visits of Palestinian masters, or the Oral Torah with its halachic corpus via τὰ ἀπομνημοὺματα τῶν ἀποστόλωη "memoirs of the Apostles?"⁷⁷⁵

The influence of the Oral Torah is evident in Coptic liturgy. My focus, however, is not on the universally recognized Jewish rituals present in all ancient churches—such as the bread and wine tradition (linked to Melchizedek) or baptism (derived from the *Mikveh* by immersion). Rather, the striking point is the presence of intricate details, articulated by the rabbis in specific ritual sections, namely the Morning and Evening Services. These correspond to Shacharit (from *shachar*, meaning morning light) and the Evening Service (*Ma'ariv*) in Jewish liturgy. Enigmatically, these precise ritual features have found their way into Coptic liturgical practices.

---

⁷⁷⁴ Bradshaw, *The Search for the Origins of Christian Worship*, 80–84.

⁷⁷⁵ The designation "memoirs of the apostles" occurs twice in Justin's First Apology (66.3, 67.3–4) and several times in the Dialogue with Trypho, chapters 89, 100-104, 106, 108 (Justin Martyr), mostly in his interpretation of Psalms

22 https://www.newadvent.org/fathers/01287.htm. Expression used by Justin Martyr in *Dal* 100,4.5; 101.3.7; 102.3.

In Chapters 3 and 4 of this book, I have demonstrated that the similarities between the Jewish Morning Service and the Coptic Morning Service are remarkable, as previously indicated, before documenting the presence of the Oral Torah in Coptic liturgy in general and in the Morning Service specifically. On multiple levels, the order of prayers is nearly identical, biblical concepts align closely, and the meticulous details in the rubrics correspond to one another. Based on this academic research, it is reasonable to conclude that these liturgical minutiae, as outlined in the following tables, are academically valid.

In the following section, I refer to Langer's[776] categorisation of the rabbinic requirements for a valid non-sacrificial liturgy. However, scholars should be aware that Langer's focus is on the halakhic parameters established by the entire rabbinic corpus for later generations of Jews. While my specifics may not be extremely relevant to the question of Coptic origins, they resonate powerfully in the liturgy of the Copts.

The sources of the Oral Torah are indicated in abbreviated form (see the list of abbreviations). The notes in the tables provide additional explanations related to rabbinic leitmotifs or specific characteristics of the Coptic Church.

---

[776] Langer, *To Worship God Properly*, 1–40.

The Creation of a Valid Non-Sacrificial Liturgy after 70 CE

A. *Laws that establish and regulate the communal nature of Prayer*

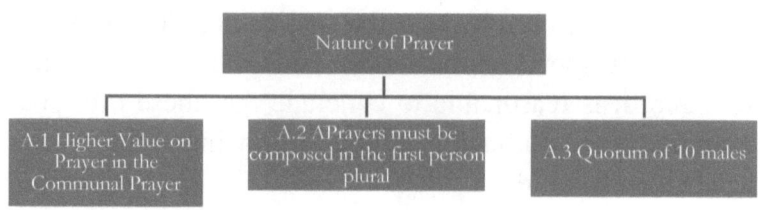

A.1 *Higher Value on Prayer in the Communal Prayer*

Rabbinic Leitmotif	Oral Thora's Source	Coptic Correlation	Rite or other sources
Higher Value on Prayer in the Communal Prayer.	B. Taanit 13b; P. Berakhot 5:2, 9b; P. Taanit 1:1, 63d.	There is no any Coptic ritual without the attending of the congregation.	Prayers in general.[777]

---

[777] *Tartib Al Bayaa* [*The Order of the Church*], edited by Samuel al-Suryāni.

A.2. Prayers (Petitions) must always be composed in the first-person plural

Rabbinic Leitmotif	Oral Thora's Source	Coptic Correlation	Rite or other sources
Prayers (Petitions) must always be composed in the first-person plural.⁷⁷⁸	B. Berakhot 29b-30a: discussing the traveler's prayer Mishnah Berakhot 7:3; B. Berakhot 49b-50a; P Berakhot 7:3. 11b-c all with reference to the invitation to the grace after meals.	Litanies اواشي⁷⁷⁹ Both Berakhot and Coptic litanies "are formulated in the plural to be used by the congregation, and the petitions are requests which concern the need of the whole congregation."	Both traditions' Morning and Evening Services.

---

⁷⁷⁸ Hedegård observes that, except for a couple of petitions in the Tefillah that are "national," many others are for the good of the community of God (peace, rain, harvest). Likewise, the Coptic petitions (litanies) focus on congregational needs, not on the individual requests. (1 SAG, intro 36).

⁷⁷⁹ See long Coptic litanies in DL for: departed (p.19); sick (23) travelers (26) sacrifices (28); all short litanies for Peace (70), Patriarchs and Bishops (71), the Place (deacon's response), Waters, Plants, Air of the Heaven and Fruits, the Assemblies.

A.3 Quorum of Ten Males

Rabbinic Leitmotif	Oral Thora's Source	Notes	Coptic Correlation	Rite other sources
A "*davar shebikedushah*"[780] or "holy matter" requires a quorum of ten.[781]	*Mishnah Megillah* 4:3. *B. Megillah* 23b *B. Berakhot* 21b This Mishnaic passage decrees those certain rituals such as reciting the Kaddish in the "Pseuque de	*Mishnah Megillah* 4:3. "When less than a quorum of ten [men], one may not lead the communal ; recitation of	*Massoudy*,[785] 13, rule no. 1, adds from the book of the Church Canons of ibn Al Assal, canon 13, that the priest should not bless the Qurban (the oblation) without the presence of a deacon [and congregation] who forewarns the congregation for prayer and calls them [to	Both traditions Morning and Evening Services.

---

[780] Langer, *To Worship God Properly*, 20.

[781] In early Coptic Christianity, it seems the expectation was for ten adult males, following Jewish tradition, without requiring individuals with specific credentials. However, without a minyan, most prayers could still be recited, and individuals remained obligated to pray even alone. Later, the Coptic system became priestly and public prayer did not absolutely require more than two participants. This topic warrants further study. Nevertheless, the requirement of a quorum (male or female) remains a liturgical principle in both traditions.

[785] Al Massoudy, *Al-Khulaji* (*The Holy Euchologion*), 16.

| | | Zimra,"[782] the repetition of the Amidah (the Eighteen Berachot), and the Priestly Blessing and many other rituals that may not be recited without the presence of such a quorum. | Shema,[783] lead the congregation in reciting the Amidah, [784] recite the priestly benediction, ritually read the Torah or prophetic portions, perform ritual blessings | pray] with reverence and staidness, Massoudy, 16, canon 13. | |

---

[782] In Jewish tradition, the Pesukei de-Zimra functions as an individual "warm-up," fostering spiritual readiness (physical readiness is achieved through washing, while spiritual readiness comes through singing the Hallel and reciting specific psalms). For the rabbinic dicta and halachic significance of spiritual preparation, see Hoffman,3–6. Similar recitations of selected passages or Psalms also exist in Coptic tradition, particularly in the Morning Doxology (HPE, 247–50), where excerpts from various psalms (Psalm 136:6; 28:2; 133:1) are found (see previous chapters). It is worthy to clarify that the Pesukei D'Zimra is not mentioned in the Mishnah and is actually fundamentally a post-talmudic phenomenon and the "washing of hands and feet" is not a part of it.

[783] "Shema" is the Jewish Creed (see Deut 6:4–9; 11:13–21 Num 15:37–41). For the Thematic correlation between both traditions see the whole Chapter 4.

[784] The Amidah is a central section of the Jewish Morning Service, also known as the 'Eighteen Berachot'. For textual parallels with the Coptic Morning Service, the whole Chapter 3.

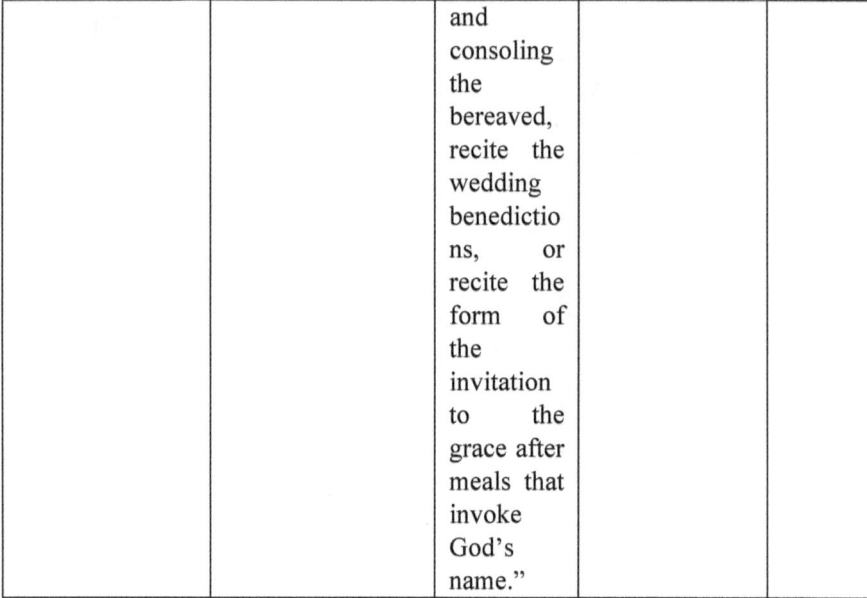

and consoling the bereaved, recite the wedding benedictions, or recite the form of the invitation to the grace after meals that invoke God's name."

B. Blessings: The Structural Framework of Rabbinic Prayer

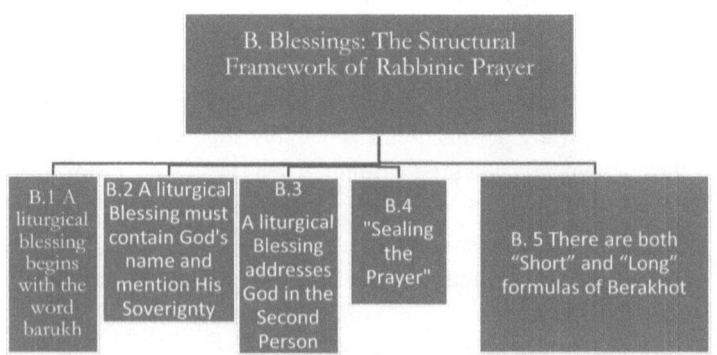

B.1. A liturgical blessing begins with the word barukh

Rabbinic Leitmotif	Oral Thora's Source	Notes	Coptic Correlation	Rite or other sources
B.1.A A liturgical blessing begins with the word "barukh."[786]	*B. Menahhot* 43b: The Babylonian Talmud ascribes to the second-century Rabbi Meir the requirements that a Jew has a basic obligation to recite a hundred blessings daily.	Questioning above quote: *Tosefta Berakhot* 6:24 and *P. Berakhot* 9:5 which both speak about performing (liturgical *mizvot*) instead of reciting blessings perhaps because the Tannaim had not yet formalized the specific blessing texts.	Evening Service: "Blessed are You. O Lord, teach me Your righteous decrees. Blessed are You, O Lord; make me to understand Your righteous decrees. Blessed are You, O Lord; enlighten me with Your righteous decrees."[787] Developed in a Christian format:	In both traditions: Morning and Evening Services, in Midnight Coptic Psalmody.

---

[786] Langer, *To Worship God Properly*, 24–25
[787] *DL*, Evening Service, 31.

			Priest, while he made the sign of the cross over the incense box. The priest made the sign of the cross three times, and while putting the spoonful of incense he says: "Blessed be God the Father, The Pantocrator. Amen Blessed be His only-begotten Son, Jesus Christ our Lord. Amen. Blessed be the Holy Spirit, the Paraclete. Amen."[788] Ϥⲥⲙⲁⲣⲱⲟⲩⲧ = barukh	

---

[788] *DL*, Evening Service, 10.

Emile Tadros 287

			In the Psalmodia book, The Hymn of the Three Children (Hos3) First six strophes start with "Blessed are You", And among many other examples.	

B.2 A liturgical Blessing must contain God's name and mention His Sovereignty

B.3 A liturgical Blessing addresses God in the Second Person

These two topics hold many elements and academic minutiae. I will devote a separate study related to the rabbinic leitmotifs.

B.4 The Beraka is to end with a benediction known as "Sealing a Prayer"

Rabbinic Leitmotif	Oral Thora's Source	Coptic Correlation
The Beraka is to end with a benediction known as	*Tosefta Berakhot* 1:9; *B. Berakhot* 46a; *B. Pesahim* 104b;	Likewise, the rule of the closing prayer or sealing

"Sealing Prayer."	a	*P. Berakhot* 1:5, 3d.	prayer is respected in many Coptic litanies.[789]
			The concept of "sealing a prayer" occurs also in the same litanies mentioned above. It occurs once after these petitions (litanies) and after the Thanksgiving Prayer, which precedes the petitions. The sealing prayer remains inconsistent: **[Stanza 1]** Through the grace, compassion, and love of mankind of your only begotten Son, our Lord, God and Savior Jesus Christ. **[Stanza 2]** Through Whom the glory, the honor, the dominion, and the worship are due unto You, with Him and the Holy Spirit, the giver of life, Who is of one essence with You. **[Stanza 3]** Now and all times and unto the age of all ages. Amen.

B.5 There are both "Short" and "Long" formulas of Berakhot

Rabbinic Leitmotif	Oral Thora's Source	Coptic Correlation

---

[789] The Coptic priest also recites it after the Thanksgiving Prayer, which comes before the petitions.

| B.5 There are both "Short" and "Long" formulas of Berakhot | Abu Dirham indicates two types of Berakhot regarding narrative length: "Those that are shaped according to the short formula and those which are shaped according to the long formula." David ben Josef ben David Abudirham (1340 CE) Sefer Ḥibbur Perush ha-Berakhot we-ha-Tefillot ("Commentary on the Blessings and Prayers") or known also as Sefer Abu Dirham, 2B, 3A, quoted by Hedegård, intro 1 SAG, 34. For the importance of the "blessing" | In the Coptic tradition, in the Morning Service, additional litanies to the long ones are also short litanies, in a form of petition. They are also recited during the ritual. For all the short litanies, see DL, 70–81.

See Table of Contents, DL, XIII. In the Coptic Morning Service, the litanies (petitions) are divided in two groups; the short litanies are for the Peace of Church, the Patriarch and Bishops, the Place (salvation of world and this city), the Three Seasons of the Year, and the Assemblies.
The long ones are for the Departed, the Sick, the Travelers, and the Sacrifices. |

| | in Jewish liturgy.[790] | |

---

[790] Millgram, Jewish *Worship*. 89, 94.

Bibliography

Qumran
1QH
1QS
4Q408
4Q503
4Q504
4Q506
4QS

Philo of Alexandria
Agr. 80f
Agr., 78–82
Ebr., 105–121
Ebr., 94.
Plant., 126
Plant., 126, 135
Post., 103–111
Post., 106
Som II 268
Spec. Laws 1.1.1–1.2.11
V. Moses. II, 256
Som. I 35, 37
Virt. 72–75.

Mishnah and Talmud Tractates
(B = Babylonian Talmud; M= Mishna); P = Palestinian Talmud; T = Tosefta)
B. Berakhot 21b
B. Berakhot 29b-30a
B. Berakhot 40b
B. Berakhot 49b-50a
B. Megillah 23b
B. Menahhot 43b
B. Pesahim 104b
B. Suk. 46a
B. Ta'anit 13b
M Megillah 4:3

M. Berakhot 7:3
M. Edu. 8:7 (Eduyyot)
M. Pe'ah 2.6
M. Yad 4:3 (Yadayim)
P Berakhot 7:3. 11b-c
P. Berakhot 5:2, 9b
P. Berakhot 9:1
P. Berakhot 9:5
P. Ta'anit 1:1, 63d
T. Berakhot 1:9
T. Berakhot 6:24

Jewish/Christian sources
1 and *2 Enoch*
Apocalypse of Elijah
Apostolic Constitutions VIII, 12:27
Arabic- Coptic *Synaxarium.*
Didascalia Apostolorum
Epistle of Barnabas.
Gospel of Thomas (P. Oxy. 1)
Letter of Aristeas
Oxy. 6.903
Seder Amram Gaon (Part 1)
Shepherd of Hermas
The Alexandrian Synodus
The Apostolic Constitutions
The Egyptian Church Order
The Gospel of the Hebrews

Patristic Sources
Athanasius, *Festal Letters,* 2:7, 2:29
Athanasius, *Hist. Arian,* 81; *De Fuga* 24; *Homilies on Second Thessalonians.*
Augustine, *Against the Donatists,* 5:23[31]; 5:26[37]).
Basil the Great, *The Holy Spirit*, 27:66
Chrysostom, John, *Commentary on the Psalms*, 66
Clement of Alexandria, *Miscellanies,* 1:1

Clement of Alexandria, *Strom* 1.11.2, *Strom,* 6, 14; *Protrepticus* I,5*(PG* VIII,57); *Paedagogus* II, 4; *PG* VIII, 440–1. Paedagogus II, 6 (PG VIII, 441)
Cyprian of Carthage, *Letters* 75:3
Cyril of Alexandria, *de Ador., in Spir. et Verit*, 12
Dionysius (of Alexandria): *The Second Canon*; *Ep. ad Fab.* (Ed. Feltoe, 58).
Epiphanius of Salamis, *Medicine Chest Against all Heresies*, 61:6.
Eusebius, *Historia Ecclesiastica* 2.16.1; 5.11.1
Irenaeus, *Against Heresies*, 1:10:2; 3:4:1; 3:3:1–2
Justin Martyr in *Dal* 100,4.5; 101.3.7; 102.3
Macarius, *De Caritate*, 29
Origen, *On First Principles; Luc Homily,* 39
Origen, *The Fundamental Doctrines*, 1:2
Papias in Eusebius's *Church History*, 3:39 (fragment); 4:21
Synesius, *Ep.*, 67 (the 'Sacramental Curtain')
Vision of. Theophilus

Liturgical Books

Abdallah, Alfonso. *L'Ordinamento Liturgico [Al Tartib Al Taksi]*. Cairo: Centro Francescano Di Studi Orientali Christiani, 1962. (Arabic-Italian).

Al Massoudy, Abdel Massih Saleb Al Baramoussy *Al-Khulaji* [*The Holy Euchologion*]. Cairo: Al Baramous Monastery, No publication year. (Coptic-Arabic).

Azmy, Abraham. *The Book of Holy Pascha: From Last Friday of The Great Lent to Resurrection Feast Liturgy.* Cairo and Connecticut: Saint Mark's Printing, 2010. (Coptic-Arabic-English).

Book of The Seven Canonical Hours [Arabic: *Ajbiyah*]. Mississauga: Canadian Coptic Centre, no publication year. (English).

Coptic Synaxarium. Edited by St. George Coptic Church. Chicago: St. Antonio Press, 1999. (English).

Hedegård, David. *Seder R. Amram Gaon, Hebrew Text with*

Critical Apparatus Translation with Notes and Introduction (Part I). Lund: Lundstedts Universitets, 1951. (English).

Kronheim, Tryggve. Seder R. Amram Gaon (Part II). Lund/Sweden: CWK Gleerup, 1974

Tartib Al Bayaa [*The Order of the Church*], edited by Samuel al-Suryāni, 2000 (Coptic–Arabic). 3 Vols. Cairo: Al Naam Press, 2000. (Coptic-Arabic).

The Book of Khedmat Al Shamas wa Al Alhan [*The Book of the Liturgical Responses of the Deacon and Hymns*]. Cairo: Gamayet Nahdet Al Kanayess, 1951. (Coptic-Arabic).

The Divine Liturgy, The Anaphoras of Saints Basil, Gregory, and Cyril. No city: Coptic Orthodox Diocese of Southern United States, 2007. (Coptic-Arabic-English).

The Holy Psalmody [*Al Abssalmodieh Al Mokadessa*]. No publisher, no city, no year (rare book). (Coptic-Arabic).

The Holy Psalmody. Edited by Saint Mary and Saint Antonios Coptic Orthodox Church. New York: no publisher, no year. (Coptic-Arabic-English).

Secondary Literature

Abel, E. L. "The Psychology of Memory and Rumor Transmission and Their Bearing on Theories of Oral Transmission in Early Christianity", The Journal of religion, Vol.51 (4): 270–281, 1971.

Al Makary, Athanasius. Salwat Raf Al Bokhour fi Asheya wa' Baker [Office of Evening and Morning Incense]. Cairo: Dar Nobar, 2006 (Arabic).

Amélineau, Émile. *La Géographie de l'Egypte à l'Époque Copte.* Paris: Imprimerie Nationale, 1893.

Anderson, G. A., Clements, R., & Satran, D. (2013). *New Approaches to the Study of Biblical Interpretation in Judaism of the Second Temple Period and in Early Christianity: Proceedings of the Eleventh International Symposium of the*

Orion Center for the Study of the Dead Sea Scrolls and Associated Literature, Jointly Sponsored by the Hebrew University Center for the Study of Christianity, 9-11 January 2007 (1st ed., Vol. 106). Brill.

Atiya, Aziz. "Copto-Arabic Literature." In *Coptic Encyclopedia*, 5:1460–67.

———. "Copto–Arabic Synaxarion." In *Coptic Encyclopedia*, 4:2171–90.

———. "Eusebius of Caesarea." In *Coptic Encyclopedia*, 4:1070–71.

———. "Ibn Kabar." In *Coptic Encyclopedia*, 4:1267–68.

———. *The Copts and Christian Civilization*. Salt Lake City: University of Utah Press for the Frederick William Reynolds Association, 1979.

———. "Sawirus Ibn Al-Muqaffa." In *Coptic Encyclopedia*, 7:2100–103.

Awadallah, Mankarious. *Manaret El Akdas [The Lighthouse of the Holies]*. Cairo: Al Mahaba Press, 1979. (Arabic).

Badawy, Alexander. *Coptic Art and Archaeology: The Art of the Christian Egyptians from the Late Antique to the Middle Ages*. Cambridge: MIT Press, 1978.

Bagnall, Roger. *Early Christian Books in Egypt*. Princeton: Princeton University Press, 2009.

Bardy, G. "Les premiers temps du Christianisme de langue copte en Égypte." in L. Vincent (ed) Mémorial Lagrange. Paris 1940, 203–16

Barnard, Leslie W. *Studies in the Apostolic Fathers and their Background*. New York: Schocken Books, 1967.

Barnstone, W. *The other Bible: Jewish pseudepigrapha, Christian apocrypha, Gnostic Scriptures, Kabbalah, Dead Sea scrolls* (Rev. ed.). San Francisco: Harper, 2005.

Barrett, C. K. *Jesus and the Gospel Tradition*. London: Spck, 1975.

Barucq, André. *L'Expression de la Louange Divine et de la Prière dans la Bible en Egypte*. Cairo: IFAO 1962.

Basilios (Archbishop). "Baptism." In *Coptic Encyclopedia*, 2:336–39.

———. "Book of Canonical Hours." In *Coptic Encyclopedia*, 2:446–49.

———. "Euchologion." In *Coptic Encyclopedia*, 4:1066–67.

_____ and, René-Georges Coquin. "Lectionary." 5:1435–37.

———. "Orientation towards the East." In *Coptic Encyclopedia*, 6:1846.

Bauer, Walter. *Orthodoxy and Heresy in Earliest Christianity*. Trans. and ed. R.A. Kraft et al. Philadelphia: Fortress, 1971.

Baumstark, Anton. *Comparative Liturgy*. London: A. R. Mowbray, 1958.

Bautch, Kelley Coblentz. *A Study of the Geography of 1 Enoch 17–19: "No One Has Seen What I Have Seen."* Leiden and Boston: Brill, 2003.

Beaugé, Charles. "Un Réformateur copte au XIIe siècle." In *Revue des Questions Historiques*, t. 106, 1927, pp. 5–34.

Beckwith, R. T. "The Jewish Background of Christian Worship." In *The Study of Liturgy*, edited by J. Cheslyn, G. Wainwright, E. Yarnold, and P. Bradshaw, 68–80. London and New York: SPCK, 1992.

Beckwith, John. *Coptic Sculpture, 300-1300*. London: A. Tiranti, 1963.

Bell, H. Idris, and T. C. Skeat. *Fragments of an Unknown Gospel and Other Early Christian Papyri*. London: British Museum, 1935.

Bell, H. Idris, and Walter E. Crum. *Jews and Christians in Egypt: The Jewish Troubles in Alexandria and the Athanasian Controversy, Illustrated by Texts from Greek Papyri in the British Museum*. London: Oxford University Press, 1924.

Berkovitz, A. J., and Letteney, M. Rethinking "Authority" in Late Antiquity: Authorship, Law, and Transmission in Jewish and Christian Tradition. *1st ed.*, Routledge, 2018.

Bernat, David. "Circumcision." In *The Eerdmans Dictionary of Early Judaism,* edited by J. Collins and D. Harlow, 471–74. Grand Rapids: Eerdmans, 2010.

Blouin, Katherine. *Le Conflit Judéo-Alexandrin de 38–41.* Paris: L'Harmattan, 2005. (French).

Borsai, I. "À la Recherche de l'Ancienne Musique Pharaonique" *Cahiers d'Histoire Égyptienne* 11 (1968):25–42

Bourguet (du), Pierre. *L'Art Copte.* Paris: A. Michel, 1968.

Boyarin, D. "Introduction: Judaeo-Christianity Redivivus." In *Journal of Early Christian Studies,* vol. 9, no. 4: 417–19, 2001.

Bouyer, Louis. *Eucharist: Theology and Spirituality of the Eucharist Prayer.* Translated by Charles Underhill Quinn. Notre Dame: University of Notre Dame Press, 1968.

Bow, Beverly. "Melchizedek's Birth Narrative in 2 Enoch 68–73." In *For a Later Generation: The Transformation of Tradition in Israel, Early Judaism, and Early Christianity,* edited by Randal A. Argall et al., 33–42. Harrisburg, PA: Trinity Press International, 2000.

Bradshaw, Paul. "Ten Principles for Interpreting Early Christian Liturgical Evidence." In *The Making of Jewish and Christian Worship,* edited by P. Bradshaw and L. A. Hoffman, 3–22. Notre Dame: University of Notre Dame Press, 1991.

———. *The Search for the Origins of Christian Worship: Sources and Methods for the Study of Early Liturgy.* New York: Oxford University Press, 1992.

———. and Hoffman L. A. *The Making of Jewish and Christian Worship.* University of Notre Dame Press, 1991.

Broadhead, Edwin Keith. *Jewish Ways of Following Jesus: Redrawing the Religious Map of Antiquity.* Tübingen: Mohr Siebeck, 2010.

Broyles, Craig. *Psalms*. Grand Rapids: Baker Books, 1999.

Brownlee, William Hugh. *The Midrash Pesher of Habakkuk*. Missoula: Scholars Press, 1979.

Burmester, Oswald H. E. *The Egyptian or Coptic Church: A Detailed Description of her Liturgical Services and the Rites and Ceremonies Observed in the Administration of her Sacraments*. Cairo: Société d'Archéologie Copte, 1967.

Butcher, Edith. *The Story of the Church of Egypt: Being an Outline of the History of the Egyptians under their Successive Masters from the Roman Conquest until Now*. London: Smith, Elder, 1897.

Butler, Alfred J. (Alfred Joshua). *The Ancient Coptic Churches of Egypt*. Clarendon Press, 1884.

Cannuyer, Christian. "L'Ancrage Juif de la Première Église d'Alexandrie." In Le *Monde Copte*, 23: 31–46.

Castellino, Giorgio. *Le Lamentazioni individuali e gli inni in Babilonia e in Israele*. Torino: Società Editrice Internazionale, 1939.

Charlesworth, James H. *The Old Testament Pseudepigrapha*. London: Darton, Longman & Todd, 1983.

Chazon, Esther. "The Function of the Qumran Prayer Texts." In *The Dead Sea Scrolls: Fifty Years after Discovery, Proceedings of the Jerusalem Congress,* edited by L. H. Schiffman et al., 217–25. Jerusalem: Israel Exploration Society, 2000.

———. "When Did They Pray?" In *For a Later Generation: The Transformation in Israel, Early Judaism, and Early Christianity*, edited by Randal A. Argall et al., 42–52. Pennsylvania: Trinity Press International, 2000.

Church of St Mary in Choubra Committee. *St Mark in Prayers and Hymns* and *Liturgical Books of the Coptic Church*. Cairo: Ramses Press, 1968. (Arabic).

Clugnet, Leon. *Dictionnaire Grec-Français des Noms*

Liturgiques en usage dans l'Église Grecque. Paris: A. Picard, 1895

Cody, Aelred. "Coptic Calendar." In *Coptic Encyclopedia,* 2:433–36.

———. "Doxology." In *Coptic Encyclopedia,* 3:923–24.

Collins, John. *"Pseudo-Hecataeus."* In *The Eerdmans Dictionary of Early Judaism,* edited by J. Collins and D. Harlow, 718. Grand Rapids: Eerdmans, 2010.

Cooney, John D. (John Ducey). *Late Egyptian and Coptic Art: An Introduction to the Collections in the Brooklyn Museum.* Brooklyn Museum, Brooklyn Institute of Arts and Sciences, 1943.

Coquin, René-Georges. "Les Canons d'Hippolyte." In *Patrologia Orientalis,* 31:273–443.

Crum, W. E. *Catalogue of the Coptic Manuscripts in the British Museum.* London: British Museum, 1905.

———. *Coptic Monuments: Catalogue Général des Antiquités Égyptiennes du Musée du Caire.* New Jersey: Gorgias Press, 2009.

Crusé, Christian. *The Ecclesiastical History of Eusebius Pamphilus, Bishop of Caesarea, in Palestine.* Translated by C. Crusé. New York: Thomas N. Standford, 1856.

Danby, Herbert. *Tractate Sanhedrin, Mishnah and Tosefta: The Judicial Procedure of the Jews as Codified Towards the End of the Second Century, A. D.* London: Society for Promoting Christian Knowledge, 1919.

Daoud, Moawad. *Kamous Al Logha Al Keptia* [*Dictionary of the Coptic Language*]. Cairo: The Printing Shop of the Egyptians, 1999. (Coptic-Arabic).

Davis, Stephen J. *The Early Coptic Papacy: The Egyptian Church and Its Leadership in Late Antiquity.* Cairo and New York: American University in Cairo Press, 2004.

Deiss, Lucien. *Springtime of the Liturgy.* Translated by Matthew O'Connell. St. Paul, MN: The Liturgical Press, 1979.

Delamarter, Steve and James Charlesworth. *A Scripture Index to Charlesworth's The Old Testament Pseudepigrapha.* London and New York: Sheffield Academic Press, 2002.

Den Heijer, Johannes. "History of the Patriarchs of Alexandria." In *Coptic Encyclopedia*, 4:1239–42.

deSilva, David. "Circumcision." In *The Dictionary of Scripture and Ethics,* edited by Joel Green Collins, 139–40. Grand Rapids: Baker Academic, 2011.

Dix, Gregory. *The Shape of the Liturgy.* London: Dacre Press, 1949.

Dugmore, C. W. (Clifford William). *The Influence of the Synagogue Upon the Divine Office.* Faith Press, 1964.

Dunlop, Laurence. *Patterns of Prayer in Psalms.* New York: The Seabury Press, 1982.

Eisenstein, Judah. "Shema." In *Jewish Encyclopedia*, 11:286–87.

El Masry Iris. *Story of the Copts: The True Story of Christianity in Egypt.* Los Angeles: St. Antony Monastery, 1987.

Elman, Yaakov, and Israel Gershoni. *Transmitting Jewish Traditions: Orality, Textuality, and Cultural Diffusion.* New Haven: Yale University Press, 2000.

Eusebius of Caesarea. *Ecclesiastical History.* Edited by E. Schwartz and T. Mommsen. Leipzig: J.C. Hinrichs, 1903.

Evetts, Basil T. E. "History of the Patriarchs of the Coptic Church of Alexandria (S. Mark to Benjamin I)." Arabic text edited, translated and annotated by B. Evetts. In *Patrologia Orientalis*, 1:103–214.

Fakhry, Ahmed. *The Necropolis of al-Bagawat in Khargah Oasis.* Cairo: Service des Antiquités de l'Egypte, 1951.

Falk, Daniel K. *Daily, Sabbath, and Festival Prayers in the Dead Sea Scrolls.* Leiden: Brill, 1998.

Fairman, H. W. "Fouilles Exécutées à Baouît.". Par Jean Maspero. Notes Mises En Ordre et Éditées Par Étienne Drioton. Premier Fascicule. Cairo: 1932.

Feldman L. H and J.L. Kugel (Ed.). *Outside the Bible: Ancient Jewish Writings Related to Scripture;* 3 vols. Philadelphia: Jewish Publication Society; Lincoln: University of Nebraska, 2013.

Fiensy, David A. *Prayers Alleged to Be Jewish: An Examination of the Constitutiones Apostolorum.* Chico, CA: Scholars Press, 1985.

Fillion, Louis-Claude. *La Sainte Bible Commentée d'Après La Vulgate.* Vol. 4. Paris: Librairie Letouzey et Ané, 1921. (Latin-French).

Flusser, David. "Psalms, Hymns and Prayers." In *Writings of the Second Temple Period: Apocrypha, Pseudepigrapha, Qumran, Sectarian Writings, Philo, and Josephus*, edited by Michael E. Stone, 551–77. Assen and Philadelphia: Van Gorcum, 1984.

Fonrobert, C. E. "The Didascalia Apostolorum: A Mishnah for the Disciples of Jesus." *Journal of Early Christian Studies*, vol. 9, no. 4: 483–509, 2001.

Fowler, Montague. *Christian Egypt, Past, Present, and Future.* London: Church Newspaper Company, 1902.

Frederick, Vincent. "Murqus Ibn Qanbar." In *Coptic Encyclopedia*, 6:1699–700.

Frey, Jörg, and Jacob Cerone. *Qumran and Christian Origins*. Baylor University Press, 2022.

Futato, Mark. *Interpreting the Psalms: An Exegetical Handbook.* Grand Rapids: Kregel, 2007.

Gayet, Al. (Albert). *L'Art Copte : École d'Alexandrie, Architecture Monastique, Sculpture, Peinture, Art Somptuaire.* E. Leroux, 1902.

Gee, John. "Some Neglected Aspects of Egypt's Conversion to Christianity." In *Coptic Culture: Past, Present and Future,* edited by Mariam Ayad, 43–57. Stevenage, UK: Coptic Orthodox Church Centre, 2012.

Gerhardsson, Birger, and Eric J. Sharpe. *Memory and Manuscript: Oral Tradition and Written Transmission in Rabbinic Judaism and Early Christianity; with, Tradition and Transmission in Early Christianity*. Grand Rapids, MI: William B. Eerdmans, 1998.

Ginzberg, Louis. "Amram Ben Sheshna." In *Jewish Encyclopedia*, 1:536–37.

Girgis, Waheeb. *Al Kalemat Al Younanya Al Mostakhdama fi al Logha al Keptya [Greek Words in Coptic Usage]*. Cairo: Society of Anba Gregorios, 2010. (Arabic).

Goodenough, Erwin Ramsdell. *Jewish Symbols in the Greco-Roman Period.* Pantheon Books, 1953. Griggs, C. Wilfred. *Early Egyptian Christianity: From its Origins to 451 CE*. Leiden and New York: Brill, 1990.

Graf, Georg. *Eine Reforversuch innerhalb der Koptischen Kirche im Zwölften Jahrhundert*. Paderborn, 1923.

Grossmann, Peter. ""Architectural Elements of Churches." in *CE*, vol.1, 194–226.

Gruen, Erich. "Judaism in the Diaspora." In *The Eerdmans Dictionary of Early Judaism,* edited by J. Collins and D. Harlow, 77–96. Grand Rapids: Eerdmans, 2010.

Hachlili, Rachel. "The Origin of the Synagogue: A Re-Assessment." Journal for the Study of Judaism in the Persian, Hellenistic, and Roman Period, vol. 28, no. 1, Brill, 1997, 34–47,

Hall, Robert G. "Epispasm." In *Bible Review* 8/9 *(*1992), 52–57.

Hamilton, Alastair. *The Copts and the West, 1439–1822: The European Discovery of the Egyptian Church*. Oxford and New York: Oxford University Press, 2006.

Harrington, Hannah. "Purity and Impurity." In *The Eerdmans Dictionary of Early Judaism*, edited by J. Collins and D. Harlow, 1120–23. Grand Rapids: Eerdmans, 2010.

Heinemann, Joseph. *Prayer in the Talmud: Forms and Patterns*. Berlin and New York: Walter de Gruyter, 1977.

Hinge, G., and A. Krasilnikoff. "Introduction." In *Alexandria: A Cultural and Religious Melting Pot*, edited by G. Hinge and A. Krasilnikoff, 9–21. Aarhus: Aarhus University Press, 2009.

Hoffman, Lawrence A. "Reconstructing Ritual as Identity and Culture." In *The Making of Jewish and Christian Worship*, edited by P. Bradshaw and L. A. Hoffman, 22–42. Notre Dame: University of Notre Dame Press, 1991.

———. "Introduction to the Liturgy: Why the *P'sukei D'zimra*?" In *My People's Prayer Book: Traditional Prayers, Modern Commentaries*, 3, 1–15. Woodstock, VT: Jewish Lights Publishing. 1997.

———. *The Canonization of the Synagogue Service*. Notre Dame: University of Notre Dame Press, 1979.

Horbury, William and David Noy. *Jewish Inscriptions of Graeco-Roman Egypt: With an Index of the Jewish Inscriptions of Egypt and Cyrenaica*. Cambridge University Press, 1992.

Horst, Pieter Willem van der and Judith Newman. *Early Jewish Prayers in Greek*. Berlin and New York: Walter de Gruyter, 2008.

Hurtado, Larry W. *The Earliest Christian Artifacts: Manuscripts and Christian Origins*. Grand Rapids: Eerdmans, 2006.

Ibn Kabar, al-Shaykh al-Mu'taman Shams al-Riyasah. *Misbah al-Zulmah fi Idah al-Khidmah* [*The Lamp that Lights the Darkness in Clarifying the Service*]. Cairo: Mina Press, 1993. (Arabic).

Idelsohn, A. Z. *Jewish Liturgy and Its Development*. New York: Schocken Books, 1967.

Isizoros, Bishop. *Al Kharida Al Nafeessa Fi Tareikh Al Kenissa* [*The Precious Pearl of the Church History*]. Cairo: Al Mahaba Press, 1991. (Arabic).

Jacobs Joseph, Hirsch Emil G. "Curtain." In *Jewish Encyclopedia*, 4: 390–394.

Jacobson, Issachar. *Meditations on the Siddur: Studies in the Essential Problems and Ideas of Jewish Worship.* Tel Aviv: Sinai, 1966.

Jacquet, Louis. *Les Psaumes et le Cœur De l'homme: Étude Textuelle, Littéraire et Doctrinale.* vol. 2. Gembloux: Les Presses Duculot, 1975.

Jahvist, no first name. "Haggadah." In *Jewish Encyclopedia*, 6:141.

———. "Halakah." In *Jewish Encyclopedia*, 6:163.

Jaffee, M. S. "How Much 'Orality' in Oral Torah? New Perspectives on the Composition and Transmission of Early Rabbinic Tradition." *Shofar (West Lafayette, Ind.)*, vol. 10, no. 2: 53–72, 1992.

James, Jamie. *The Music of the Spheres: Music, Science, and the Natural Order of the Universe.* Copernicus Press, 1995.

Jones, C. et al. *The Study of Liturgy.* Oxford University Press, 1978.

Josephus, Flavius. *The Jewish War, Books I–III.* St. Translated by St. J. H. Thackeray. Loeb Classical Library. London and New York: Heinemann and Putman's Sons, 1927.

Kamil, Jill. *Christianity in the Land of the Pharaohs: The Coptic Orthodox Church.* London and New York: Routledge, 2002.

Kanawaty, George. *Al Massiheya wa' Al Hadara' Al Arabeya* [*Christianity and the Arabic Civilization*]. Cairo: Dal Al Thakafa, 1992. (Arabic).

Kasher, Aryeh. *The Jews in Hellenistic and Roman Egypt: The Struggle for Equal Rights.* Tübingen: J. C. B. Mohr, 1985.

Katz, S. T. "Issues in the Separation of Judaism and Christianity after 70 C.E.: A Reconsideration.", *Journal of Biblical Literature*, vol. 103, no. 1, 1984.

Keel, Othmar. *The Symbolism of the Biblical World: Ancient Near Eastern Iconography and the Book of Psalms.* Crossroad, 1985.

Kerkeslager, Allen. "Jewish Pilgrimage and Jewish Identity in Hellenistic and Early Roman Egypt." In *Pilgrimage and Holy Space in Late Antique Egypt,* edited by D. Frankfurter, 99–122. Leiden and Boston: Brill, 1998.

Khalil, Samir. "Gabriel V." In *Coptic Encyclopedia*, 4:1130–33.

Klijn, Albertus. "Jewish Christianity in Egypt." In *The Roots of Egyptian Christianity*, edited by B. Pearson and James Goehring, 161–78. Washington, DC: The Catholic University of America Press, 2007.

Knibb, Michael. *"Ethiopic Apocalypse of Enoch."* In *The Eerdmans Dictionary of Early Judaism,* edited by J. Collins and D. Harlow, 585–87. Grand Rapids: Eerdmans, 2010.

Kohler, Kaufmann. "Easter." In *Jewish Encyclopedia,* 5:29.

———. "Korban." In *Jewish Encyclopedia,* 7:561.

——— and H. G. (Hyman Gerson) Enelow. *The Origins of the Synagogue and the Church.* Arno Press, 1973.Kruger, Michael J. *The Gospel of the Savior: An Analysis of P. Oxy. 840 and Its Place in the Gospel Traditions of Early Christianity.* Leiden and Boston: Brill, 2005.

Kuhn, Magdalena. *Koptische Liturgische Melodien: die Relatie Zwischen Text und Musik in der Koptischen Psalmodia.* Uitgeverij Peeters, 2011.

Kulik, Alexander and others (eds). *A Guide to Early Jewish Texts and Traditions in Christian Transmission.* Oxford: Oxford University, 2019.

Kuvatova, Valeria. "Iconography of the Procession of Virgins, Chapel of Exodus (Egypt): Origins and Parallels." in

Cultural and Religious Studies, June 2019, Vol. 7, No. 6, 306-318

Laporte, Jean. *la Doctrine Eucharistique chez Philon d'Alexandrie*. Beauchesne, 1972.

Landsberg, Max. "Sheliah Zibbur." In *The Jewish Encyclopedia*, 11:261.

Langer, Ruth. *To Worship God Properly: Tensions between Liturgical Custom and Halakhah in Judaism*. Cincinnati: Hebrew Union College Press, 1998.

———. *Cursing the Christians? A History of the Birkat HaMinim*. Oxford University Press, 2012.

———. "Revisiting Early Rabbinic Liturgy: The Recent Contributions of Ezra Fleischer." Prooftexts, vol. 19, no. 2, Johns Hopkins University Press, 1999, pp. 179–94.

———. *Jewish Liturgy: A Guide to Research*. Rowman & Littlefield, 2015.

——— and Richard S. Sarason. "Re-Examining the Early Evidence for Rabbinic Liturgy: How Fixed Were Its Prayer Texts?" *On Wings of Prayer*, edited by Nuria Calduch-Benages et al., vol. 44, Walter de Gruyter GmbH, 2019, pp. 203–32,

Lanne, Emmanuel. "Le Grand Euchologue du Monastère Blanc." In *Patrologia Orientalis*, 17: 269–406. (French).

Lauterbach, J. Z. 1973. *Rabbinic Essays. NY:* Ktav Pub. House,

Leclercq, H. "Alexandrie (Archéologie)" *DALC* (1924) vol. 1, 1098–1182.

———. "Alphabets Vocaliques des Gnostiques." *DALC* (1924) vol. 1, 1268–1288

———. "Egypte" *DALC* (1924) vol. 4, 2476–2500.

Leonhard, C. "Ruth Langer. Cursing the Christians? A History of the Birkat HaMinim." *Studies in Christian-Jewish Relations*, vol. 7, no. 1, 2012.

Leonhardt-Balzer, Jutta. *Jewish Worship in Philo of Alexandria*. Mohr Siebeck, 2001.

Leslie, Laurence. Psalms, Translated and Interpreted in the Light of Hebrew Life and Worship. New York: the Seabury Press, 1982.

Liesen, Jan. "'With all your heart': Praise in the Book of Ben Sira." *Ben Sira's God*, 2002, vol. 321, Walter de Gruyter GmbH, 2002, pp. 199–213.

Leo Depuydt: "Catalogue of Coptic BRILL Manuscripts in the Pierpont Morgan Library". In *Der Same Seths*. Ed. Schenke Robinson, G., Schenke, G., & Plisch, U.-K. (2012). (Vol. 78, pp. 1224–1230), 2012.

Levine, Lee. *The Ancient Synagogue: The First Thousand Years*. New Haven: Yale University Press, 2005.

Macomber, William. *Catalogue of Christian Arabic Manuscripts of the Franciscan Center of Christian Oriental Studies*. Jerusalem: Franciscan, 1984.

McKenzie, Judith. *The Architecture of Alexandria and Egypt, c. 300 BC to AD 700*. New Haven, Conn: Yale University Press, 2007.

McKinnon, James W. *Music in Early Christian Literature*. Cambridge University Press, 2012.

Malaty, Tadros. *Introduction to The Coptic Orthodox Church*. Ottawa: Saint Mary Church, 1987.

——. *The Church: House of God*. Alexandria: Saint George Coptic Church, 1994.

——. *Tradition and Orthodoxy*. Alexandria: Saint George Coptic Church, 1979.

Mallon, Alexis. *La Grammaire Copte*. Beyrouth: Imprimerie Catholique, 1926. (French).

Martin, Matthew J. "The Necropolis Of El Bagawat in The Khargah Oasis: Some Implications for The History of Judaism and Early Christianity in Egypt." *in Orientalia Lovaniensia*

Analecta 133. Leuven - Paris - Dudley: Uitgeverit Peeters en Departement Oosterse Studies, 2004.

Maspero, Gaston. *Guide de Visiteurs au Musée du Boula*q. Boulaq (Cairo), 1883.

Meinardus, Otto. *Two Thousand Years of Coptic Christianity*. Cairo: American University in Cairo Press, 1999.

Menassa, Youhanna. *Tarikh Al Kenissa Al Keptya* [*The History of the Coptic Church*]. Cairo: Al Mahaba Library, 1983. (Arabic).

Mettaous, Bishop. *Al Thalathat Kodassat* [*The Three Liturgies*]. Cairo: Diocese of Beni Souef, 1993. (Arabic).

———. *Rouhaniet Taks Al Kodass Fi Al Kenissa Al Keptia* [*The Spirituality of the Mass in the Coptic Church*]. Beni Souef: Lagnet Al Tahrir, 2010. (Arabic).

———. *Rouhaniet Al Tasbeha Hassab Taks Al Kanissa al Keptya* [*The Spirituality of the Praise According to the Order of the Coptic Church*]. Cairo: Diocese of Beni Souef, 1989. (Arabic).

———. *The Spirituality of The Rites of The Holy Liturgy*. https://accot.stcyrils.edu.au/wp-content/uploads/2020/07/The-Spirituality-Of-The-Rites-Of-The-Holy-Liturgy-In-The-Coptic-Orthodox-Church.pdf

Millgram, Abraham. *Jewish Worship*. Philadelphia: Jewish Publication Society of America, 1975.

Mingana, Alphonse. *The Vision of Theophilus: The Book of the Flight of the Holy Family into Egypt*. New South Wales: St. Shenouda Monastery, 2012.

Modrzejewski, Joseph. *The Jews of Egypt: From Rameses II to Emperor Hadrian*. Princeton: Princeton University Press, 1997.

Moule, Charles Francis Digby. *Worship in the New Testament*. London: Lutterworth, 1964.

Muftah, Ragheb, et al. "Coptic Music." In *Coptic Encyclopedia*, 6:1715–47.

Muftah, R. *Al Musika al Kepteya*. In *Bulletin de l'institut des Études Coptes*, 42–53. Le Caire : 1958. (Arabic).

Neusner, Jacob. *The Oral Torah: The Sacred Books of Judaism: An Introduction*. San Francisco: Harper & Row, 1986.

———. *The Tosefta*. Vol. 2. Peabody, MA: Hendrickson, 2002.

Nickelsburg, George W. E. "Stories of Biblical and Early Post-Biblical Times." In *Jewish Writings of the Second Temple Period: Apocrypha, Pseudepigrapha, Qumran, Sectarian Writings, Philo, and Josephus*, edited by Michael E. Stone, 75–80. Assen and Philadelphia: Van Gorcum, 1984.

———. "The Bible Rewritten and Expanded." In *Jewish Writings of the Second Temple Period: Apocrypha, Pseudepigrapha, Qumran, Sectarian Writings, Philo, and Josephus*, edited by Michael E. Stone, 149–52. Assen and Philadelphia: Van Gorcum, 1984.

Newlandsmith, E. *The Ancient Music of the Coptic Church*. London: New Temple Press, 1931.

Oegema, Gerben S. "The Reception of the Book of Daniel in the Early Church." In *Apocrypha*, edited by Gerben Oegema and James Charlesworth, 243–52. Downers Grove: InterVarsity, 2010.

Oesterley, W. O. E, et al. *Myth and Ritual*. London: Oxford University Press, 1933.

———. *The Religion and Worship of the Synagogue: An Introduction to the Study of Judaism from the New Testament Period*. Pitman and Sons, 1907.

———. *The Psalms*. vol. 1. London: Society For Promoting Christian Knowledge/ NY: the MacMillan Company, 1939.

Orlov, Andrei. "Slavonic Apocalypse of Enoch." In *Eerdmans Dictionary of Early Judaism,* edited by J. Collins and D. Harlow, 587–90. Grand Rapids: Eerdmans, 2010.

Paget, James Carleton. *Jews, Christians and Jewish Christians in Antiquity*. Tübingen: Mohr Siebeck, 2010.

Pearson, Birger Albert. "Enoch in Egypt." In *For a Later Generation: The Transformation of Tradition in Israel, Early Judaism, and Early Christianity*, edited by Randal A. Argall et al., 216–32. Harrisburg, PA: Trinity Press International, 2000.

———. "Earliest Christianity in Egypt: Further Observations." In *The Roots of Egyptian Christianity*, edited by B. A. Pearson and James Goehring, 97–112. Washington: The Catholic University of America Press, 2007.

———. "Jewish Sources in Gnostic Literature." In *Jewish Writings of the Second Temple*: *Apocrypha, Pseudepigrapha, Qumran, Sectarian Writings, Philo, and Josephus*, edited by Michael E. Stone, 443–81. Assen and Philadelphia: Van Gorcum, 1984.

———. *Gnosticism and Christianity in Roman and Coptic Egypt*. New York: T. & T. Clark International, 2004.

———. *Gnosticism, Judaism, and Egyptian Christianity*. Minneapolis: Fortress, 1990.

Penner, Jeremy. *Patterns of Daily Prayer in Second Temple Period Judaism*. Leiden and Boston: Brill, 2012.

Porter, Stanley E., and Andrew Pitts. *Christian Origins and Hellenistic Judaism: Social and Literary Contexts for the New Testament*. Brill, 2013.

Rafael (Bishop). *Isnaou Hada L'Zikri* [*Do This in Remembrance of Me*]. Cairo: Youth Bishopric, 2012. (Arabic).

Rénaudot, Eusèbe. *Historia Patriarcharum Alexandrinorum Jacobitarum a D. Marco usque ad finem saeculi 13. Cum catalogo sequentium patriarcharum & collectaneis historicis ad ultima tempora spectantibus. Inseruntur multa ad res ecclesiasticas jacobitarum patriarchatus Antiocheni, Aethiopiae, Nubiae & Armeniae pertinentia. Accedit epitome historiae Muhamedanae ad illustrandas res aegyptiacas. Omnia collecta ex autoribus ... persicis*. Apud F. Fournier, 1713.

Reif, Stefan C. *Problems with Prayers: Studies in the Textual History of Early Rabbinic Liturgy.* Berlin and New York: Walter de Gruyter, 2006.

Rey, Jean-Sébastien. "The Dead Sea Scrolls as Background to Postbiblical Judaism and Early Christianity," Revue de Qumran, Vol. 22, No. 2 (86), Peters Publishers, 2005.

Roberts, Colin. *Manuscript, Society, and Belief in Early Christian Egypt.* London and New York: British Academy by Oxford University Press, 1979.

Robertson, M. "The Reliability of the Oral Tradition in Preserving Coptic Music, III. A Comparison of Four Recordings of the Confession of Faith from the Liturgy of Saint Basil" *Bulletin de la Société d'Archéologie Copte,* Tome XXVII. Le Caire: 93–105

Roncaglia, Martiniano. *Histoire de l'Église Copte,* 1. Beirut: Dar Al-Kalima, 1966.

Rouwhorst, G. "Jewish Liturgical Traditions in Early Syriac Christianity." Vigiliae Christianae, vol. 51, no. 1, 1997.

Ruelle, Émile. *Aristoxène, Éléments Harmoniques* : Texte traduit du Grec en Français sur les Sept manuscrits de la Bibliothèque Nationale par, Collection des Auteurs grecs relatifs à la musique. Paris, 1871.

Runesson, Anders. *The Origins of the Synagogue: A Socio-Historical Study.* Stockholm: Almqvist & Wiksell, 2001.

Ryken, Leland, et al. "East." In *Dictionary of Biblical Imagery,* edited by Leyland Ryken, James Wilhoit, and Tremper Longman, 225–26. Downers Grove: InterVarsity, 1998. [In this *Dictionary* editors do not mention the author of each article.]

Schiffman, Lawrence H. *Texts and Traditions: A Source Reader for the Study of Second Temple and Rabbinic Judaism.* Hoboken, NJ: Ktav, 1998.

———. *Understanding Second Temple and Rabbinic Judaism.* Jersey City, NJ: Ktav, 2003.

Schimmel, Harry C. *The Oral Law: A Study of the Rabbinic Contribution to Torah She-be-al-peh*. Jerusalem and New York: Feldheim, 1971.

Schnabel, Eckhard J. *Early Christian Mission*. Downers Grove and Leicester: InterVarsity, 2004.

Seeman, Chris. "Jewish History from Alexander to Hadrian." In *The Eerdmans Dictionary of Early Judaism*, edited by J. Collins and D. Harlow, 25–53. Grand Rapids: Eerdmans, 2010.

Seybold, Christian. "Historia Patriarchum Alexandrinorum." In *Corpus Scriptorum Christianorum Orientalium*, 8, 1–120. Louvain: Secrétariat du Corpus, 1964. [Severus' text in Arabic with no comments from the author].

Shisha-Halevy, Ariel. "Sahidic." In *Coptic Encyclopedia*, 7:194–202.

Shivtiel Avihai, and Friedrich Niessen. *Arabic and Judeo–Arabic Manuscripts in the Cambridge Genizah Collections*. New York: Cambridge University Press, 2006.

Smit, P. B. *Felix Culpa: Ritual Failure and Theological Innovation in Early Christianity*. Leiden: Brill, 2021.

Spurgeon, C. H. (Charles Haddon). *The Treasury of David: Containing an Original Exposition of the Book of Psalms; a Collection of Illustrative Extracts from the Whole Range of Literature; a Series of Homiletical Hints upon Almost Every Verse; and Lists of Writers upon Each Psalm*. I.K. Funk & co., 1882. (Vol.3).

Strauven, P. and J. Van Reeth. "De Harmonie der Sferen en het Ontstaan van de Muzikale modi", Handelingen - Koninklijke Zuid-Nederlandse maatschappij voor taal- en letterkunde en geschiedenis. 2008.

Srawley, J. H. *The Early History of the Liturgy*. Cambridge: Cambridge University Press, 1947.

Stapert, Calvin. *A New Song for an Old World: Musical Thought in the Early Church*. Grand Rapids: William B. Eerdmans Publishing Co., 2007.

Stern, Henri. "Quelques Problèmes d'Iconographie Paléochrétienne et juive." in *Cahiers Archéologiques*, XII, 1962, pp. 99–113.

Stern, Sacha. *Calendars in Antiquity: Empires, States, and Societies*. 1st ed., Oxford University Press, 2012.

Stock, Brian. *Listening for the Text: On the Uses of the Past*. Baltimore: Johns Hopkins University Press, 1990.

Stone, Michael E. *Jewish Writings of the Second Temple Period: Apocrypha, Pseudepigrapha, Qumran, Sectarian Writings, Philo, Josephus*. Assen and Philadelphia: Van Gorcum, 1984.

Shwartz J. "Nouvelles Études sur des Fresques d'El Bagawat." in *Cahiers Archéologiques*, 13, 1–11.

Thackeray, H. St. J. *The Letter of Aristeas*. London: SPCK, 1918.

Tadros, Emile. *The Long Vocalisms in the Coptic Songs and Its Ancient Musicological Concepts*, (Arabic), Cairo, 2001 – I.S.B.N. 977-5607-66-3.

_____. Contribution à l'Étude des alphabets vocaliques et des syllabes dans la pratique des Chants Liturgiques Coptes. https://www.musicologie.org/publirem/tadros_01.html

Teppler, Y. Y., Birkat HaMinim: Jews and Christians in Conflict in the Ancient World. Tübingen: Mohr Siebeck, 2007. Trans. Susan Weingarten. Tübingen: Mohr Siebeck, 2007.

Vanbeek, Lawrence. "1 Enoch among Jews and Christians: A Fringe Connection." *In Christian–Jewish Relations through the Centuries*, edited by Stanley E. Porter and B. W. Pearson, 93–115. Journal for the Study of the New Testament Supplement Series, 192. Sheffield: Sheffield Academic Press, 2000.

Verhelst, S. *Les traditions Judéo-Chrétiennes dans la liturgie de Jérusalem : spécialement la Liturgie de saint Jacques frère de Dieu*. Peeters, 2003.

Villard (de), Ugo Monoret. *Les Couvents près de Sohag*. Vol. I, Milan, 1925.

Villecourt, Louis. "Les Observances liturgiques et la discipline du Jeûne dans l'Église Copte." *Le Muséon*, vol. 36, 249, 1923.

Viaud, Gérard. *Les Pélerinages Coptes en Egypte*. Cairo: Institut Français d'Archéologie Orientale, 1979. (French).

Wahle, Stephan. "Reflections on the Exploration of Jewish and Christian Liturgy from the Viewpoint of a Systematic Theology of Liturgy." In *Jewish and Christian Liturgy and Worship: New Insights into Its History and Interaction*, edited by A. Gerhards and C. Leonhard, 169–84. Leiden and Boston: Brill, 2007.

Wainwright, Geoffrey. "The Periods of Liturgical History." In *The Study of Liturgy,* edited by J. Cheslyn, G. Wainwright, E. Yarnold, and P. Bradshaw, 61–68. London and New York: SPCK, 1992.

Watson, John H. *Among the Copts*. Brighton and Portland: Sussex Academic Press, 2000.

Werner, Eric. *The Sacred Bridge: Liturgical Parallels in Synagogue and Early Church*. Columbia University Press, 1970.

Wessel, Klaus. *Coptic Art*. Translated by Jean Carroll and Sheila Hatton, McGraw-Hill, 1965.

Wilken, Robert Louis. *Judaism and the Early Christian Mind: A Study of Cyril of Alexandria's Exegesis and Theology*. New Haven: Yale University Press, 1971.

Will, Ernest. (Lee I. Levine, ed.). The Synagogue in Late Antiquity. (A Centennial Publication of The Jewish Seminary of America). The American Schools of Oriental Research, Philadelphia, 1987." *Syria. Archéologie, Art et Histoire*, vol. 68, no. 1, Persée: Université de Lyon, CNRS & ENS de Lyon, 1991.

Wilson, M. R. *Our Father Abraham: Jewish Roots of the Christian Faith*. W.B. Eerdmans, 1989.

Young, Frances. "Introduction: The Literary Culture of the Earliest Christianity." In *The Cambridge History of Early Christian Literature*, edited by F. M Young, L. Ayres, and A. Louth, 5–11. Cambridge and New York: Cambridge University Press, 2004.

Youssef (Bishop). *Encyclopedia of Christian Q & A*. Hamden, CT: Virgin Mary and Archangel Michael Coptic Orthodox Church, 2011.

Zanetti, Ugo. "La Distribution des Psaumes dans l'Horlogion Copte." *OCP* 56 (1990) 323–69.

www.ingramcontent.com/pod-product-compliance
Lightning Source LLC
Chambersburg PA
CBHW030510080526
44586CB00011B/140